James Ronald Leslie Macdonald

Soldiering and Surveying in British East Africa, 1891-1894

James Ronald Leslie Macdonald

Soldiering and Surveying in British East Africa, 1891-1894

ISBN/EAN: 9783337308087

Printed in Europe, USA, Canada, Australia, Japan

Cover: Foto ©Andreas Hilbeck / pixelio.de

More available books at **www.hansebooks.com**

SOLDIERING AND SURVEYING

IN

BRITISH EAST AFRICA

1891—1894

BY

MAJOR J. R. L. MACDONALD, R.E.

WITH MAPS AND ILLUSTRATIONS

EDWARD ARNOLD
LONDON   NEW YORK
37 BEDFORD STREET   70 FIFTH AVENUE
Publisher to the India Office
1897

PREFACE.

As Chief Engineer of the preliminary survey for the Uganda Railway, I had opportunities of acquiring a knowledge of the country between Mombasa and the Victoria Nyanza that do not fall to the lot of the ordinary traveller. My inquiry into the religious disturbances in Uganda gave me an intimate insight into the politics of that country; and as Acting-Commissioner I played a part in the stirring times that heralded the advent of our Uganda Protectorate. Having thus seen the old order and the new, I have ventured in this book, instead of merely confining myself to my personal experiences, to do justice to the work of others, and give a more or less connected account of the events that led up to and secured our influence and authority on the fertile uplands of British East Africa.

Such is the object of the book. It remains for me to express my thanks to those who assisted in its execution. I would acknowledge the help that was given me by my wife and sister in the earlier stages; by my friend Dr. George David Knight, who corrected the proofs; by Majors G. H.

Sim and C. B. Mayne, of the Royal Engineers, who assisted in the reproduction of the maps; and by Lieutenant H. H. Austin, of the Royal Engineers, who placed at my disposal his copies of the photographs that were taken on the preliminary survey of the Uganda Railway.

CONTENTS.

CHAPTER I.

PRELIMINARY ARRANGEMENTS AND START FROM MOMBASA.

                                                                      PAGE

Appointed Chief Engineer of the railway survey from Mombasa to the Victoria Nyanza—In London—Imperial British East Africa Company—Mr. Ernest Gedge—My staff—The estimates—My old Khalassies—Mombasa—Preparations for the survey—Mortality among donkeys—Preliminary survey—Dense jungle—Taru and Sabaki River routes—Difficulty in starting—Departure of caravans from Mombasa 1

CHAPTER II.

TO MACHAKO'S.

The second division—Waterless tract—The Wabura—Camp flooded—Tsavo River—Masai war-paths—A snake-bite, and a native remedy—First division—The donkeys—Ribi—A fight with bees—Giriama country—Cheap pineapples—Makangeni Fort—Stranded Arab contract caravan—Evicted by red ants—Lugard Falls—Alum-water—Good line for railway—Twining and Austin survey the Athi—Kilimanjaro—Invalids—Dr. Stewart—Salt and Kiboko Rivers—Disappearance of Europeans—A fatal encounter with bees—Nzoi—More bees—Panorama from Nzoi—Machako's 12

CHAPTER III.

UKAMBANI—COMPANY'S SETTLEMENT AND FIGHTING.

Ukambani—Kibwezi—Scottish Mission—Masai and Dr. Moffat—Ulu—The Wakamba—Spirits and pombe—The sacrificial goat—Organization of the Wakamba—Their war-tactics—Masai raids—Arab slave caravans—Machako's—A Company's agent in trouble with the Wakamba—Nelson and Ainsworth in Kilungu—A hostile chief—Ainsworth decides on action against the Wakamba—His success - - - - - - 34

CHAPTER IV.

MACHAKO'S TO LAKE NAIVASHA.

Food difficulties—Depots formed—Sotik and Guash Ngishu parties—Masai hunting-grounds—Our first rhinoceros—Rock-pools of Bondani—A cheetah—Pringle meets two lions—Hide-and-seek with a rhinoceros—Athi River—Partiality of hyænas for donkeys—Kikuyu—Mau escarpment—A Masai alarm and demand for hongo—Austin and myself fall ill—Naivasha—Martin arrives from Uganda—Masai become friendly—Martin announces serious fighting in Uganda—This slightly alters our plans - - - - - - - - 49

CHAPTER V.

NAIVASHA TO UGANDA.

A pause at Naivasha—A small Masai entertainment—Arrival of second food consignment under Pringle—He carries off twenty Masai women—The survey party divides—Smith and Martin—Pringle crosses Mau—An exciting encounter with natives—A Masai fight—Kariandus—Too friendly Masai—A battle with the Elmoran avoided—Lake Nakuro—Twining falls ill—We cross the equator—A nasty obstacle for the railway—A forest path—We suffer from cold—The Guaso Masa—A baboo involuntarily examines a game-pit—The Nzoia Falls—The divisions unite—Satisfactory result of their work—Small-pox—Kavirondo and Usoga—Met by Williams at Mengo—Introduced to Lugard—We visit Mwanga—Lugard decides to accompany us to the coast - - - - - - - 63

CHAPTER VI.

LUGARD'S CHRISTIAN WAR.

The civil war in Uganda—Friction between Roman Catholics and Protestants in 1889—Captain Lugard arrives—Williams' good management—The spark that caused the flame—Positions of the opposing armies—The Battle of Mengo—Victory of Protestants—Catholics take refuge in Bulingugwe—They again prove troublesome—Protestants capture the island—Unpleasant

CONTENTS

position of the Roman Catholic missionaries—Lugard proves equal to the occasion—Difficulties in Chagwe, Buddu, and with the Mohammedans—Williams captures Sese—Mwanga returns to the capital—Redistribution of territory—Discontent of the Roman Catholics - 78

CHAPTER VII.

UGANDA TO KIBWEZI.

Lugard joins the survey caravan—Wakoli—Lugard's mail-man reports his comrade has been murdered—Lugard desires war, and sends back for Wasoga contingent—Mail-man's report proves false—The Wasoga are with difficulty prevented from fighting—More donkey fatalities at Mumia's—Lugard pays me a compliment—Guaso Masa in flood—Bridging—Guash Ngishu plains—Incessant rain and no fires—Tents perched on ant-hills—Dualla and the Masai—Reach Kikuyu, where Lugard leaves us—Hear that despatches from Her Majesty's Government have missed me—Interesting talk with Masai—We dig for water—Pringle has a little excitement with a rhinoceros—Practicable railway route along the valley of the Salt River—Meet Martin with duplicates of my lost despatches—Find I must return to Uganda—Hand over my estimates to Pringle, and bid good-bye to the survey staff—Eno's Fruit Salt as a specific for cattle-raiding—Arrive at Kikuyu, and await further orders - - 92

CHAPTER VIII.

FIGHTING IN KIKUYU.

Kikuyu and the Wakikuyu—Their villages—How they raid the Masai—The Imperial British East Africa Company at Kikuyu—Dagoretti Fort—Wilson—Fort Smith—Trouble with the Waguruguru—Purkiss—He applies to me for assistance—The Guruguru expedition—Its complete success—A murderous attack on Purkiss—Refractory native sat upon—My next visit to Fort Smith—More trouble with natives—Nelson—Assault on Wyaki's village—In 1893 the Wakikuyu again make trouble—Serious attack on Fort Smith—More forts required - - 108

CHAPTER IX.

RETURN TO UGANDA, AND SHORT ACCOUNT OF THE COUNTRY.

Conflicting orders—A few hours' delay, and an unnecessary walk of 500 miles—Masai outrage on the Kiboko River—Bishop Tucker

x   CONTENTS

—My first lion—Splendid sport—Food depot at Naivasha—
A false alarm—I cross the splendid grazing-ground of the
Masai—Unexpected visitors in the forest of Mau—I scull the
whole caravan across the Nzoia River—The Nile—Uganda—
The founder of the royal race—The kingdom increases in size
—Court etiquette—Provincial chiefs—The Katikiro—Taxation
and obligatory labour—Supplies for Government caravans—
War organization—Waganda weapons—Spearmen—Their battle
array—The missionaries—What they have effected   -   -   127

CHAPTER X.

WAR AGAINST THE WAVUMA.

My work in Uganda—The Wavuma and their islands—Agriculturists and fishermen—Their industries—Outlook for the future
—Wars with Uganda—Mtesa resolves to conquer Uvuma—He
finds it difficult — The Wavuma are victorious — They wax
arrogant—Captain Williams undertakes an expedition against
them — Major Smith and myself accompany him — Roman
Catholics stand aloof—Trouble feared with the Mohammedans
—Our tactics—Pursuit of the enemy's fleet—Shoals—A land
fight—The prisoners—A cunning old fellow—The naval battle
—Difficulty in firing the Maxims—Bravery of one of our
opponents—An exciting chase—The enemy's fleet broken up—
We land on Uvuma—The Sekiwala is killed—The booty—The
chief of Uvuma submits—I am obliged to return to Uganda—
Conclusion of the campaign—Williams makes admirable terms
of peace—The Wavuma become friendly   -   -   -   145

CHAPTER XI.

SIR GERALD PORTAL'S WORK.

The Imperial British East Africa Company withdraws from Uganda
—Sir Gerald Portal on his way to the country to decide
whether the British Government shall take it over—Captain
Lugard's repartition of Uganda—Mohammedans begin to prove
aggressive—They cultivate friendship with Selim Bey—Williams
paves the way for Sir Gerald Portal—The Soudanese—Sir Gerald
Portal decides on retention of Uganda—Three problems—The
Unyoro forts—Catholics obtain extension of territory—Mohammedans threaten open rebellion—Sir Gerald Portal leaves for
the coast, and I become Acting Commissioner   -   -   -   169

CONTENTS

CHAPTER XII.

FIRST CONTEST BETWEEN CHRISTIANS AND MOHAMMEDANS.

When Mohammedanism appeared in Uganda — Mtesa — First Europeans to reach Uganda—Christian missions—The White Fathers of Algiers—Mwanga—He proves hostile to the missions —Bishop Hannington—Persecution of Christians—' Mackay of Uganda '—Mwanga deposed by united Mohammedans and Christians — Kiwewa made King — Mohammedans become masters of the country—Kiwewa deposed—Karema made King —Christians oppose Mohammedans—Mwanga, at head of Christians, takes the field—Missionaries join him at Bulingugwe — Apollo — Karema fails to grasp an opportunity — Christians under Apollo triumph—Mwanga once more King— Mohammedans prove troublesome—Apollo moves against them —Situation of opposing armies—Great battle, and a doubtful victory—Mohammedans finally overcome—Cultivation suffers —Justice is done to native Christians   -   -   -   -   179

CHAPTER XIII.

SECOND MOHAMMEDAN WAR (LUGARD'S).

Uganda in 1890—Internal and external trouble—Friction between Catholics and Protestants—Mr. Gedge represents the Imperial British East Africa Company—Lugard arrives and takes command—The second Mohammedan war—Lugard's force— His proffered terms to the Mohammedans — Battle at the Kyangora River, and victory of Christians—Kowar—Lugard, advised by the Waganda, gives up the campaign—Average rates of marching—Lugard goes to Buddu—Negotiations with the Mohammedans—De Winton—Disquieting reports regarding the Mohammedans—Negotiations prove successful -   ·   -   196

CHAPTER XIV.

EVENTS THAT LED TO THE THIRD MOHAMMEDAN WAR.

What led to the last Mohammedan war—Lugard leaves for England, and Williams is left in charge—Anxious position—His generosity —Misgivings about the Mohammedans—Robberies and murders —Mohammedan intrigues—A crisis—Both sides prepare for war—Williams succeeds in preserving peace—Arrival of Sir

Gerald Portal—General state of affairs—Trouble all around—
Enlistment of Soudanese — Unenlisted to be brought into
Uganda — Counter-orders — Kibibi — Mohammedan problem—
Mohammedans become independent, and claim more territory—
The attitude of Selim Bey—Villiers—A deadlock with Selim
Bey — Sir Gerald Portal demands an explanation — Captain
Raymond Portal—A farewell durbar—Sir Gerald Portal leaves
for the coast   -   -   -   -   -   -   -   212

CHAPTER XV.

THE LAST FORTNIGHT BEFORE THE OUTBREAK—SELIM BEY'S INTRIGUES.

Mohammedan chiefs interview Selim Bey—Their combined plot—
My first duty as Commissioner—Selim Bey tests the strength
of the new administration—Talk with Juma—Selim Bey is
sent to Port Alice for his health—Owen wishes despatches sent
after Sir Gerald Portal—Situation in Unyoro—I send Sir Gerald
Portal an account of affairs in Uganda—His reply—Selim Bey
takes up an attitude of defiance—The baraza—Sir Gerald Portal
approves of my negotiations—Mohammedan war-drums are
beaten—Selim Bey sends me a mutinous message—I decide on
a rapid initiative—Europeans consider my defeat as almost
inevitable—A busy night—Safety of the missionaries—Recall
of Sir Gerald Portal—Why I did so   -   -   -   -   226

CHAPTER XVI.

THE CRISIS—VICTORY AT RUBAGA.

An important day—An early visit from the Katikiro—My plans—I
am supported by both missions—Non-appearance of Reddie and
Gedge—I decide to act without them—I visit the Mohammedan
quarter—Fairly satisfactory result—Reason of non-arrival of
Reddie and Gedge—The Mohammedans are prepared for war—
Mr. Gedge places his caravan at my disposal—Departure of
Roman Catholic missionaries for Buddu — Disarmament of
Soudanese — Small Mohammedan settlement near the fort
cleared out—The Mohammedans decide on a bold stroke—
Topographical details—The order of battle—The battle of
Rubaga—A complete victory for us—My reserve join in the
pursuit, and I have to forego an immediate advance on Port
Alice—Fort Kampala is put in a thorough state of defence—
Excellence of my staff   -   -   -   -   -   -   242

CHAPTER XVII.

FALL OF SELIM BEY—UGANDA SAVED.

Captain Arthur—The victorious army at last returns—Disquieting news as to Selim Bey's movements—I offer terms to the Mohammedan party in the provinces—We set out—Port Alice—I place my men, and make arrangements in case I am taken prisoner—I advance with six men—The Soudanese are disarmed—Arrest of Selim Bey—His trial and punishment—The Soudanese take the oath of allegiance—The larger bulk of the Mohammedans desire war—A Protestant and Roman Catholic army is collected—Reported capture of Owen and Grant—I report to Sir Gerald Portal—He again approves of my measures—His own movements—Mr. Gedge leaves for the coast—The Soudanese reserve increases in numbers—I feel confident as to the future of Uganda - - - - - - 261

CHAPTER XVIII.

OWEN VICTORIOUS IN UNYORO—CLOSE OF THE CAMPAIGN.

The two Mohammedan parties—The Mohammedans retire before the combined Christian army—What happened in the Unyoro forts — Alarmist reports circulated by Mohammedans — The 'unenlisted' hatch plots—Owen and Grant in danger of assassination—A stroke of genius—Mohammedans seem desirous of peace—Suddenly they break off all communications, and march away—Owen follows—A successful engagement, and a satisfactory result — Distribution of land — Monseigneur Hirth—Mohammedans proceed to take their old provinces by force—I give them a threefold choice, and take rapid action—Koki—Finish of the campaign—Mohammedans cease to be of importance—Villiers—The people of Koki—Excellent work by Villiers and Reddie - - - - - - - 275

CHAPTER XIX.

CONCENTRATION AND PREPARATION AGAINST KABAREGA.

Sir Gerald Portal's views—Major Owen's report—Our number of troops—Kabarega as an enemy—How I settled about the evacuation of Salt Lake and Toru—A big scheme of immigration—Distribution of the Soudanese—Immigration successfully accomplished — I increase the military force — The various garrisons—Peaceable occupations—I become bricklayer and

sail-maker—A little excitement about slaves—A big capture—
The liberation of the Lendus—How it was managed—Smith
and Martin express surprise at the improved state of affairs—
Arrangements made for expedition against Kabarega - - 293

CHAPTER XX.

UNYORO EXPEDITION.

Arrival of Colonel Colvile—Declaration of war against Unyoro—
History of Unyoro—Major Owen defeats Chikakure—Organiza-
tion of expedition—The march—Occupation of Kabarega's
capital—Bush fighting—Kabarega starved out—Owen's dash to
Wadelai—Defeat of Kabarega—Successful close of the campaign
—Conclusion - - - - - - - - 307

GLOSSARY - - - - 323

INDEX - - - - - - 325

LIST OF MAPS AND ILLUSTRATIONS.

KILIMANJARO. (*From sketch by the Author*) - - *Frontispiece*
THE ADMINISTRATOR'S BUNGALOW. (*From photograph by Lieut.
P. G. Twining, R.E.*) - · · - *To face page* 6
LUGARD'S FALLS ON THE SABAKI. (*From photograph by Lieut.
P. G. Twining, R.E.*) - · · - *To face page* 22
BUYING FLOUR. (*From photograph by Lieut. P. G. Twining, R.E.*)
To face page 50
DEPOT AT LAKE NAIVASHA. (*From photograph by Lieut. P. G.
Twining, R.E.*) · · · · - *To face page* 64
CAMP ON THE VICTORIA NYANZA. (*From sketch by the Author*)
To face page 86
OUR SUPPLY OF FOOD. (*From photograph by Lieut. P. G. Twining,
R.E.*) · · · · - *To face page* 96
SECTION OF UGANDA RAILWAY. (*Drawn by the Author*) ,, ,, 106
A TYPICAL CAMP. (*From photograph by Lieut. P. G. Twining,
R.E.*) · · · · · - *To face page* 132
MAP OF UVUMA EXPEDITION. (*Drawn by the Author*) ,, ,, 146
UVUMA FROM UZIRI. (*From sketch by the Author*) - ,, ,, 156
PURSUIT OF ENEMY'S FLEET. (*From sketch by the Author*)
To face page 164
MAP OF MOHAMMEDAN WAR—1889-1890. (*Drawn by the Author*)
To face page 186
MAP OF SECOND MOHAMMEDAN WAR. (*Drawn by the Author*)
To face page 202
MAP OF THIRD MOHAMMEDAN WAR—POSITION AT OUTBREAK OF
HOSTILITIES. (*Drawn by the Author*) - - *To face page* 238
MAP OF THIRD MOHAMMEDAN WAR—FIRST PHASE. (*Drawn by
the Author*) - · · · - *To face page* 260

LIST OF MAPS AND ILLUSTRATIONS

A STORM ON THE VICTORIA NYANZA. (*From sketch by the Author*)
  To face page 270
MAP OF THIRD MOHAMMEDAN WAR—SECOND PHASE. (*Drawn by the Author*) - - - - - To face page 288
THE SLAVE-DEALER'S ISLAND. (*From sketch by the Author*)
  To face page 304
MAP OF UNYORO EXPEDITION. (*Drawn by the Author*) ,, ,, 316
GENERAL MAP TO ILLUSTRATE MAJOR MACDONALD'S WORK. (*Drawn by the Author*) - - - - - - At end

SOLDIERING AND SURVEYING

IN

BRITISH EAST AFRICA.

CHAPTER I.

PRELIMINARY ARRANGEMENTS AND START FROM MOMBASA.

IN August, 1891, I was at Bombay on the point of embarking for England on three months' privilege leave, the first long leave I had obtained during my seven years' service in India. During this time I had worked on the construction of one railway and the survey of two others, as well as on the defences of the North-West Frontier, and had spent an aggregate of over three years with the independent Pathan tribes across the border, amongst whom life could not be said to be monotonous. Now I was looking forward with pleasant anticipations to a short holiday at home.

On the eve of embarking I had to visit my agents to make some final arrangements, when to my surprise they handed me a telegram from headquarters asking if I would accept the post of Chief Engineer of the proposed railway survey from Mombasa to the Victoria Nyanza. After a little consideration I telegraphed my acceptance, adding that I left for England next day, and could settle details on arrival. At Aden a second telegram awaited me, placing me on duty, and directing me to proceed to London without delay and report myself to the India Office. Thus terminated my privilege leave, and commenced my connection with East Africa, which led to the wanderings and adventures that I hope to describe in the following pages. It seems to me that a short account of the hazy period in which the rule of the Imperial British East Africa Company waned, and the British Protectorate arose in its place, may prove of general interest.

On arrival in London I was passed on, with the promise of all assistance I might require, by the India Office to the Treasury, by the Treasury to the Foreign Office, and by the Foreign Office to the Directors of the Imperial British East Africa Company, whom I was destined to serve for the greater part of the succeeding year. The Directors gave me a general idea of what was wanted, and, after providing me with a somewhat bewildering mass of reports, maps, and books, asked me to furnish without delay a scheme of operations which could be carried out in about nine months, and an estimate of the cost of these operations. They emphasized the necessity of providing in the estimates for a sufficient military escort, as it was unfortunately feared that the survey would lead to hostility on the part of certain tribes.

Several days were occupied in digesting the information contained in the reports I have referred to; but my knowledge of the country to be traversed would withal have been somewhat meagre had the Directors not secured the presence of Mr. Ernest Gedge, who had but recently returned from the Jackson-Gedge Expedition to Uganda. I fear I must have considerably tried Mr. Gedge's patience by my thirst for information and by my innumerable questions. His knowledge of East Africa proved of great use to me; and after this interview I felt that I could draw up my estimates with a certain amount of confidence.

The question of military escort was one of some difficulty. The Directors of the Company had suggested a company of native infantry with a Maxim gun, and naturally great weight had to be attached to the deliberate opinions of such authorities; at the same time, a company of native infantry involved a great deal of transport, and added immensely to the cost of the undertaking, which it was necessary to keep within certain limits. After careful consideration, I decided to do without the native infantry, but to increase my survey Khalassies to forty men—an Indian survey Khalassie is a man trained as a chainman, etc.—and I felt confident that many of my old hands, who had served with me beyond the frontier in more than one tight place, would be willing to follow me to Africa. These men, being Pathans and Punjabis, could be depended on to fight if required, and would thus serve the double purpose of chainmen and guard, while there would be less difficulty in feeding them than in the case of regular troops. The Maxim I also decided to dispense with, as it required special ammunition; and it did not appear economical to carry, for a gun that we might not want to fire, some ten loads of ammunition, which would be absolutely useless for the rifles with which our men were to be armed.

While reducing the cost of the expedition in this respect, it was found necessary to increase the European staff in view of the great extent and little-known nature of the country that had to be examined in the brief space of nine months. The final result was the production of a scheme which allowed for the survey expedition taking the field for nine months in two completely self-contained divisions, with the necessary provision for transport, commissariat, and stores. My staff consisted of three Royal Engineer officers accustomed to railway survey work, one of whom was to be of sufficient standing to command the second division when detached. The subordinate establishment amounted to forty-six Indians, including surveyors, draftsmen, hospital assistants, and Khalassies. Two of the Company's local officers, with a due complement of headmen, askaris, porters, and donkeys, were placed in charge of the transport.

The commissariat arrangements allowed for depots of food to be formed at Tsavo, Kibwezi, Machako's, and a point on the Sabaki River, and a stock of trade goods for the purchase of provisions beyond Machako's. For defence we had the Indian Khalassie guard and a certain proportion of the transport caravan armed with Snider carabines; in addition to this, the estimate allowed for the cost of passages, instruments, working out the reports and plans, etc. The calculated cost fell within the limits laid down by superior authority; and I am happy to say that the actual expenditure, when the survey closed its operations, came to a little under the figure I had given.

The estimate and scheme of operations were accepted by the Directors of the Company and by Government; but it was one thing to approve of the scheme, and another to sanction expenditure. In the multitude of offices, as of counsellors, there may ultimately be wisdom, but the immediate and most apparent result is delay. However, I was permitted to engage my staff and make a few other arrangements, which did not mean spending money.

For my second in command, I was fortunate in securing Captain J. W. Pringle, R.E., who had seen a good deal of active service in Burmah, and done much work on the North-West Frontier of India. We had been associated in some trans-frontier work beyond Peshawar, and there I had learned to appreciate his sterling qualities. At this time he was at home on leave, and agreed to join me without delay. In Lieutenants P. G. Twining and H. H. Austin, both of the Royal Engineers, I obtained two valuable assistants, who had previously served under me on two railway surveys, and whose zeal and capabilities I thus thoroughly understood. With such a staff, I felt that if the survey failed I must blame myself alone.

The two latter officers were in India, and to Lieutenant Twining was entrusted the task of collecting the necessary Indian subordinates and Khalassies—a task which he carried out satisfactorily. As I had anticipated, my old Khalassies came forward willingly to serve in what must have appeared to them a most remote and unheard-of region. Throughout the expedition they did their work loyally and well, and bore its hardships with patience and cheerfulness. I am glad to say that, with but one exception, a poor fellow who died of fever at Fort Smith, all ultimately returned in safety to their homes.

Meanwhile, I had been occupied, with the assistance of Captain Pringle, in making out complete lists of instruments, stores, and provisions required; and so when, after several weeks of exasperating delay, the authorities suddenly told me one Monday morning that all the survey stores must be purchased, packed, and embarked on the British India steamer *Madura* by the following Saturday, we were just able to do it by working like slaves during that week. Captain Pringle and I left London on November 6th by P. and O. express for Brindisi, and reached Aden on the 17th of the same month. At Aden we were joined by the Indian contingent under Lieutenant Twining, and the combined staff then embarked on the *Madura* for Mombasa.

The voyage was very pleasant, the sea being so smooth that not even the worst sailor amongst us could complain; while Captain Avern kept us amused by countless dry anecdotes of the early days of the Company's rule, when the law of the survival of the fittest had not weeded out the bad bargains amongst the numerous staff at Mombasa. The only port we called at was Lamu, where we anchored for the day at the mouth of the creek, about one and a half miles below the old

Arab town. On the north the land lay low, and was covered with scrub, amidst which rose groves of palms; but the most interesting sight to an engineer was the old Arab battery, which was supposed to guard the entrance. It bore a distinct resemblance to those quaint old engravings showing the siege-battery of the wars of the Parliament, and might well be preserved as an interesting relic. On the south rose a small rounded hill, on which the shifting sands were constantly laying bare skeletons of victims in some great fight, the details of which must be for ever hidden in the legendary past. Near the town a few German merchants, evidently imbued with the traditional characteristics of their Fatherland, have settled. I had been obtaining information from Captain Avern regarding the exports and imports of the East African ports, and asked him what the imports of Lamu consisted of. 'Pilsener beer and soft soap,' was the reply. And the exports? 'Empty Pilsener beer-bottles.'

From Lamu a single day's run brought us off the port of Mombasa, and we at last saw a panorama of a portion of the country in which our labours were to lie. I must say that the prospect, with its dense vegetation and graceful palm-groves backed by the Rabai Hills, was far from cheering from the standpoint of a railway survey, though wonderfully beautiful from an artistic point of view. We could see at a glance some of the difficulties that lay before us if the tangled mass of wood extended far into the interior. But such thoughts were swiftly banished as we threaded our way between the coral reefs that line the coast, and slowly sailed into the harbour itself. We glided past the low palms of English Point, and past the fine old castle, towards the line of imposing Arab houses glistening white in the sunlight, which fronted the harbour on the south. In the farther distance could be seen the comfortable-looking buildings of the Freretown Mission, half concealed by shady trees.

The anchor was scarcely dropped, when a number of the Company's employés came on board and gave us a warm welcome to Mombasa. We were soon busily occupied in landing men and stores, but it was not till the following day, November 25th, 1891, that we had our people comfortably camped in a mango tope at Kilindini. Mr. Berkeley, the Company's administrator, put his own bungalow at the disposal of the officers; indeed, throughout our stay on the coast he showed us such hospitality and kindness as it is seldom one's lot to receive.

Mombasa is an island blocking the mouth of a bay which runs far inland, and is separated from the mainland by a channel about 500 yards wide, and fordable at low tide, while north and south extend deep and sheltered harbours. The smaller of these, Mombasa, lies to the north, and was the more used, while to the south lies Port Ritz, a magnificent natural harbour in which we could anchor a fleet several times as large as our East African squadron. The Arab town of Mombasa was at one time of even greater importance than when we saw it, and had, with its castle, been the scene of much fighting between the Arabs and Portuguese in the seventeenth century. The grim old castle could tell many tales of gallant deeds, perhaps not chronicled in despatches, and bears over its gateway an inscribed slab which tells how it was recaptured by the Portuguese after many futile assaults. In 1891 it was an imposing pile, though so ruinous as to have little defensive value, and was occupied by a company of Zanzibar troops, who displayed the Sultan's red flag from the lofty flagstaff. The actual town was clean and in good order, which said much for the Company's administration. There were a good many native shops, and a useful co-operative store which had been started by the Directors for the convenience of their employés. But the days of retrenchment had already set in, and masses of engineering plant which had never been erected, or had fallen into disuse, were stacked about the place, and had rather a depressing effect on the visitor.

At Mombasa we found that considerable preparations had been made for the survey before our arrival. Two of the Company's officers had been told off for transport duties. One of these, Mr. Jackson, had joined us at Lamu, but the other was somewhere between Machako's and the coast on the Athi or Sabaki River. A fair number of porters were already engaged, and 120 donkeys had been purchased; but as they had been kept on the island, which is not healthy for transport animals, about 50 or 60 had died before we landed, and others were evidently desirous of following the bad example thus set. Hyænas also attacked the donkey sheds on more than one occasion, and caused a good many casualties, so that in donkey transport we were not up to the mark. Depots were being formed at Tsavo, Kibwezi and Machako's, and Lugard's first stockade on the Sabaki River, near Makangeni, had been temporarily occupied, while an officer was engaged in cutting a road from Makangeni to Lugard's second stockade on the same river.

But much still remained to be done before we could start for the interior. Our complement of porters was incomplete, and in view of the mortality of the donkeys it was essential to still further strengthen the porter transport. Then all the survey kit, stores, and provisions had to be separated into loads of 65 lbs. gross, in such a way as to allow for two independent field divisions, and this involved no little labour. Many of the things we did not want during our work in the coast regions were sent off by contract caravan to Machako's, three hundred miles up country, to await our arrival, but we had still a considerable quantity of baggage to carry with us.

While this was being done at Mombasa, Captain Pringle and I led two small preliminary parties into the coast hills.

Our objects were to reconnoitre for a feasible ascent on to the first step of the interior plateau, some fifteen miles inland, to see if a system of triangulation beyond this was feasible, and also to gain a little experience, however slight, of what caravan work was like. Pringle went south-west, while I headed directly west. Our experiences are not worth entering into minutely; suffice it to say that we found a railway route, and that triangulation was impossible in the time at our disposal, owing to the hills being so densely wooded.

The discomforts of this preliminary canter were considerable; it rained on the average twice a day, and on one occasion my camp went astray. We laboriously cut our way through dense jungle to the summit of a commanding hill, only to find that the view did not extend to a greater distance than fifty yards. We realized the pleasures of chaining a base in long wet grass, full of holes and pools of water in which the chainmen not infrequently took an involuntary bath, a proceeding not conducive to accuracy in measurement. To add to my discomfort, my interpreter was a fraud as regards his knowledge of English, and supplemented it by a barbarous lingo which he called Hindustani, but which had little resemblance to the Hindustani spoken in India. When we got back to Mombasa after five days of this sort of thing, we both agreed that survey work in the interior could not be classed as altogether amusing!

By December 17th our arrangements were complete. Captain Pringle in command of the second division, to which were attached Lieutenant Austin and Mr. Jackson, was to survey the ordinary caravan route viâ Taru and Teita to Tsavo, and there await the arrival of the first division under my charge. This division, at the special request of the Directors, was to investigate the route viâ the Sabaki River, which had been favourably reported on by Captain Lugard.

On December 18th the second division got under way, and

the start was most trying to the temper, though not without its ludicrous aspect. Every detail had been arranged the day before; but the Swahili porter, as long as he is within reach of the drink-shops of the coast, is a mortal on whose action no reliable forecast can be based. A good many men were absent, and others paraded late; some objected to their loads, while others energetically seized a box or a bale and vanished into the surrounding jungle. Ultimately, after much noise and not a little unparliamentary language, the division marched off, with its drums beating; and then Twining and I picked up and collected the remaining loads, and sent twenty of our men to carry them to Pringle's camp, which was for that night to be on the mainland, just beyond the ford.

The donkeys had now to be got off, and this was even more difficult. They were laboriously loaded; and then, when the first one started, the whole crowd would follow with a rush, all trying to proceed in a close body along a narrow path that was only meant for one. The result was a sort of football scrimmage, during which most of the animals succeeded in getting rid of their loads, to the accompaniment of frantic braying. The whole comedy was then enacted again from the beginning, and each scrimmage saw the donkey caravan about a hundred yards on its way. With this by no means rapid rate of progression, it is hardly necessary to say that when the donkeys got to the ford the tide had risen so much that, after nearly drowning one, we had to pronounce the passage impossible for that day. The loads were sent to Pringle's camp, and the donkeys returned to their sheds triumphant. Next morning they were handed over to Pringle, who reported that nearly all his missing porters had also turned up, and that he would move inland the following day.

I determined to await the next mail from home, as it might contain further orders. The first division moved into camp at English Point on December 23rd, preparatory to a start next day, as I did not wish to run the risk of having my caravan demoralized by the Christmas festivities at Mombasa. On the 24th we marched to Coroa Mombasa—a line of three small hills about seven miles from English Point—without so much trouble as had attended the departure of the other division, but still with the loss of a few deserters. Having thus seen both divisions away from Mombasa, we may fittingly close this preliminary chapter.

CHAPTER II.

TO MACHAKO'S.

THE second division, under Captain Pringle, was proceeding by the recognised trade route viâ Taru and Teita, which was well known to all the porters, and after a few days these settled down to their work very satisfactorily. The donkeys, too, got used to their loads, and did well. As far as Taru water could be obtained every march, except in years of great drought, and as the present season was very wet, there was no difficulty in this respect. Beyond Taru, however, there was a waterless stretch to Maungu—a rocky hill some thirty-five miles distant by road. The ordinary trading caravan generally did this in one march, doing as much as possible by night, and having one or more halts in the middle. But this procedure was of course impossible in the case of the survey, and we estimated that it would take about three days to march across and survey this inhospitable tract. As we could depend on water at both ends, we required to carry a supply for two days only. At a pinch the men's water-bottles held enough for one day, and empty kerosene-oil tins in rough wooden cases were provided to hold rather more than a day's supply. These were carried on the donkeys, which had so far travelled rather light.

As a matter of fact, the water question between Taru and Maungu was much simplified by heavy rain, and Pringle was able to camp for one night by a pool of rain-water. His reserve in the kerosene tins thus easily tided him on to Maungu, where there was a large rocky pool about 1,000 feet above the camping-ground. Another march led to Teita, a flat-topped cultivated hill. Beyond Teita rose the Bura Hills, also densely inhabited by the Wabura, who are practically the same tribe as the Wateita, so accurately described by the late Joseph Thomson in his book 'Across Masai-land.' These people have generally had a good reputation, frequently travel to the coast, and in recent years have freely engaged as porters.

In 1892, however, the Wabura became rather defiant, and Captain Nelson, of Starvation Camp fame, was sent by the Company to punish them. He had only a small and indifferent force, and in advancing up the steep and rugged hills met with stubborn resistance. The Wabura more than once stood till Nelson got within twenty yards, and made warm practice with their arrows, even in face of his breech-loading rifles; progress was so slow that he found he could not reach the summit by sunset, and so encamped for the night in a strong position half-way up, where during the darkness he was more than once attacked. The following day he pushed on to the summit of the range, and the Wabura immediately submitted, as Nelson was now complete master of the situation. Since this one lesson they have remained very friendly, and have supplied food for passing caravans.

From Teita, where some interesting work was done, Pringle pushed on to Ndi, where he camped on the bank of a mountain stream, swollen to a torrent by the recent rains. Ndi is on the plain just at the foot of the Bura Hills. It is now the site of a small post for the purchase and storage of grain for the transport service to Uganda.

In the middle of the night there was a sudden alarm, and the officers hurried from their tents to find that the mountain stream had burst its banks higher up, and was now rushing furiously through the camp, and threatening to sweep away everything before it. All hands were turned out, and had to work for several hours in partial darkness before the stream could be diverted. Standing nearly the whole time in water, officers and men raised banks and dug channels till the worst was over. Next morning the camp presented a woeful appearance, being ankle-deep in mud, and, in spite of every effort, some of the tents and huts had disappeared in the confusion. The trees round the camping-ground were festooned with damp clothing, hung out to dry; but a few hours of warm sunshine soon revived the spirits of the party. Without further adventure the second division reached the Tsavo stockade on January 11th, 1892, and encamped comfortably to await the arrival of the first division, which was marching up the Sabaki.

With the exception of the cultivation near the coast, and on the summits of the Teita and Bura Hills, the whole country traversed had been jungle. Sometimes, indeed, it was thin and open, and frequented by game, but for the most part close, with, in many places, great masses of impenetrable aloe thickets. The trees were small and thorny, and of a somewhat monotonous and depressing colour. A little sport had been obtained by Mr. Jackson, but the other members of the division had shot nothing up to date, and were rather inclined to think the East African shikar had been overrated. Mr. Jackson, however, consoled them with the assurance that they would change their opinion when they saw the Masai plains.

The Tsavo River rises in the snows of Kilimanjaro, flows through a gap between the Bura and Kyulu Hills, and joins the Athi River a few miles below the Company's stockade. At ordinary times it is fordable, with a width of about fifty to sixty feet, but in the rains it appears to attain a depth of over twenty feet, and a width of over a hundred. It is a fine stream, abounding with fish, of which three or four varieties were caught. The upper course of the river is through open grass plains, where game is abundant, but after passing through the line of hills already mentioned, it enters a jungle region in which numerous rocky outcrops occur. The banks of the river are well defined, and clad with luxuriant vegetation which marks the course of the river by a band of vivid green, contrasting strongly with the more sombre thorn jungle.

Along each bank of the river runs a Masai war-path, the route of this warlike tribe when raiding coastwards. The Company's stockade was originally located on the Tsavo River to bar these paths, and appears to have answered its purpose. A thrilling report of his engagement with the Masai was furnished by the founder of the stockade. He had only a small force at his disposal, but, from his account, sallied forth and attacked a returning war-party laden with spoil. The battle was severe, and the Company's representative apparently performed every military evolution that is mentioned in the drill-book, with the result that he defeated the Masai with great loss, and captured their flocks and herds. This gentleman, however, although of undoubted capacity, had the reputation of being highly proficient in the use of the longbow, and subsequent reports from other sources gave a very different account. Apparently, a few of his men stumbled on a small Masai outpost, and both made strategical movements to the rear. The Commandant sent a small party to see what the Masai meant to do, and then picked up a few goats and sheep which these left behind. The bloodshed was a picturesque detail subsequently introduced. Which report is true I cannot venture to say, but the latter is the one commonly believed.

When we saw it, the Tsavo post was very strong, but had a weak garrison. A formidable stockade enclosed quarters for the Commandant, and one or two storehouses and huts for the garrison, and as it was built on the bank of the river, the water-supply was secure, and the ground was fairly clear for about a couple of hundred yards.

Captain Pringle had no sooner established his division at Tsavo, than he started with a small body to survey a route south of the hills towards Taru. A Wakamba cattle-track made marching easy, but there was little water till the Voi River was reached. On his way back to Tsavo one of his porters was bitten by a poisonous snake, and in a short time the poor fellow's leg swelled up till he was quite unable to walk; he rapidly grew worse, and appeared, in the course of a few hours, to be a doomed man. One of his compatriots, however, applied some native remedies, the nature of which he carefully concealed. The porter had to be carried back to camp on an improvised stretcher, but ultimately recovered, whether on account of the secret remedy, or because the bite was less poisonous than had been imagined, it is impossible to say.

Meanwhile, the first division had a more difficult task before them. We had been congratulating ourselves that we had got off with less trouble than the other division—a clear case of hallooing before we were out of the wood. Just after daybreak on Christmas morning, 1891, the caravan started on a long march to Ribi, which is a small mission-station on the coast hills. The path lay through jungle and forest, and after the recent rain was marshy in places, while early in the day a nasty mangrove swamp had to be crossed. This, though pestilential enough, offered little difficulty to the porters, and Twining, with this portion of the caravan, pushed ahead, and reached Ribi without mishap.

It was very different with the poor donkeys, which, as has already been mentioned, were weak, the stronger having been handed over to the second division to carry water through the

Taru Desert. They had very light loads, not exceeding 60 to 70 lbs., but even so it became apparent that progress would be extremely slow. It required nearly two hours to cross the mangrove creek, and though the loads were passed over by hand, it took a lot out of the animals. The rest of that day was like a nightmare. Every few yards a donkey or two would lie down, and the numerous pitfalls and bog-holes along the path appeared to offer irresistible attractions to the weary beasts. By mid-day, what with picking up donkeys, hauling them out of swamps, and readjusting loads, the Somali drivers were in a state of complete exhaustion, and more than half the day's march was yet before us. I had, however, a few Swahilis with me, and we struggled forward till sunset, when I pushed on to camp in order to send men back for the loads. This, as it turned out, was unnecessary, as Twining had already thought of it, and I met the party he had despatched on its way to our assistance. All the loads were in by 10 p.m., but not a single donkey arrived in camp till next morning, even the stoutest of the lot spending the night about two miles off. Next day we found that two of them were dead, and several others were evidently on their last legs; indeed, though we halted at Ribi, we lost one or two the following night. It was certainly a merry Christmas!

At Ribi we were joined by Mr. Foaker, who had marched down the Sabaki River, but his accounts of that route were far from encouraging. He had been obliged to cross numerous swamps, some of them breast-deep, and had generally had a poor time. Much as I would have liked to keep him with us for the transport work, I decided to send him to Mombasa to pick up a few more porters, and then, by rapid marches, to rejoin us at Tsavo. On December 27th we left Ribi, and the caravan marched off well, Twining and I staying behind to survey.

After covering about a couple of miles, we heard a terrific

row going on in front, but, knowing that there could be no danger from natives in this peaceable region, we were not much alarmed. Soon after, a Swahili met us with the information that the caravan had been set upon by bees. When we got up to the scene of the uproar, we found that the caravan had passed on, and a man who had been left to mark the place for us, so that we might avoid it, assured us that it had got through with nothing worse than a few stings. We made a détour till we thought all danger from the hostile glade was over, and then Twining marched off to the left, to continue his work. He soon came rushing back, and at first we all burst out laughing, concluding he, too, had encountered bees. We soon found, however, that it was no laughing matter, for he reported having found a man being stung to death. We two Europeans, with a couple of native volunteers, at once went to the rescue. A buzzing crowd of angry bees completely hid the unfortunate man. We seized him by his arms and legs, and made the best speed we could out of the glade, pursued fiercely by the angry insects, and it was not till we were some way off that they relinquished the pursuit. The sufferer was one of the Indian Khalassies, who, while escaping, had evidently fallen and stunned himself. He was a terrible sight. Although his clothes had protected most of his body, his face, hands, and neck were a mass of stings, which it took some time to extract. He was conscious, but quite blind, and his mouth was so swollen that he could not speak. We judged, however, from a gash on the forehead, that he had fallen against some hidden root and half stunned himself. We dosed him with spirits, and, having made a litter, sent him off to camp.

It now transpired that several loads had been left amongst the bees, which swarmed over nearly an acre of ground. To recover these loads was a difficult matter. The Swahilis were prepared to expose their half-naked bodies when a man's life was in danger, but did not think it essential to do so for the sake of a few bales of cloth, and suggested waiting till nightfall, when the bees would be asleep. But this would not do. There was plenty of combustible material at hand, so we lighted a large fire on the edge of the glade, and threw green stuff on it till we got a cloud of smoke; then a short rush was made, and another fire lighted some five or six yards farther on. This operation was repeated till, under the cloud of pungent smoke, we were able to secure the loads. This would have appeared sufficient mishap and delay for the day, but we had not seen the end of our troubles. While searching for the loads, we found two donkeys which had been stung to death, and on arrival in camp discovered that our surveyor, Sergeant Thomas, had been so badly stung that he was suffering from slight fever.

As the donkey caravan was now practically useless, I sent it back next day to the coast with Sergeant Thomas and the crippled Indian, and a message asking Mr. Berkeley to try and give us instead some more porters. Sergeant Thomas had orders to rejoin us at Tsavo, marching by the Taru route; but when he reached Mombasa, after spending a night in the swamp, he got so ill that he had to remain in hospital for nearly a month, and as a consequence did not pick us up till we reached Machako's.

Being now quit of the donkey incubus, the caravan pushed on more rapidly. Our route lay northwards through the Giriama country, the inhabitants of which are hard-working and industrious, the owners of considerable flocks and herds, and now that, under the Company's protection, they were secure from Galla raids, they appeared to be a flourishing community. Some of their villages were large, and all were more or less enclosed by stockades, with intricate gateways. The country itself varied a good deal; sometimes our way lay through heavy forest, and again amid bush jungle, in which were the scattered clearings of the inhabitants. We seemed incessantly climbing up and down small spurs and ridges, and there was a good deal of cross-drainage, but the only important streams were the Zovoni and the Fuladoya Rivers. The former was a broad but fordable river, with a very rocky bed; the latter, which is supposed to be the river known as the Voi near Teita, was narrow, deep, and sluggish.

Fuladoya itself is a cluster of large villages, occupied partly by runaway slaves, partly by Wagiriama, and the climate is distinctly feverish. Nineteen out of the twenty-two Indians, and nearly a third of the Swahilis who accompanied the first division, were down with fever. Twining, too, was very seedy. The only redeeming feature of the place was the supply of magnificent pineapples, which could be bought in large numbers at the not exorbitant price of four a penny. Just beyond Fuladoya rose the hill of Mangea, and our route lay along the southern base of this striking hill through uninhabited country. The northern slopes, which are well watered, were peopled more or less densely; but a railway-line that way was manifestly hopeless. Two long marches— the second of which lay for miles through the densest growth of cactus and aloe that it has ever been my lot to encounter —now brought us to Makengeni, on the Sabaki River. In many places the path was so narrow, and so enclosed by walls of this impenetrable vegetation, that it was with difficulty that laden porters could get along at all, while frequent pools of black stagnant water poisoned the air.

At Makengeni are the ruins of an old stockade, the first of a series of seven, built by Captain Lugard between the coast and Kikuyu, of which only the sixth is now occupied. It must have necessitated no little labour to construct, and could, even when we saw it, have been without much work rendered defensible. The Sabaki at this point is a shallow river, about eighty yards wide, with a sandy bed, while great walls of shady forest stretch along either bank. Makengeni itself is a small settlement of runaway slaves, who produce only sufficient food for their own consumption, and live in constant dread of raids by the natives beyond the Sabaki.

We found stranded at this old stockade an Arab contract caravan, with stores for the survey depot at Kibwezi, which ought to have reached their destination by this time. A number of the men had deserted, for the Sabaki route is most unpopular with porters, and they had more loads than they could carry. The Arab chief of Takaungu, against whose party military operations became necessary in 1895, had taken the contract, but, as he had received half his price down, did not seem in any hurry to forward the goods. Bags of rice formed the majority of the loads; there were also a few tins of clarified butter for the Indians, while the remainder consisted of trade goods, for the purchase of food up-country. I found out how many porters were deficient in the Arab caravan, and took over rather more than this number of loads of rice to issue as rations, and this enabled the caravan to accompany us on our onward march.

While encamped at Makengeni we had a very unpleasant visitation. We were awakened in the middle of the night by a tremendous noise, and on getting out of my tent I found about half the caravan in a state of nudity, apparently executing a dance round the fires, but not singing the cheery song that generally accompanies this performance. In fact, their exclamations were the reverse of cheerful. It transpired that one-half of the camp had been invaded by an army of large red ants. These ants march in regular columns, with advanced guard, scouts, and flankers, and constitute a formidable and well-drilled army. They had at once attacked the sleeping men, and, needless to say, in a very brief space of time had cleared the camp. Those whose quarters had escaped were busy barring the further progress of the ants by lines of fires and red-hot embers, while the sufferers were engaged in picking the ants off each other. This operation is not by any means easy, as the ant will part with its body rather than release the hold it has obtained with its powerful jaws. As a consequence, the first proceeding is to tear off the body, and then pick off the head and jaws, which remain fixed in the flesh. In three-quarters of an hour or so the legions of ants had marched on, and the camp resumed its normal condition. The progress of these insects through grass causes a curious hissing sound not unlike that of a snake. On one occasion, while sitting by the roadside with Mr. Jackson, we were startled by this ominous hiss, and sprang to our feet, imagining we were attacked by a snake, but were relieved to find it was only the noise made by the advance guard of a column of these red ants.

There was not much of incident in our march from Makengeni to the second stockade, a small earthwork about fifty miles up the river. We met the road-cutting officer, a perfect wreck from fever, returning to the coast. He warned us against a wounded buffalo near the path, but it did not put in an appearance, somewhat to our disappointment. Twining, who was ahead, stumbled one day on a hippopotamus grazing in a small glade, but the great beast got off safely to the river. During the march I suffered from my second attack of fever, and both Indians and Swahilis were frequently down with it. Our first night from Makengeni was marked by the desertion *en masse* of one headman, two askaris, and twenty of our porters; seventeen of them, however, were subsequently recaptured by Mr. Fitzgerald. We saw little game, but I succeeded in bagging a rather rare antelope.

At the second stockade we found a small garrison of Beluchis; they had only been there about three months, but looked in a most miserable condition from frequent attacks of

LUGARD'S FALLS ON THE SABAKI.

fever. The mere sight of them was sufficient to cause two-thirds of the Arab contract caravan to at once bolt for the coast. We threw out a cordon of Indians to prevent further desertions; but the Arab headman asked us to call them in, as he had none but thoroughly reliable men left, who could be depended on not to desert. No sooner had the cordon been removed than, with the exception of half a dozen, away went the rest of his men. The Arab now wished me to take over his loads; but this I refused to do, as the contract was that they were to be delivered at Kibwezi, still 100 miles distant. The end of it was that he stacked his goods in the stockade and left them there, we afterwards learned, without a guard, for no sooner had we marched on than the Arabs and Beluchis returned to the coast. After some weeks, however, a relief-party from the coast recovered the loads intact. We were compelled to leave some of our own goods as well, as strong cutting-parties were necessary to clear a road, and the captured deserters had not yet reached us.

The country now changed considerably. The Sabaki was enclosed on the left bank by a well-defined escarpment, and on the right bank numerous rocky spurs ran down to the water's edge. The jungle was for the most part very dense, and for seven weary days we had laboriously to cut our way. The river was full of rapids, and there was one fine fall, which, as it had no name, we called after Captain Lugard, who has written so much about the Sabaki. Really, Mr. Pigott was the first European to follow the course of the Sabaki as far down as Mangea, but Lugard traversed the whole valley from Malindi, at the coast, to the Athi. There was little game, though we bagged a few partridge and guinea-fowl, and saw some water-buck. One day, too, the advanced party was confronted by two lions, but we could not get a shot. At the junction of the Athi and Tsavo Rivers—the Sabaki is only that portion of the main river below this junction—we discovered a letter from Pringle stuck on a stick, and found that he had cut a road for us to his camp. We reached the Tsavo stockade seven days later than the second division, and were not sorry to have got quit of the Sabaki fever, jungle, and swamp. A small party was at once sent back to the second stockade to bring on the loads we wanted; and we set to work on the plans and reports that we had agreed to forward to the Directors from this point, which was about 145 miles from Mombasa by the Taru route, and longer by the Sabaki.

One little incident regarding the water in the Sabaki may be worth mentioning. The river was in flood, and the water full of mud, which would not settle as sand does. As we had some alum with us, we used this to clear the water, and, after one or two successful experiments, entrusted the job to our native servants. A few days afterwards we experienced most uncomfortable internal symptoms. At first we could not imagine whence they proceeded, but, on testing the beautifully clear drinking water furnished by the process, we found that our servants, delighted with the method, had used such a liberal supply of alum that the water possessed astringent powers of the most alarming strength. Disguised in the form of tea, we had not noticed this, beyond thinking that the quality of tea we had been supplied with was most inferior. Moral: Do not allow a Swahili to clear your drinking water with alum.

So far the survey had been successful in finding a good line—that via Taru; the only drawback was want of water, which necessitated a considerable estimate for tanks, etc., at more than one station. The Sabaki route, with a terminus at Mombasa, was not a success. Though the Sabaki Valley afforded a good grade from Makengeni, the country between that point and Mombasa was more than unfavourable, and would have necessitated gradients that utterly discounted any advantage in the Sabaki section. Malindi did not offer a suitable terminal harbour, and the country between Malindi and Makangeni was, from reports, very difficult, owing to what appeared to be settlements in the soil and slips. With Kalifi as a terminus, the prospect by the Sabaki would be better. Kalifi is a land-locked harbour, which, however, cannot compare with those at Mombasa, and is difficult in respect to water-supply. The latter objection is perhaps not so serious, in so far as it applies also to Mombasa, which must ultimately be supplied by pipes from the Rabai plateau. From Kalifi to Makengeni an easy line could have been obtained, but the Directors of the Company were perfectly right in insisting on the terminus of the line being located on the magnificent harbours of Mombasa. With this obligatory point, the line must run more or less along the trade route to Taru, and thence to Tsavo.

There was plenty of work to be done at Tsavo, and Pringle and I were kept busy from morning to night with plans, estimates, and reports. Nor were even our nights altogether periods of rest, as I was most anxious to get an observation of absolute longitude by the occultation of a star, the moon being favourable. At times we sat up till an early hour in the morning, at times were called in the middle of the night, but on every occasion at the critical moment the moon would be hidden by some untoward cloud.

Mr. Foaker joined us here, having succeeded in securing some fresh men at the coast. I sent him ahead to Machako's, 300 miles from Mombasa, to see about the arrangements being made there for the purchase of food and donkeys.

On January 24th Lieutenant Twining, accompanied by Lieutenant Austin, and carrying a food-supply for eighteen days, left to survey the Athi from its junction with the Tsavo to a point ahead of the Nzoi peak, with instructions to make for this peak, where the second point of junction had been decided on. The remainder of the caravan was to survey the ordinary route to Nzoi viâ Kibwezi, but, thanks to work on plans, etc., for the Directors, we did not get off till the 29th of the same month.

Two marches brought us to the pool of Kenani, where, close to some hog-backed granite rocks, there is an unfailing supply of water. The road had been rough and rocky in places, and mostly through jungle, as before ; but one or two glades had been passed, and in one of these Pringle bagged a zebra by a bullet through the neck. To the north-west of Kenani is a gap in the Kyulu Hills, where the Mto Andai River rises, and this gap is used by the Masai when on the war-path. I shall have more to say about these redoubtable warriors later, but at present we encountered none of them. From the top of one of the rocks at Kenani we got our first view of the magnificent snow-peaks of Kilimanjaro. From where we stood they had the most peculiar effect, and seemed, indeed, to be floating in the clouds. The higher summit resembled strongly, though on a vast scale, one of those ribbed marble domes so often to be seen in India, while the other was rocky, with only patches of snow here and there. Almost every day, as we marched towards Nzoi, these grand peaks were visible behind us, though gradually fading away into the dim distance.

During our march to Kibwezi, Pringle and I suffered from fever, and Mr. Jackson, who had been taken ill at Kenani, became rapidly worse, and had to be carried. Fortunately for him, there was a doctor at the newly-founded Scottish Mission at Kibwezi, and he was thus enabled to receive proper treatment. Dr. Moffat did all in his power, but finally, to our great regret, it was decided that Mr. Jackson must abandon the survey expedition, and return to England.

Dr. Stewart and his staff, who had accomplished wonders here in a short time, gave us a warm welcome. In something like nine months this energetic Scotchman had marched to

Machako's, decided against settling there, and, returning to Kibwezi, had laid out and nearly completed the mission-station, to the establishment of which he had so unselfishly given up his time. Very useful roads had been made, and a church was well begun, and many large and comfortable dwellings were already finished. The site he had chosen was certainly a beautiful spot; it lay in the middle of a large park-like glade, on the bank of the Kibwezi stream, which here issued in considerable volume from underneath an overlying mass of lava, and ran parallel to the station. To the north lay the rugged and wooded slopes of the Bwinzau Mountain, and the whole horizon to the west was bounded by the Kyulu Hills, over which appeared the gleaming snows of Kilimanjaro. Everywhere, within easy reach, grew splendid timber, and the surrounding Wakamba settlements were flourishing, and produced a great deal of food, while, the distance from the coast being only 200 miles, it was easy to obtain supplies from Mombasa. The only objection to the site was its low altitude, 3,000 feet above the sea, which in these latitudes is hardly sufficient to enable Europeans to form a colony.

After a short halt in this pleasant spot we pushed on. The exit from the station lay over a rough mass of lava blocks, and when we remarked to the Wakamba that the road might be improved, we were told they had given up attempting to do so, as every time they cleared the road the goats brought back the lava blocks. Our first camp was on the shoulder of Bwinzau, from which we could see the striking peak of Nzoi, marking our immediate objective. The forest land now became more open, while across the great plain that lay between us and the Ulu Mountains ran the Kiboko and Salt Rivers, both large streams. To the north-north-west we could see open grassy uplands with bare rocky hills; these uplands were the forerunners of the great Masai Steppes. The Kyulu

Hills, which had so far bounded our western horizon, ended abruptly, and a well-marked depression, in which rose a jumbled mass of lesser heights, separated them from the mountains of Ulu—the land of plenty. The banks of the Salt and Kiboko Rivers are the haunt of great quantities of game, and here can be obtained the somewhat scarce oryx. Near these rivers are several Masai war-paths, of which more hereafter.

These shooting-grounds have been responsible for the mysterious disappearance of two Europeans. Two gentlemen started from Kibwezi to shoot, and after passing Bwinzau marched off towards the Kyulu Hills, with three natives. After going a short distance they killed a hartebeest, and, leaving two of their followers to get this to camp, pushed on with one boy. They went so fast that the lad could not keep up with them, and eventually lost sight of them altogether. In the meantime the men with the hartebeest returned to camp, whither next day they were followed by the boy, who reported having made many fruitless efforts to find his masters, and had finally been obliged, through fear of wild animals, to spend the night in a tree. Information of the disappearance of the Europeans was at once sent to Kibwezi, when search-parties were organized, and scoured the country, but without effect. The two men, who, it was ascertained, had gone on with only one rifle and not more than four or five cartridges, could not be found, nor was even a trace of them discovered. They may have perished of thirst and been devoured by animals, they may have been killed by lions or slain by Masai, but which of these possibilities actually befell them none can tell.

Two more marches brought us to the Wakamba villages at the foot of Nzoi, where we encamped to await the Athi party, who had not yet arrived. On the latter of these two marches, however, we met with a sad accident, which caused the death of one of our followers. In the neighbourhood of Wakamba settlements the trees are hung with hollow logs, used as beehives, and the Wakamba bee is as pugnacious as the coast variety. The caravan marched close under one of these trees, and the angry insects swarmed down and attacked the rear. The result was the usual stampede. I was behind with a small party surveying, and on arriving on the scene discovered that one unfortunate sick Msoga, who had been riding a donkey, was missing. The donkey, without its rider, had rejoined the rear guard, who had halted well out of reach of the swarm. My gun-bearer and I went back past the fatal tree to see if the poor fellow was there, but there was no sign of him, and we hoped he had slipped into the grass and got out, but on rejoining the rear guard we learned he was still missing. Two natives, an Indian and a Swahili, volunteered to go back with me to search for him in the grass. We set to work quartering the ground near the tree; the bees swarmed down on us, and it was quite impossible to avoid being stung; all we could do was to keep the brutes out of our eyes. After a short time it became too hot for my companions, and they left. It was becoming too hot for me, too, when I stumbled on the Msoga, and, picking him up, ran for it. Some of the rear guard then dashed in to our assistance, and the sick man was carried off about 300 yards, when the bees relinquished the pursuit. The poor fellow, who wore only a loin-cloth, was terribly stung. His body, owing to the innumerable stings left in him, instead of smooth black skin, appeared covered with close brown fur. We dosed him with brandy, removed the stings, and carried him to camp, some two miles distant, when he was placed in the hands of the hospital assistant. But all the latter's care was of no avail, and in about five hours the Msoga died.

It was February 10th when we reached Nzoi, and next day the Athi party marched in, not from the east, as we had expected, but from the north. For five days they had marched along a Wakamba path, which they had found on the right bank of the Athi River, above its junction with the Tsavo. During these days they advanced rapidly, but, unfortunately, the friendly path crossed the river and plunged into the jungle to the eastward, towards the Wakamba settlements on the Tiwa, and Twining's party had then to cut their way through dense bush, when progress was necessarily slow. About January 6th they struck a large tributary of the Athi, which appeared to flow from the direction of Nzoi peak, and the small party, when provisions were nearing an end, marched up this stream for a day. Finding, however, that it trended too much to the west, they struck across country. Next night they camped in the jungle, and the last issue of rations was made. Owing to ravines and bush, the country was extremely difficult, but as their food was practically exhausted two very long marches were made, and then, to Twining's relief, they came upon the Keite River, with numerous Wakamba settlements upon its banks. Here, discovering that they had passed Nzoi, the officers, through dense population and abundant cultivation, marched up the Keite River towards Kilungu, and then south to Nzoi. Round Nzoi there are a great number of small villages, and the friendly Wakamba were soon swarming into the camp, and eagerly bartering supplies of all sorts for trade goods. After the never-changing—except for the couple of days at Kibwezi—diet of rice and beans on the march from the coast, it is not to be wondered at that the men appreciated the plenty of Nzoi, where they could obtain flour and fresh Indian corn, sweet potatoes, bananas, sugar-cane, fowls and eggs *ad libitum*. Nor was there any difficulty about purchasing all they wanted, for, in addition to our issue of beads in lieu of rations, nearly every one of the Swahilis had his own little store of trade goods.

While halted here we determined to ascend Nzoi peak, from which it was evident that a valuable round of angles could be obtained. The natives told us there was one possible track from this side, and pointed out what appeared from the camp a narrow crack running up the stupendous cliffs at an angle of 45° or more; they assured us that we must face this, or else make a détour of one day's journey north or east. They were willing enough to point out the path or track from below, but when we asked for guides we found that superstitious fears held them back. A spirit of exceptional powers was supposed to reside on this lofty peak, and they feared to provoke him by intruding on his barren crags. At last, after a good deal of talk and a handsome present, two daring men, who evidently thought we were relations of the dread spirit of Nzoi, agreed to accompany us. The summit of the peak was 2,400 feet above the camp. For the first thousand feet the ascent was over a steep slope strewn with enormous boulders, but above this rose sheer precipices of twelve to fourteen hundred feet. We made an early start, and after surmounting the first slope were glad to rest in a cool cave at the foot of the precipice. We could now see the line we had to take. A more or less broken ledge ran up the face of the precipice at a steep angle; at some places it gave barely foothold, and at others it opened to a width of thirty feet. At one spot we could see that the ledge ceased, and the climber would have to work along the face of the precipice as best he could, by means of little projections or weather-worn footholds. In spite of these difficulties, however, the path looked practicable. Pringle and I were making the ascent with a few men carrying a theodolite, etc. While resting in the shady cave, and admiring the masses of maidenhair fern that clung to its damp walls, we heard a familiar sound above us, and, looking up, saw a swarm of bees, streaming in and out of a large hole in the cliff. As the hole was close to one of the worst portions of the ascending ledge, strict silence was enjoined on all. We Europeans removed our boots, to get a secure foothold, and the whole party crept quietly along the face of the precipice. But, cautious as we thought we were, there was enough noise to attract the attention of the suspicious bees, and soon an angry cloud swarmed out. Pringle and I, with the guides and a couple of gun-bearers, were in front, then a gap, and a little behind the party with the instruments. The bees cut us in two, and the rear party beat a hasty retreat, while we in the van made the best pace we could up the steep ledge. A false footstep meant a fall that must have been fatal, but there was no time to think of our footing, with the angry buzzing swarms at our heels. Fortunately for us, the retreating rear made so much noise that the bees devoted the main portion of their attention in that direction, and we succeeded in reaching the protection of a patch of vegetation growing in a cleft, and here lay still to regain our breath. It was, however, rather disconcerting to think that there might be similar foes above us, and that we had not yet accomplished one-third of the precipitous ascent. Luckily, our fears were not realized, and in due course we reached the top of the cliff, and found ourselves on a flat ridge, waist-deep in genuine bracken. To attain the actual summit was now easy, and we were rewarded by a view that could not readily be surpassed. At our feet lay the camp, looking small and insignificant, with Liliputian inhabitants; beyond, amidst the light-green gardens and fields, wound the Nzoia River like a silver thread; while the valley was enclosed by a wooded range, on the north side of which, broken by a mass of rugged rocky mountains, stretched a broad, open expanse of grass towards the Kapote steppes. To the south-west was the forest region we had lately crossed, with Bwinzau standing out clear and distinct, and the Kyulu Hills becoming blue in the distance. Beyond these, again, half hidden in horizontal clouds, gilded with the level rays of the afternoon sun, beautiful as ever, and dwarfing in its gigantic proportions all the intermediate hills, stood out the great snowy dome of Kilimanjaro. It was getting late, and we had to think of the descent. Our guides said it would be madness to attempt passing the swarms of bees until after sunset, when they retire indoors; on the other hand, it was clear that it would be equally insane to descend certain parts of the ledge in the dark. We thought of making a détour, but were assured it would mean two days' marching, for which we were hardly prepared. A compromise was finally decided on, and we crept down before sunset to the friendly clump of bush near the bee cave, and waited there till after sunset. One man then went softly forward, and returned with the welcome news that the bees had retired for the night. With unshod feet, and the greatest care that not a stone should be dislodged, we glided past in the fast-gathering darkness, and were one and all glad to stand once more amid the boulders at the foot of the cliffs. It was not seven o'clock when we left the precipices behind us, but so difficult was the path in the gloom that it was past eleven before we reached our halting-place, a thousand feet below; indeed, had not our comrades in camp sent out a search-party with lanterns to our aid, we should have been still later.

After a few days' halt at Nzoi, the expedition again advanced in two parties, Pringle resuming charge of the second division. He descended the Keite River, then struck across to the east of the Ulu Mountains, and followed up the Machako's River Valley, everywhere finding a wealthy and peaceful population. The first division surveyed the passes that form the main trade route, and both divisions were encamped outside the Company's post at Machako's on March 21, 1892, having thus safely accomplished half the long journey to the lake.

CHAPTER III.

UKAMBANI—COMPANY'S SETTLEMENT AND FIGHTING.

THE country of Ukambani, the home of the many sections of the industrious and enterprising Wakamba, extends from the extreme eastern settlements between the Tiwa and Tana Rivers to the edge of the Kapote Steppes, and is roughly bounded north and south by the Athi and Tsavo Rivers. Though the whole of Ukambani covers about 15,000 square miles, the greater portion of this area is uninhabited, and only occasionally visited. The Wakamba mostly live on the banks of highland streams, or in the mountainous districts, at altitudes varying from 3,000 to 6,000 feet. With the eastern section of the tribe beyond the Athi River we had nothing to do; indeed, we only met small parties of them proceeding with flocks and herds of cattle, goats and sheep, to the markets at the coast. On the other hand, we saw a good deal of the western districts included in the main divisions of Kikumbuliu and Ulu. The former, situated to the south of Kibwezi, is small and comparatively insignificant as regards population. The people live in scattered bush villages on the banks of the Kibwezi and Kikumbuliu streams; they cultivate their land to a very fair extent, and in favourable seasons produce a large supply of food for passing caravans; but, though owners of considerable flocks of sheep and goats, they possess comparatively few cattle. Exposed as they are to

Masai raids from the north and south, and isolated from the main sections of the tribe, they no doubt do not wish, even though they have made a sort of treaty with them, to put temptation in the way of their raiding neighbours. The treaty is on the whole wonderfully binding on the Masai, but, nevertheless, the presence of a small war-party in the neighbourhood of Kikumbuliu causes great trepidation in the district.

Kibwezi was, from the earlier reports, supposed to produce an inexhaustible supply of food, but this is only true for favourable seasons. In the autumn of 1892, owing to want of rain, there was a famine in the land, and the small following of the Scottish Mission could with difficulty obtain supplies, while caravans had to carry their own from Ndi to Ulu. This Scottish Mission has done some valuable work amongst these Wakamba, but, on the whole, I doubt if the missionaries themselves are satisfied with the results. Mr. George Wilson, now in Uganda, constructed a portion of the Mackinnon road with Wakamba labour, and after a few months found that these natives were ready enough to work for him, but the mission schools, in which the Wakamba were taught trades, were not so successful. At first numbers of children turned up, but the parents, farther advanced even than European nations in this respect, not only expected that free education should be granted, but insisted that the children should also be paid for their attendance. It seems a pity that the headquarters of this valuable mission should not have been made in Ulu, where the natives seem not only more enterprising, but more intelligent.

Kibwezi was the scene of much excitement in the autumn of 1892. A fortnightly mail-service to Kikuyu had been organized, and the mail-bags were carried by Wakamba from the mission-station to Nzoi; but numbers of Masai appeared near the route, and the service became one of much danger, so much so, indeed, that Dr. Moffat had himself on more than one occasion to accompany the mail-runners to give them confidence. Ultimately, after a successful Masai attack on a native caravan at the Kiboko River, the risk became too great, and the mail-service had to be suspended. The Masai, encouraged by this, threatened to attack the mission-station, where a few cattle had been collected. This was a real danger to the new settlement. Dr. Moffat, however, showed an undaunted attitude, and made no elaborate preparations for defence, thus infusing confidence into the Wakamba and discouraging the enemy. For some months the position was one of anxiety, but ultimately the war-clouds passed away, and the mission was left to pursue its avocations in peace.

Ulu, *par excellence* the headquarters of the Wakamba, is a very different country from Kikumbuliu. It is a mass of bare and rocky mountains, intersected by numerous fertile valleys, well watered on every side. Many of the passes resemble Scottish glens, but the grassy hills, diversified by outcrops of rock, on the whole are more like those common amongst the smaller spurs of the Himalayas. On the lower slopes of the mountains, and dotted along the banks of the streams, are the numerous clusters of beehive huts which form Wakamba villages, while on every side are cultivated fields and signs of prosperity. Ulu is divided into a good many sections, amongst which may be mentioned Nzoi, Kilungu, Dhovoni, Maka, Iveta, etc. One of the most powerful of these is situated in the mountains, about a day's march east of Machako's. But the people of Maka on the extreme north-west, overlooking the Kapote plains, have perhaps the greatest reputation for hardihood. The Wakamba as a whole, however, would be much stronger if, instead of each village having a separate chieftain, they were all united, as a few of them indeed are, under one paramount ruler.

The Mkamba is a tall and well-made man. He considers

clothing, in the usual acceptance of the term, superfluous, and goes about much as Nature made him, but even in his nakedness has a certain etiquette as regards ornaments and deportment. He wears a band round the head, and from this is suspended, in the centre of the forehead, a polished brass plate or a small round looking-glass. On his neck lies a string of beads, and his glossy black arms are encircled by polished copper and brass bracelets, and probably a similar ornament adorns his leg below the knee. His ankles are covered by a sort of spat neatly made of white beads, which is most effective against the dark skin; a band of iron wire encircles his waist, and a dressed skin or piece of cloth hangs from one shoulder. His teeth are filed into points, thus detracting from the beauty of his appearance, which otherwise is not unpleasing. As weapons he has a short sword and a long bow, the arrows for which are carried in a well-made quiver hanging from one arm. The women, like the men, consider superfluous clothing unnecessary; a large belt of beads, often blue, encircles the waist, and from this, before and behind, hangs an apron. The one in front is nearly square, and is made of leather, beautifully ornamented with beaten brasswork or beads, while that behind is long and narrow, and ends in two swallow-tails. A few strings of beads round the neck, and a few bangles and perhaps anklets, complete the ladies' attire. The younger women have pleasant faces, but the older specimens could not be called comely by the most friendly critic.

Their marriage customs are something like those of the Wateita. To obtain a wife is mainly a matter of purchase, but not entirely so; in any case, the preliminaries having been settled, the would-be husband has first to pay down a certain sum to the parents of his bride, and, this being done, he has to carry her off with a pretence of force. The bride and bridegroom meet at some pre-arranged spot, and the former's friends, armed and ready, lie hid in the bushes. The bridegroom seizes the girl and bears her off to his hut, pursued by an apparently furious party of her kinsmen; but when the hut is reached, all the pretence of hostility is dropped, and a great carousal, at which vast quantities of beer are drunk, completes the ceremony.

A child when born is smeared over with the blood of a chicken as a sort of rude baptism, though what this is held to signify is not quite clear, and a certain ceremony also attends the period at which the teeth are filed. The dead are mostly dragged into the bushes and left to the wild animals, chiefs being the only people who receive burial.

The Wakamba are, like most savages, very superstitious, and believe in a great many spirits, mostly malevolent. Every large tree and curiously-shaped rock has its attendant spirit, who is propitiated from time to time, but generally only when some advice or counsel is wanted. On such occasions the suppliant approaches the mysterious spot, and, in an attitude of humility, offers a large bowl of the strongest beer possible, as well as other gifts, and then, after invoking the aid of the mighty spirit, retires till next day. The unseen power, having thrown his attendant medicine-man into a trance, makes merry with the pombe, holding high festival during the night. Towards morning, if satisfied with the quantity and quality of the beverage—small beer is worse than useless on these occasions—he vouchsafes certain information to the medicine-man regarding the affairs of his client. However, scepticism is already abroad in the land, for one old chief informed us that he feared the propitiatory offering found its way down the material throat of the medicine-man, instead of gratifying the ethereal taste of the spirit, and even hinted that the prophetic trance of the former was just what might have been expected to result from excessive indulgence in the potent pombe.

We had one rather interesting experience in Kilungu, due to the superstition of the natives. Some old woman, one of the numerous mothers-in-law of a petty chieftain, dreamed a dream of ill omen, in which a dog climbed on to the roof of the hut and howled at the moon, whereupon the roof fell in and the family escaped with difficulty from the débris. As is the custom in such a case, the villagers resolved, through the medicine-man, to consult the spirits as to whether the evil might perchance be averted. An immense gourd of powerful beer was placed at twilight under a sacred tree, and, in fear and trembling, the villagers waited till the dawn, when they hurried to the medicine-man to learn the fate of the community. They were told a tale of imminent disaster, but learned that the evil might even yet be turned away if divers gifts to their spiritual counsellor were immediately presented, and a goat of a certain colour offered up that day. The presents were easily obtained, and at once produced, but, alas! amongst the flocks of the village there was no goat that was in every respect what was required.

As luck would have it, our rear guard was just passing with a few sheep and goats, and one of these proved to be the identical animal desired by the unseen powers. With a rush, the men of the village seized and bore off the victim in triumph to the kraal, and closed the gate. This being reported to me, I sent back ten men to obtain restitution of the stolen property, with as little fuss as possible; but by the time they reached the village the whole of the inhabitants were found to have been celebrating, in pombe, their success in averting the evil of the dream, and were not in a condition to listen to reason or to prudence. They swarmed out of the enclosure, and opposed a hostile front to our little party, answering my message with derisive jeers; then, without a word of warning, they let fly their poisoned arrows, and fled back to their huts. These arrows, however, did no damage, for much pombe loosens the bowstring, and our men, rushing forward, captured the chief, who, first in council, had also evidently been foremost at the beer-gourd, and was so drunk that he could not run away. The great man was brought back to camp, and put in the guard-tent to sleep off the effects of his liquor.

Soon Kilungu bowmen were swarming in the bushes round the camp, and another chief, a brother of the prisoner, came to see us. He presented us with an ox, as compensation for the double assault made on our party, and expressed a hope that his brother might be liberated. We showed him the erring brother sound asleep in the guard-tent, and promised that he should be set free in the morning, provided his people made no further disturbance during the night. This proving quite satisfactory, the ambassador returned and informed the warriors that all was well, and despatched them to their huts. He himself, however, came back to our camp, where our headmen entertained him, and all ended happily.

The prisoner was set free next morning, and swore that the medicine-man was a liar, and had wrongly interpreted the old woman's dream; for was it not the possession of the spotted goat, and not the want of it, that had nearly brought ruin on his people? How he and his medicine-man settled the matter I did not hear, but the interview that followed must have been entertaining to the onlookers, if not to the priest.

On another occasion we pitched our tents under one of their sacred trees, in ignorance of its character, and not a single villager would sell us anything. They held aloof, firmly believing that the result of our foolhardy and sacrilegious conduct would be the annihilation of the whole caravan by the offended spirits. When, next morning, we marched off alive and well, they concluded they had made a mistake, and I fear for the future that shrine lost some of its sanctity.

The Wakamba are not generally supposed to excel in

bravery, but I am inclined to think that their warlike qualities have been unnecessarily underrated. That they are man for man less brave than their neighbours, the Masai, is of course undisputed; but the mere fact of their owning such numbers of cattle in the vicinity of these noted cattle-lifters shows that they cannot be absolutely deficient in pluck. One fact that militates against their being a great power is their organization in small village communities, which in peace time are not grouped under a recognised head, and which thus fail in cohesion in time of war. It is true that when war with the Masai is imminent the Wakamba, if there be time to do so, hastily elect a chief or chiefs to lead their soldiers; but often the Masai raids are so sudden that there is no time for preparation, and in any case the hastily raised body of Wakamba is wanting in combination and discipline. They are in a better position when they raid the Masai, as deliberate preparations and a concerted plan of operations can then be made.

It may appear somewhat strange that a people so often overcome by small war-parties of Masai should, when they quit the rôle of defender for that of assailant, be able to successfully turn the tables on their enemies; but the Wakamba make up for lack of warlike discipline by craft and cunning. At all times, day and night, they have scouts located in the outlying hills north of Machako's, anxiously looking out for Masai war-parties on the Kapote plains. These scouts are also greatly assisted by their hunters, who follow the antelope even into the plains beyond the Athi River. Should any of these discover that the Masai kraals are greatly weakened in Elmoran by the departure of strong war-parties to distant raiding-grounds, word is at once passed to the Wakamba, who assemble a force of fighting men and elect their war-leaders. This force is then divided into two or more battalions, and moves north, under cover of the hills, to the edge of the great grass plains on which are dotted the low black kraals of the enemy.

The Wakamba then wait till dark, when, by a rapid and noiseless march, they approach the hostile kraal. But they know better than to dream of surprising the ever-vigilant Masai, and it is now their craft comes in. With much uproar, one battalion advances on the kraal, and the alarm is hardly sounded before the Masai Elmoran spring out to confront the foe. The battle is soon being hotly waged, but the Wakamba battalion, avoiding too close a combat, retires slowly, covered by flights of poisoned arrows, which whistle through the darkness. The impetuous Masai warriors, eager to flesh their spears, press forward in triumph, and are led farther and farther from the kraal by the cunning foe.

Meanwhile, the other division of the Wakamba creeps round and falls on the now undefended village camp. Short work is made of the few feeble old men who attempt to defend it, and women and children, cattle, sheep, goats, and donkeys are hastily driven off. After having allowed sufficient time for this manœuvre, the first Wakamba battalion makes some show of resistance, and thus prevents the Elmoran from detailing any large number to recover the cattle, and under shelter of the darkness and confusion a good deal of the booty is often triumphantly carried off. They are not, however, always so successful, for the Masai, having learnt caution from previous raids, sometimes divide their force, and the Wakamba find great spears flashing up to oppose both their parties, and are forced to retire discomfited.

On the other hand, the Masai freely raid the Wakamba, and cause great loss in cattle, if not in life. The Wakamba scouts are sometimes caught napping, or more frequently the raiders make such a rapid advance that no preparations can be made to offer a combined resistance. In such a case each little Wakamba village thinks only of its own safety. The women and children flee to the mountains, and the men, instead of assembling to resist the invaders, endeavour to drive off their flocks and herds to the same haven of refuge. When each village is thus playing for its own hand, the disciplined Masai find it an easy matter to cut off some of these isolated parties, and retreat with their spoil, with hardly the loss of a single man. These raids are often carried out successfully by parties of only a couple of hundred; but they are mostly confined to the outer Wakamba districts, for the Masai, after an experience they had some years ago, are chary of becoming entangled in the mountain gorges.

On that occasion they raided deep into the mountains, and reached Kilungu. They had been successful, and had collected a large number of cattle, for the Wakamba, as usual, had offered only a feeble resistance. The Masai, however, had proceeded too leisurely, and those of the Wakamba who had got their property to the safety of the rocks and caves now joined those who had been caught *en route;* and as the Masai, encumbered with herds of cattle, began to retire, the Wakamba bowmen made good practice from every bush and clump of jungle that commanded the road. Again and again the Masai charged to the flank and rear, and as often the Wakamba fled, but only to return and ply afresh the death-dealing bow.

So far the invaders' road had not been blocked in front, but as they toiled up the rugged gorge that opens on to the grasslands of Kapote, near the great rock pools of Bondani, they found the Wakamba warriors of Maka perched on the rocks which commanded the outlet, and drawn up across the gorge itself. To contend against the Parthian tactics of those behind, fight this fresh foe in front, and at the same time control the great herd of cattle, was manifestly impossible. For some time the Masai Lagonani attempted to save his spoil; but his wearied followers were now falling fast, for the great war-shield could protect only one side of the body, and the arrows were raining down from every direction. At last he gave the order to abandon the spoil, formed up the remainder of his party, and charged the men of Maka like a whirlwind. The great spears flashed and fell, and the Wakamba line was at once broken before that mighty rush. Only about one-third of the Masai war-party emerged on the grass plains, but these at once reformed and faced about. The Lagonani, however, saw they were too exhausted to renew the fight, and the remnant of his party retired in good order and unmolested, for the Wakamba considered them, wearied and disheartened although they were, too formidable to attack in the open. The Wakamba loss had not been small; but they had absolutely beaten the Masai, and since that day the inland districts have suffered but little from raids.

It is otherwise with the valleys that are not protected by difficult passes, but open directly on to the plains. Nzoi, which in the spring of 1892 was a land of plenty, was in the following autumn practically a desert. The valley of the Machako's River to the east of the mountains had been laid waste, and the Wakamba settlers on the banks of the Athi had fled across the river towards their brethren of the Tiwa. Two years later the actual district of Machako's was attacked, though on this occasion the damage was much less.

Ulu had long been a favourite halting-place for Arab slave-caravans, as not only could food be cheaply obtained, but the Wakamba had captives for sale, and, for a consideration, were always ready to look after sick and ailing slaves. Once the Company's rule extended to Machako's, the slave-dealer often found it convenient to leave a large number of slaves among the Wakamba, where they learned the language, and otherwise qualified themselves to pass as Swahilis at the coast the following season. When the survey caravan passed Nzoi in the spring of 1892, it was joined by several of these unfortunates, who claimed safety and freedom. Needless to say, as many as we could find were liberated. A month or so before the Company's representative at Machako's had succeeded in breaking up a large slave-caravan; and this is only one of many instances of good work done in the interior by the much-abused East African Company.

The Company's first station in Ulu was at Nzoi; but this was shortly afterwards transferred to Machako's, when a small earthwork inside a thorn zeriba was built. In 1889 Captain Lugard arrived at this post and doubled its extent, without altering the site. In 1892 there was a talk of abandoning this station. The argument for evacuation was that, as Machako's and Fort Smith, in Kikuyu, are only fifty miles apart, and both are situated in good food-supplying districts, it was expensive and unnecessary to maintain both. But it would have been very false economy to abandon Machako's and retain Fort Smith, for the former had secured a valuable hold on the peaceable and industrious Wakamba; while the latter, situated in the most treacherous district between the coast and the lake, exercised little influence outside gunshot of the fort itself. Fortunately Mr. Berkeley, at that time the Company's Administrator at the coast, decided to retain Machako's as a station; and I am glad to think that my representations to him had some little weight in dissuading him from abandoning a place which has done more than any other in East Africa to secure a peaceful hold over a fine country and an enterprising tribe.

The early days of the Company's rule at Machako's were not free from bloodshed; but the true facts of the case will never be known. The Directors were at first unfortunate in their choice of an agent at this important point, and friction with the Wakamba followed. The district of Maka was attacked and looted, and there was trouble even in the more immediate neighbourhood of the station itself. The agent had requisitioned a tall tree as a flagstaff, and the Wakamba were to bring it in, but some difference of opinion arose, and the Company's agent went out with a few men to settle the matter. He said that he was treated with insult and hostility, and had to retire to the fort, which was subsequently attacked in the most determined way by the Wakamba. The gallant agent, however, was equal to the occasion, and repulsed the attack, inflicting great loss on the assailants.

His version of the story is not entirely reliable, as will be understood when it is mentioned that he was the same gentleman who had the apocryphal battle with the Masai at Tsavo. The Wakamba account is that, although there was a dispute about the carriage of the tree, they decided to meet the wishes of the European, and detailed large parties to work in relays and carry the heavy flagstaff to the fort. These parties the garrison mistook for a hostile force, and opened fire, whereupon some of their young men fired a few arrows, and the whole party, who did not wish for or expect hostilities, retired hastily to the mountains. The truth probably lies somewhere between these accounts, as the Wakamba are not as guileless and bland as they would wish to make out.

In the winter of 1892 the Kilungu district became unsettled, and interfered with trading caravans to such an extent that Captain Nelson and Mr. Ainsworth had to lead out a small punitive expedition to bring it to order. By good management, this result was accomplished without much fighting; but, unfortunately, Captain Nelson contracted a chill, which aggravated an attack of dysentery, from which he died on his return to Kikuyu.

In 1893 the more consolidated district to the south-southeast of the station became troublesome. The chief of this district was a strong man, and had gradually absorbed in his own person almost all the power that in other Wakamba districts is distributed amongst the petty chiefs. Not only this, but he set to work to extend his influence over the Machako's district itself, and issued an ultimatum to the people of that district, forbidding them to work for, or in any way recognise, the Europeans, under pain of war.

This was a sad blow to the Company's agent, Mr. Ainsworth, who by dint of great patience and tact had gradually been inducing the Wakamba to labour on roads and buildings, as well as to accept contracts as carriers. At the time this decree was issued, his garrison was so weak that he could not undertake extended operations, and, moreover, could not obtain help from the more powerful garrison in Kikuyu, as they had their hands full with one of the periodical outbreaks which occur in that country. Still, he saw that some effort must be made, as the ultimatum was regarded by the Wakamba as a challenge to the Europeans, to whom they had looked for protection. Inaction was already telling heavily on the labour market, and Mr. Ainsworth determined to take the field. A small Swahili caravan arrived at the time from the coast, and Mr. Ainsworth persuaded them to join him. With a force of under 100 men, he made a long march into the hostile district, and by the celerity of his movements had crossed a difficult pass before he encountered much resistance. Then, however, the enemy showed fight, and from behind every sheltered spot the Wakamba bows were busy.

Mr. Ainsworth pushed steadily and rapidly forward towards the large kraal of the dominant chief, the Wakamba not standing their ground nor hazarding a close combat, but pursuing their usual Parthian tactics. The Company's force was now hampered by several wounded, and the sun was sinking low towards the western mountains when the objective was reached. The kraal was a large one, and defended by a formidable thorn zeriba. To open a way through this, Mr. Ainsworth detailed a party which pursued their work while covered by the fire of their comrades. Once an opening had been made, one rush put them in possession of the enemy's headquarters, and the campaign was over.

Next day the hostile chiefs made submission, and paid a fine in cattle, and Mr. Ainsworth returned to Machako's in triumph, having by his bold march and sharp action firmly established the Company's rule in Ukambani. Other districts had been watching the result of this conflict, and no doubt had reverse, instead of victory, been the fate of the Company's flag, there would have been far more serious trouble, for Wakamba, like people nearer home, worship the rising sun.

Since this the Wakamba have remained good friends with the Europeans, and are fast becoming accustomed to work and wages. Mr. Ainsworth can justly pride himself on the results of his two years' rule. In the spring of 1892 we could not obtain a single Wakamba porter, while in 1894, when I required about twenty men to help me by carrying food, the Wakamba fairly tumbled over each other in their eagerness to enlist. Wakamba have also been obtained in considerable numbers to carry loads from Tsavo to Machako's, and even from the coast; and a militia has been formed to guard the passes against Masai raids. Altogether, the future of Ulu is a most promising one.

CHAPTER IV.

MACHAKO'S TO LAKE NAIVASHA.

OUR arrangements for the more difficult work ahead commenced in earnest at Machako's. We found that Mr. Foaker had not been idle, and had already collected nearly all the food and some of the donkeys that we required; but we were destined to spend nearly a month in further preparations. Kikuyu was the usual point of departure for caravans towards the lake, but this season the locusts had proved so destructive that only with difficulty could portable food be secured. There was no famine in Kikuyu, as the magnificent fields of sweet-potatoes were untouched, but potatoes do not by any means form a portable food. Even if dried and made into flour, the result is not satisfactory if the weather be wet, and so I had decided to load up with millet flour from Ulu, where the supply was cheap and abundant.

A brief description of our food difficulties may be interesting. From Machako's to Kikuyu is four ordinary marches, from Kikuyu to Kavirondo about twenty-four; so that the usual caravan time from Machako's to the cultivated districts of the lake is twenty-eight marches, while viâ Sotik fifteen days from Kikuyu carries a caravan through the foodless tract.

As it was evident that we could not make a satisfactory survey of the route if we marched at ordinary caravan pace, it was necessary to provide much more food than would have been required by a trading expedition, and I estimated we should need rations for about forty-five days. Our limited transport could not carry anything like the amount, which worked out to about 36,000 lbs., so we decided to form two depots. The first was at Fort Smith, in Kikuyu, and in this, by three trips from Machako's, we stored 36,000 lbs. of flour. The second was afterwards made at Lake Naivasha, five days' march from Kikuyu, and required two trips to stock it. From Lake Naivasha the Sotik party branched off west, with fifteen days' supplies, while the Guash Ngishu party, with thirty days' rations, marched along the meridional rift. To carry out these arrangements Twining was sent to Kikuyu as receiving officer; another officer remained at Machako's to pack and forward the supplies, and Mr. Foaker, as transport officer, travelled backwards and forwards with the bulk of the caravan. Those of us not engaged on this work made two short trips to explore the country round the Ulu Hills, for up to now we had not succeeded in finding a railway route from the Salt River to Machako's which would not prove very costly.

Pringle and I started off on the more important investigation, and marched to the south with the object of finding a route between the Kapote Steppes and the Salt River Valley, and so avoiding the intricate jumble of hills which constitutes Ulu. In two marches we made the rock pools of Bondani, and during the second day understood at last what the great Masai hunting-grounds were really like. We had hardly left the cultivated tracts when game began to swarm on every side. Gazelle and hartebeest predominated, but on the distant grassy ridges we could see zebra and ostriches. Early in the day we had each bagged a hartebeest, and put our small caravan in good humour at the prospect of abundant meat diet.

Soon, on topping a low spur, we saw a few hundred yards

"BUYING FLOUR."

away our first rhinoceros, lazily cropping the luxuriant grass. The caravan halted, and Pringle and I had a hasty consultation as to the advisability of stalking him. The wind was very uncertain, and came in fitful puffs, now one way and now another, and, neither of us in these unfavourable circumstances appearing particularly keen to push matters to a conclusion, we marched on, determined to wait for a more suitable opportunity. The rhinoceros in the meantime became alarmed and disappeared.

Shortly afterwards, it being my day off duty, I went ahead to look for a camping-ground, and came on two more of these animals. They made off across a small dry nullah-bed, and then stopped to investigate us. The ground was not very favourable, but I tried a stalk, and got a somewhat long shot. Whether the rhinoceros I selected was hit or not is hard to say; anyhow, both made off, and very quickly put several miles between us. Soon after I reached the pools of Bondani. A small reef of rock crossed the nullah-bed, and above this were several fine ponds, the only water for miles round. A few mimosa-trees lined the watercourse, and numerous tracks showed this to be a favourite game resort.

There was a nice camping-ground on short turf near the pool, surrounded by shady trees; but, unfortunately, in these a few objectionable beehives were visible. A man was despatched to see if they were tenanted, as, if so, previous experience indicated the advisability of pitching our tents a little farther off. The man approached one of the trees, and beat a hasty retreat, to the great delight of his comrades, who had watched his movements with interest from a safe distance. But on his arrival he reported, not bees, as everyone expected, but a leopard, reposing under the shade of a tree.

This was a great piece of luck, and, hastily taking my rifle, I began a cautious stalk. We got close to the tree, and, sure enough, there was the leopard; but I could not get a clear

4—2

view. So, retracing our steps, we made a little détour, and gained, unobserved, a small mound, within fifty yards of the tree. From this I got a good shot, and disabled the animal, which, however, required two more bullets to despatch it. Then we found that my luck was greater than I had anticipated, for the animal proved to be a cheetah, and not a true leopard. This, according to the authority of Mr. Jackson, who had for years devoted himself to sport in these regions, was only the second cheetah which had been bagged in East Africa.

The remainder of our caravan soon came up, and camp was pitched. Pringle then went out, burning to beat my day's record, and he very nearly did so, for at no great distance he stumbled across two lions, which were lying in the grass on the look-out for game. Unfortunately, they vanished over a small rise before he could use his rifle. That evening we saw abundance of game all round the camp, and had some sport, putting up another rhinoceros and a leopard, but failing to bag either.

Next day we marched over undulating ground towards the bluff shoulder of the Maka Mountains, which on the Kapote side form the sentinels of Ulu, and from whose summits the Wakamba warriors are ever on the outlook for Masai. During this march Pringle bagged a rhinoceros. The grass was so long that stalking was easy; but its length was a positive disadvantage at close quarters, as it prevented his firing kneeling, and to make accurate shooting from the shoulder, with a heavy double eight-bore rifle, is a matter of some difficulty. The huge animal did not succumb to the first shot, and the subsequent proceedings were interesting and exciting for both parties. Finally the eight-bore won, and Pringle was justly proud of his first rhinoceros, which proved to have very fair horns.

The rhinoceros is a stupid beast, and somewhat blind;

but, on the other hand, it has a keen sense of smell. Thus, it is essential to stalk from down-wind; otherwise, if at a distance, it may make off, or if near it may charge. But with the wind in one's favour it is astonishing how close one can get without alarming him. We had a good deal of experience with these animals later on, as the caravan was frequently stopped by them, and was charged on no less than five occasions. A caravan passing a solitary rhinoceros to windward affords a very amusing spectacle. The great beast scents the caravan at once, but cannot quite make it out, so he stands facing it, and wagging his enormous head from side to side in ludicrous uncertainty. Then up goes his tail, and he comes tearing down, only to pull up again after twenty or thirty yards to repeat his investigations. To give time for reflection and vary the monotony, he then trots along parallel to the caravan, till, on an extra strong whiff of scent, he wheels round, and again makes a headlong charge for a few yards. This somewhat stupid, though distinctly entertaining, performance is repeated until, in most cases, the caravan has passed safely, and the rhinoceros is left in his uncertainty. Sometimes, however, the caravan is of such length, or so slow, that a charge home comes off; then the porters drop their loads and scatter, and the rhinoceros gallops through the line and away up-wind, with his tail in the air, and no damage done.

Our little party, having passed Maka, got on to the headwaters of certain tributaries of the Salt River, and found, as we had hoped to do, that the difficulties to a railway on this line were, comparatively speaking, slight. As we had rations for only ten days with us, we had now to retrace our steps. On the homeward journey it was my turn to bag a rhinoceros, which had not, however, such good horns as the one that fell to Pringle's rifle. At Bondani we found the same abundance of game, and between that and Machako's I had my first experience of a charging rhinoceros. I was following the banks of a dry nullah, keeping parallel to the caravan at a distance of about a mile, in hopes that it might drive some antelope my way. Our range of vision was not extensive, owing to the lie of the ground; but this was an advantage, as it meant that game must come pretty close before sighting us. Happening to glance uphill, we were suddenly aware of a rhinoceros about 100 yards away, and making straight for us like an express engine. I had only a double ·500 Express with hollow bullets, which would have produced no effect, so judged discretion the better part of valour. My few followers hastily retired at a pace I could not hope to equal, so I plunged into the nullah-bed, and ran, as I thought, about thirty yards out of the line. On climbing up the steep bank, I came almost face to face with the rhinoceros, who had evidently changed his direction a little, so I had somewhat hurriedly to scurry out of his way. He passed quite close, offering me a splendid shot, had I possessed a suitable rifle. On reaching the far bank of the nullah, he wheeled round, and investigated me for a few minutes, before he resumed his way to windward. Pringle, who was trying to circumvent the wily ostrich on a hill a little way off, enjoyed the performance immensely, as he could see the unceremonious way in which we had to make room for his excellency the rhinoceros.

On our return to Machako's, a similar small expedition went out to the north-east, and reached the Athi River. They, too, found the country traversed a sportsman's paradise. They came across lots of hippopotami in the Athi, and bagged two of them, and so the porters came back laden with meat. On returning to Machako's, the caravan had the wind behind, and our olfactory nerves gave us notice of their approach before they came in sight, as the meat, after a few days in the sun, was, to say the least of it, rather high.

Meanwhile Foaker had done his work well, and about two-thirds of the necessary rations were already stored at Fort Smith. The standing camp at Machako's was accordingly broken up about the middle of March, and the whole caravan, laden with as much flour as it could carry, made for Kikuyu, across the grass plains of the Athi. Game swarmed on every side, but was difficult to stalk, as there was so little cover. Still, we were not altogether unsuccessful. On reaching the Athi, I decided to camp for a day on the banks of the stream, more especially as Pringle and I had each killed a hippopotamus, and the meat would be a welcome addition to the porters' fare. Pringle had also come across four lions at the Stony Athi, which is a few miles south of the real Athi, and had a shot, but without result. Next morning parties of men with ropes and knives went out to retrieve the two dead hippopotami, and the white men separated into two shooting-parties. Pringle and Austin stuck to the Athi River, and though they had no luck with large game, made a phenomenal bag of guinea-fowl. Foaker and I struck off towards the Stony Athi, and bagged two gazelles and a hartebeest, as well as a few guinea-fowl. We also sighted a few water-buck, but, as they also saw us, we could not get a shot. On return to camp we found that one of our sentries had shot a hartebeest, as it strolled along the river bank, within a hundred yards of the encampment.

Another long march amidst countless herds of game brought us to the edge of the Kikuyu Forest. A strong boma was at once built with branches and bushes, not against the warlike Masai or treacherous Wakikuyu, but to protect our donkeys from the hyænas, which simply swarmed there. The hyæna, which is generally considered a timid, and even cowardly, animal, is comparatively bold and aggressive in Masailand, where the inhabitants are accustomed to laying their dead outside the camp to be devoured by these foul scavengers. The trait in these hyænas that troubled us most was their marked partiality for donkeys. When Foaker and Twining first reached this camp with the donkey caravan newly-raised at Machako's, they arrived so late in the evening that they had not time to make a donkey enclosure. Instead, they trusted to large fires all round the encampment, in the centre of which the donkeys were picketed. But a thunderstorm came on and put out the fires, and the Swahili sentries, of course, abandoned their posts and got under cover, according to their custom. Then the hyænas got, and took, their opportunity, with the result that the camp was soon in an uproar. The frightened donkeys broke loose from their pickets, and rushed all over the place, even into the officers' tents, in their frantic efforts to escape their pursuers. Soon the men turned out, the hyænas retired, the donkeys were collected, and the fires relighted. But three several times during the night was this performance repeated.

Thanks to the boma, we passed a quiet night on this occasion, and next day entered Kikuyu, crossed the narrow forest belt, with its grand trees and open glades, and entered what appeared one great expanse of potato-fields. The narrow tapering spurs seemed covered with potatoes far in excess of the requirements of the natives. Dotted about amongst the cultivation stood patches of dense forest, and in the heart of each patch nestled a native village. At this time the natives were friendly, and crowds turned out to watch us pass, and brought food and delicacies for sale. But we did not stop to trade; we soon reached Fort Smith, where we were hospitably received by the founder, Major Eric Smith, and his indefatigable assistant Mr. Purkiss. On the natural glacis north of Fort Smith our camp was pitched, and, while the native market made glad the hearts of our followers with abundance of good things, we adjourned into the fort, where we were regaled on mutton-chops and vegetables that would not have disgraced an English table.

At Fort Smith the survey expedition was once more reunited. Twining, who had been far from well when he left Machako's, was now quite strong, and had done some valuable work towards the north. Austin still suffered from occasional attacks of fever, and Pringle was rather out of sorts; but, taking us all round, the officers were prepared for any amount of work, and the Indians and Swahilis were in good condition.

We reached Fort Smith on March 24th, and three days later marched for Naivasha, where I intended to make a temporary depot. Pringle, with a few men, remained behind to bring on a second lot of food, and also to extend the survey towards Ngongo Bagas. This he did very successfully, and combined sport with work in bagging two more rhinoceroses. One of these was only wounded, and made for some interlaced bush, into which Pringle followed it. Had the animal charged, escape would have been impossible, but Pringle, to his satisfaction, found that the first bullet had done its work, and the enormous animal lay dead.

Two days' march brought us to the edge of the great Kikuyu escarpment, where we had intended to camp, trusting that the heavy rains would have filled a small natural tank which Twining had found there. It did contain a little water, but it was so fouled by game, that we decided to push on down the escarpment to the Kedong River. The view from the summit of the pass was grand. In front the ground fell steeply down to where the Kedong wound its way amidst clumps of mimosa 1,400 feet below us; beyond stretched the level meridional trough, with its bright grassy glades and patches of forest, to where the dark wall of the Mau escarpment seemed to reach the sky; midway rose the extinct volcano of Suswa, with its immense crater, from which one wall had apparently been blown away, while to the northward lay the equally imposing volcanic mass of Longonot, appearing to block our road to Naivasha. The steep sides of the escarpment at our feet were strewn with masses of rock and volcanic débris, half hidden by the waving grass, while north and south extended great unbroken forests of majestic trees.

The descent proved difficult for our train of 120 donkeys laden with flour, and the sun had set before the last rocky step of some 500 feet was reached, although the advanced porters were already pitching camp on a beautiful spot on the banks of the Kedong. In the fast-gathering darkness the donkeys stumbled along, and one after another slipped from the path and rolled down the precipitous slope, tearing the bags of flour to pieces. I saw this could not continue, or all our food-supplies would be strewn on the mountain-side, so halted and unloaded the donkeys. They were then sent on to camp, and Twining was directed to send back porters to carry in the bags of flour. Though the distance was only about a mile, this took time, and I foolishly remained out to see it done. The survey work that day had been very trying; and as the descent was a difficult one for the railway, I had seen to it myself, and got wet through climbing about amongst the rocks and bushes. Now the cold Kedong wind, which always arose after sunset, chilled me to the bone, and brought on an attack of sickness, which a few days later prostrated me.

About 11 p.m. all was safe in camp, and we discussed a possible visit from the Masai, as numerous fires had been seen in the darkness at no great distance. Sure enough, early next day, before I was out of bed, I heard the Masai hongo song echoing through the camp, and my interpreter rushed in to say that the Masai were advancing in thousands. I gave a few hasty orders, and, hurriedly dressing, rushed out, to find the Indians steadily standing to their arms in camp, on the borders of which an excited mass of Swahilis were drawn up between us and the Masai hordes. On passing the Swahilis the anticlimax was reached, for all the fuss had been made over seventeen wretched Masai who were facing our formidable force.

The usual palaver followed. The Masai warriors sat down behind their shields, and their Lagonani stepped forward and addressed us, emphasizing his points by expressive waves of his knobkerry. The subject of his speech was, of course, a demand for hongo, or transit dues. Our interpreter then borrowed his knobkerry, and replied that transit dues were a relic of barbarism, and never levied by civilized nations, and that we declined to pay, although we were delighted to make the acquaintance of such a fine-looking Lagonani and his Elmoran.

After a little further speechifying, to which we turned a deaf ear, the Lagonani abruptly turned to his followers, and remarked that it was not seemly that Masai warriors should sit baking in the sun like dried fish, and that, as we would give them nothing, they might as well return to their kraal. With a parting hint to us that their war-strength on mobilization came to more than seventeen spears, he retired with true Masai dignity. Our caravan men were by no means exultant over this meeting, and most of them thought we had made a mistake in not paying hongo. In fact, I believe that but for the presence of the Europeans and Indians this strong caravan, mustering nearly 200 breechloading rifles, would have paid tribute to those seventeen wretched spearmen.

I had another heavy day's work on the Kikuyu escarpment before I was satisfied that a railway line could be made, and at sunset returned to camp, feeling rather exhausted. Next day we moved on to the second Kedong camp, when I became rapidly worse. I suffered from intense nausea, and cholera-like symptoms soon reduced my strength. Finally, late at night, repeated doses of chlorodyne sent me to sleep, and next morning I thought I was all right. We again marched on, and as a precautionary measure I bestrode a donkey; but

I had not ridden far, when I found Austin by the roadside suffering from a very severe attack of fever. His plight was worse than mine, so I handed him over the donkey, and walked on to camp. As soon as the sun had set, and the cold night wind arose, my yesterday's symptoms returned even more violently. Chlorodyne appeared to have little effect, and my comrades began to feel seriously alarmed. Finally I got to sleep, and arose to find myself decidedly weak; but we could not halt, and so marched past the rugged shoulder of Longonot, towards the beautiful lake of Naivasha, which lay below us half shrouded in the morning mist. I had to ride a donkey all day, and the march to the border of the lake appeared a very long one.

At last we reached a spot that satisfied my requirements for a temporary depot, and next day a strong boma was built, in which our loads of food and goods were stored. I was now undoubtedly on the mend, though unfit for much rough work; and while Austin, Sergeant Thomas, and I remained at Naivasha, with forty rifles to guard the depot, and survey round the lake, Twining and Foaker returned with the bulk of the caravan to bring on Pringle and the balance of our food. In a few days I was sufficiently recovered to undertake, with Austin, an expedition round the lake, while Sergeant Thomas, with twenty rifles, remained at the depot. Our first march was to the south, through alternating grassy glades teeming with game and beautiful clumps of mimosa swarming with guinea-fowl.

The next day's march was very much the same, and brought us west of the lake, through similar country, but marked by numerous little volcanic peaks, whose slopes were strewn with volcanic ash and obsidian. Game was still abundant, and the lake shores were dotted with ducks and geese, while from beyond its border of rushes resounded at intervals the hoarse grunt of the hippopotamus.

Leaving Austin in camp, I pushed eastward, as I wished to examine more closely the great escarpment of Mau, which now towered above us. Making my way with a few men through the jungle that covered the lower slopes of the grotesque volcanic peaks, I struck a fault, which had left its mark, like a railway cutting, amongst the hills. Following this, I suddenly found myself on a plain of open grass, stretching to the wooded foot of Mau. This plain was known to the Masai as Ndabibi, and was evidently more or less swampy after the rains. We pressed on towards Mau, and I got some useful work done, when it began to rain in torrents. On our way back to the camp, I revisited the railway cutting to see if I could pick up any guinea-fowl, and so witnessed a most beautiful sight. In the cutting, not thirty yards from me, was a fine leopard with a small gazelle in his mouth. As he saw me he gracefully climbed the opposite side, still carrying the gazelle, and disappeared into a bush. Of course I had not a rifle handy—in fact, both my gun and rifle were in their cases, to protect them from the wet—and thus I could only look on and admire this wonderful display of graceful strength and agility.

On arriving in camp I found a messenger had come from Sergeant Thomas, to say that James Martin had arrived with a caravan from Uganda, and wished to see me, as he was the bearer of important news. I accordingly started back for the depot with six men, leaving fourteen with Austin, who was to continue the survey round the lake. This he successfully accomplished, though he met a good many Masai, who of course demanded hongo, and were refused. This, however, did not cause any ill-feeling—in fact, the Masai became so friendly that, when one of his Indians went astray, they fed the wanderer like a fighting-cock, and three days later brought him back to the depot. These friendly Masai were suitably rewarded, and left us vowing that we were real good fellows, though somewhat ahead of the times in regard to transit dues.

Martin's news was really serious. There had been severe fighting in Uganda, and the communications between that country and the coast were completely severed. Martin had waited some seven weeks in Usoga and Kavirondo endeavouring to open communication with Lugard, but without success. The latter was reported beleaguered at Kampala, and Bagge and De Winton were supposed to have been killed by the enemy.

This was indeed bad news, if matters were as reported, for we could not hope to reach Uganda under two months. A message was sent by Martin to Pringle to bring on all our reserve ammunition from Kikuyu, and the now unnecessary presents we were taking to Mwanga, King of Uganda, were returned to store.

CHAPTER V.

NAIVASHA TO UGANDA.

MEANWHILE we awaited at Naivasha the arrival of our second food consignment under Pringle, who, as I mentioned before, had also been warned to bring on all our reserve ammunition. The Masai of Naivasha were in a very destitute condition, or, rather, the old men and women were, for the warriors were for the most part absent raiding. We had no difficulty with the few who remained, except on one occasion when they amused themselves by chasing two of our men, who had gone out to purchase milk. The Masai came too close to camp while pursuing the interesting pastime, and we turned the tables by chasing them. They got away, but were so hard pressed that they dropped two spears, which we secured. Matters then adjusted themselves, and an amicable arrangement was made, by which they bound themselves to refrain from such national amusements as frightening porters, and we returned the spears to their owners.

A few days later Pringle's caravan put in an appearance. He had experienced a little trouble from the Masai of Kedong, who carried off three of his donkeys. He retaliated by securing about twenty women, who were trading in camp, and threatened to carry these off, unless the missing property was returned. As next day this was not done, he marched off with his prisoners, and demanded six donkeys for the trouble that had been caused. This brought the Masai to their senses, and the six donkeys were soon produced. The women were then liberated, and, being evidently struck with Pringle, insisted on his spitting on each individually in token of friendship.

From Naivasha we were to proceed to Kavirondo in two divisions. One, equipped with porter transport throughout, was to proceed through Sotik under the command of Pringle, accompanied by Austin and Sergeant Thomas. The other, with a mixed transport of porters and the donkeys, was to follow me, by what is known as the Guash Ngishu route, my assistants being Twining and Foaker. Before separating we called for volunteers, in case military operations should be necessary to assist Lugard in Uganda, and enrolled, and commenced to drill, a fine body of porters and askaris.* On April 17th, as all our arrangements were complete, we moved the two divisions into separate camps in readiness for the march, and next day we parted company, having arranged to meet at Mumia's, in Kavirondo, if possible, by May 18th. Previous to this, and in order to still further facilitate Pringle's movements, Sergeant Thomas had been sent on in advance, with a certain number of food loads, to the top of Mau, there to await the arrival of the Sotik column.

Here I may as well say a few words about the original discovery of the two routes we were on the point of examining, in case I should appear to claim the credit that rightly belongs to Smith and Martin.

The earlier travellers, Joseph Thomson, Jackson and Gedge, and Bishop Hannington, had, with one exception, reached Kavirondo by travelling north along the meridional rift to Baringo, and then west across Kamasia and Elgeyo.

* I thought it only right to call for volunteers, as the survey caravan had originally been enlisted for the journey to Kavirondo and Lake Victoria.

DEPOT AT LAKE NAIVASHA.

This route was known to be well-nigh impossible for a railway, and was rather circuitous, even for caravan work. Jackson and Gedge had on their outward journey endeavoured to strike due west from Naivasha, but got involved in trackless forest, in which they wandered for seventeen days, laboriously cutting their way through the undergrowth or following elephant-tracks. Their provisions were exhausted, and the whole caravan was only saved from collapse by stumbling across a few Wanderobbo, who guided them into the cultivated districts to the westward. This great forest barrier extends in a long belt between the summit of Mau and the eastern shores of the Victoria Nyanza, separating the Masai grazing-grounds on the east from the cultivated regions near the great lake. To find some shorter route across this belt was one of the objects of every one of the Company's earlier exploring expeditions.

Smith, who led an expedition to Usoga before he founded the new fort of Kikuyu, set himself the task of finding some direct route due west of Naivasha. He formed a food depot there, and while the bulk of his caravan were engaged in stocking it with provisions, he started away himself, with only ten followers, to search for a path to Sotik. He selected a line to the south of Jackson's route, found an old Masai track, and after great hardships reached the borders of the inhabited outskirts of Sotik. He then returned for his caravan, led them along this new route, and reached Sotik without having passed more than a few days in the forest. The people of Sotik and Lumbwa were suspicious, but not hostile, and Smith reached South Kavirondo without opposition.

On his return he travelled along the Guash Ngishu route, which had meanwhile been discovered by Martin, but sent his assistant, Newman, with about 100 men, along the Sotik route. The latter was led astray by Lumbwa guides, and at night his camp was attacked. The people had appeared friendly, and so no boma or zeriba had been made, and the surprise was complete. A third of the caravan were killed, and at the first rush Newman himself was wounded. He, however, rallied his men and drove off the enemy. Hampered as he now was with wounded, he reached Kikuyu only with the greatest difficulty, and after days of miserable wandering in the jungle. Martin was sent later on with a strong caravan to open out this road; but though he got through safely, the result was that it was pronounced too dangerous a route for small caravans, though a very tempting one, as the cultivation of Sotik could be reached in fifteen days from Kikuyu.

While Smith had thus succeeded in finding a short, albeit a dangerous, route through Sotik, Martin had been equally successful on the Guash Ngishu. Lugard, who had preceded him to Uganda, had tried a road west of Nakuro, but after one day in the virgin forest thought better of it, and struck off to Baringo, whence he made his way westward a little south of Thomson's line. Martin followed Lugard as far as Nakuro, and then kept along the foot of Mau till he reached the point where the Kamasia range branches off, and there he attempted the ascent. He struck an old Masai road, used in former days, when the Wakwavi still grazed their cattle and built their kraals on the grassy uplands of Guash Ngishu, and, following the general line of this path, emerged in a few days on these magnificent open downs. From this point there was little difficulty in reaching Kavirondo. To Martin, then, belongs the credit of discovering this easy route, which is now the recognised caravan road to Uganda.

Smith had provided us with rough sketches of both routes, and Martin was able to give us Masai guides, so that we of the survey party had no difficulty in finding the way.

Pringle crossed Mau at an altitude of over 10,000 feet, and found himself in a damp, cold region, where the morning mists were not dispersed until the sun had risen well above the horizon. Here some of his party reported that they had seen true grouse—an interesting discovery if correct. From Mau for several days the line led over rolling and well-watered downs, the southern counterpart of Guash Ngishu, and, like the latter, the ancient home of large settlements of Wakwavi. Then followed several days of dense forest, rendered still more difficult by the heavy rains that fell daily, till at last he reached the populous district of Sotik, with whose inhabitants he was much struck. In bearing they resembled the Masai, and in physique and good looks they far surpassed these doughty warriors.

Everyone had prophesied that he could not traverse Sotik and Lumbwa without fighting, and the prophets proved very nearly right. The highlanders were suspicious, and not altogether friendly, and on one occasion bloodshed was only averted by Pringle's good management and military precautions. One night in particular there was very nearly a battle. The tribesmen had crept up to the camp in great numbers, and so confident were they of success that they called out to the Swahilis that their last hour had come. Each of our divisions had been provided with a portable magnesium search-light and a number of signal rockets, and Pringle now brought these harmless adjuncts into play, with the result that the would-be enemy hesitated, and finally decided to postpone their attack. Next day the division pursued its way unmolested, but similar night alarms were of frequent occurrence.

The most narrow escape that my gallant second in command experienced occurred, however, in broad daylight. The heavy rains had flooded most of the rivers, and, if the current was too swift to allow of the use of his Berthon boat, Pringle had frequently to halt and build a bridge before his caravan could cross. On one of these occasions he had left camp with some

5—2

half a dozen followers, and was examining the river bank, with a view to finding a convenient bridge site, when he noticed an unusual number of armed natives coming up. He at once sent a man back to warn Austin, but meanwhile held his ground, as a retreat would probably have precipitated an attack. Austin promptly sallied out with fifty armed men to his leader's assistance, and arrived none too soon, for Pringle and his small party of five were already surrounded by a mass of excited spearmen, who, however, awed by the white man's fearless bearing, hesitated to strike the first blow. On Austin's appearance they hastily retreated, and bloodshed was again averted. After this and similar experiences the survey division was not sorry to reach the more peaceable regions of South Kavirondo, where they were warmly welcomed by one of Smith's old friends. Ugowe Bay was examined for a harbour, and Pringle then marched for Mumia's, which he reached on the exact day settled on beforehand, after an exciting journey of about 250 miles.

I must now ask my readers to return to the division under my personal command, which marched northwards from Naivasha on April 18th. Martin had told us that there were great numbers of Masai on the Gilgil and towards Lake Elmenteita, and warned us that we must be careful, or we might lose some loads, as had happened to him. On the second day we encountered the first of these Masai. I was surveying behind the caravan, when I suddenly saw a commotion in front, and a fast increasing line of Elmoran forming across our path. It appeared that they had lost a few goats, and suspected that we had appropriated them. On discovering that we were not the culprits, they came to the conclusion that the inhabitants of a neighbouring kraal were the evil-doers, and hurried off to retaliate. This led to a fight, the preliminaries of which we were able to watch.

The rival Elmoran formed up a few hundred yards apart,

and in front of the lines a body of old men eagerly discussed peace proposals to a vigorous accompaniment of knobkerry. Every minute or two some impatient warrior would dash forward from the line, and, with loud war-cry and brandished spear, make for the enemy's line, only to be headed off, caught, and led back to his own party by one of the older men who were endeavouring to arrange matters. We approached within about fifty yards of one party of combatants, and watched the scene with the greatest interest. The rival factions of Elmoran had turned out in such a hurry that they had been unable to don their full war-paint, and thus presented a somewhat heterogeneous appearance; but all carried the great shield and deadly spear. Finally, as the Elmoran got more and more impatient, and the peace negotiations were evidently of no avail, one of the old men came up to us, and civilly asked us to move off to a greater distance, as the fight was about to come off, and it might be dangerous for us two Europeans, with our half-dozen followers, to remain so close to the combatants. We retired a little, and suddenly a roar proclaimed that the pent-up bodies of Elmoran had been loosed on each other.

When the battle was over, our camp was visited by the victorious party, who appeared in high good-humour. They did not ask for hongo, somewhat to our surprise, and we were inclined to think highly of our visitors until, on packing up next morning, we found that an artificial horizon and Twining's indiarubber bath were nowhere to be found.

The following march brought us to Kariandus, a recognised camping-ground on a small stream of the same name, which flows into the south-eastern corner of Lake Elmenteita. Before we had pitched our tents, Masai were swarming round us, but each warrior had the point of his spear covered with a ball of cotton-wool, as a sign of peace. All were extremely desirous of shaking hands with the Europeans, so much so that this token of amity became rather fatiguing. I now requested the Lagonani to tell his warriors to keep outside the camp until our preparations for the night were finished and our loads stacked, after which I assured him we should be delighted to welcome them and show them round. The Elmoran, however, declined to move, and so, to their intense surprise, the Indians quietly shouldered them away. This staggered them considerably, as a Swahili would never dream of jostling a Masai warrior, and the Elmoran, not approving of our reserve, sullenly withdrew.

Soon our porters, who had gone to draw water, came back to camp with the news that the Masai had occupied the stream, and declined to allow them near it. This had to be stopped at once, so I went out with Foaker and twenty men. As we descended one side of the ravine, we could see the Masai forming up on the other, until we were confronting each other, with only a few hundred yards between us. Being anxious to avoid a conflict, I now went forward, accompanied by an interpreter, and two Masai advanced to meet us half-way. The discussion that ensued was very interesting.

I asked the Lagonani to refrain from molesting our porters, but he said if we came into Masailand we must put up with Masai customs, and that one of these was to play with any Swahilis they might come across. I replied that this was hardly friendly conduct, and that their ancient customs must be set aside as far as my men were concerned, to which the answer was that, if we wished to fight over such a trifle, the Masai would be most happy to oblige us. My argument then was that, although we wished for peace with all men, we were prepared to defend ourselves, and make it hot for those who interfered with us. I pointed out that the Masai we had already come across had been friendly, and that we had not molested them, and asked whether he wished for peace or war. He now pretended that he was not the leading Lagonani; and sent his man back to call the real article, but I heard him give the message 'Mboto Elmoran.' My knowledge of Masai was sufficient to enable me to understand that this meant 'Call out the warriors,' so I pressed him for a definite answer to my question. He said it was for me to choose, but to this I demurred. I drew his attention to the fact that he stood to lose most, being the owner of many cattle, which would be highly acceptable to my porters, so I thought he should pronounce for peace or war. He then, to my intense satisfaction, decided there should be peace, and we shook hands over it, and withdrew our opposing troops. This conclusion having been arrived at, the Masai loyally adhered to their word, and, though next day we marched northward amidst hundreds of them, we had absolutely nothing to complain of, and at each successive kraal were hailed with cheery greetings.

At Kampi Ambaruk we left the Baringo road and struck west for Lake Nakuro. The camp of Ambaruk was once the scene of a great fight between a Swahili trading caravan and the Wakwavi section of Masai. All day the Swahilis held this post against repeated attacks, until their ammunition gave out; then they bolted, only to be run down and speared by their savage foe. After a long march we reached the north end of Nakuro, and camped near a mimosa wood which lay at the base of a small rocky hill. From this latter we had a splendid view of Lake Nakuro, which looked very gloomy, almost surrounded as it is by sombre, rocky hills. From our natives we learned of another smaller lake called Nakuro Ndegi, more to the north, but, as it was evidently not on our railway route, and since opinions as to its exact position were very conflicting, we did not go out of our way to search for it.

Twining had been suffering from fever the last two days

and now became so bad that he could not walk: not that his temperature was abnormally high, but because his limbs were affected and became powerless. This was a serious matter, as we could not halt long on account of our limited supply of food. We did remain one day at Nakuro, but he got no better, so, for the fourteen days he was thus disabled, we had to carry him. This made my work harder than ever, as Foaker was not an engineer, and could therefore help me but little. To add to our difficulties, it rained every day but one between Naivasha and Kavirondo, and this constant wet was bad for poor Twining, and retarded his recovery. However, he bore it very cheerfully on the whole, and, once he began to recover strength, was eager to resume his work; this, naturally, I would not allow till he was well.

One long march from Nakuro over open grass brought us to a beautiful hilly country, diversified by alternations of splendid forest and beautiful glades of fresh green grass. Through this we marched for three days, crossed the equator, and reached the edge of the great forest of Mau, at the Eldoma Ravine. About fifteen miles to the right we could see some scattered settlements of Wakamasia, and once we got a peep of the fair lake of Baringo. The ravine was a nasty obstacle for the railway, being about 700 feet wide and 200 feet deep, though the stream that flowed in this enormous channel was only some twenty yards in width. The sides were clad with beautiful trees, amidst whose green foliage could be seen here and there gray masses of rock. Here we halted a day, while I made an exploration up the course of the stream to search for a narrower crossing. But my labour was in vain, for the ravine soon divided into two branches, each apparently as formidable as the original. On this occasion we came upon fresh spoor of a herd of buffalo, and I followed them up for some time, though without success.

We then crossed this great chasm, and plunged into the

gloomy forest. The road appeared to enter by a dark tunnel into a solid mass of foliage, and, though the mid-day sun shone outside, we marched along in a dusky twilight. Now and again we emerged on to a small glade, of a few acres in extent, only to disappear again into another mass of forest. Though Martin's caravan had but recently passed, we were obliged in many places to cut away creepers and branches that had descended across the path. In places, too, some mighty tree had fallen, crashing across our road, and formed a barricade of trunks and branches that completely blocked the way, and would have required a day's work to cut through. In such cases we had to go round the obstacle, cutting through the interlaced undergrowth.

To render things more unpleasant, it rained steadily, and everything was sopping wet. Each branch that was moved treated us to a shower-bath, and in places the well-worn path was little better than a quagmire, through which we slipped and stumbled in tenacious mud from nine to twelve inches in depth. Twining's litter required the greatest care, as the bearers could not make sure of their footing, and frequently our sick comrade was within an ace of being shot out down the hillside.

For two days we passed upward through this wonderful forest, and felt, short as the experience was, that we could sympathize with Stanley's months of similar toil. Sometimes we got a glimpse of the scenery down some mountain valley, and could see the tall trees, heavy with their masses of waving gray moss that gave them a hoary appearance of age; but, as a rule, we were completely enclosed in a screen of foliage. Then we saw a bright light in front of us, and emerged, not by gentle gradations, but quite suddenly, on an open expanse of green, rolling downs, looking doubly brilliant in comparison with the gloomy forest that now stretched as a wall behind us.

We had reached a height of about 8,000 feet above the sea, and the incessant damp and wet made it bitterly cold. Our unfortunate porters felt it more than we did, and one poor fellow died of pneumonia, while the whole camp seemed suffering from coughs and colds. After a couple of days in these high altitudes, we struck the upper waters of the Nolosegeli, and were standing on the watershed of the great lake which was our goal. Still travelling over luxuriant grass downs, we steadily descended, steering for the lofty truncated cone of Mount Elgon, visible on the distant horizon. Game, which had been scarce at the higher altitudes, now became abundant, but we noticed that the graceful Thomsonii of Masailand had been replaced by the more sombre-coloured klipspringer.

Gradually the blue line of hills on our left, which marked the boundary between the pasture-land of the Guash Ngishu and the cultivated regions of the lake, approached our line of march, till we reached their detailed outposts—the so-called three hills of Nandi. Here we had to leave Martin's route, as the Guaso Masa was in full flood, and impassable without extensive bridging. Keeping to the left, through open jungle of wild fig, we crossed a considerable tributary of the river, and pitched our camp at the foot of the hills, once more on the route of our distinguished predecessor, Joseph Thomson.

Twining had now recovered, and so I sent him direct through Kabras to Mumia's, while Foaker and I, with a small caravan, followed the course of the Guaso Masa—'the river of wealth'—until it joined the Nzoia, which in point of size probably ranks second amongst the feeders of the Victoria Nyanza. We continued our way down this river, passing pools swarming with hippopotami, and soon discovered signs of inhabitants in the numerous game-pits that lined the hippo tracks. In addition to these pits, heavy logs, with great spears attached to them, were hung in the trees, ready, by a trigger arrangement, to drop on any unsuspecting animal passing underneath. These and the pits were too numerous to be pleasant. One of our baboos, who stepped off the path, suddenly disappeared with a yell; but fortunately that particular hole was not furnished with the usual pointed stake, and our draftsman escaped with nothing worse than a fright and a shaking.

We found one splendid fall on the Nzoia, where the river plunged over a precipice about sixty feet high, and then in a succession of bounds descended another seventy or eighty feet, shrouded in a misty veil of spray. The roar was audible for miles, and at the fall itself the ground appeared to tremble under our feet. The grandeur of the scene was enhanced by a smaller stream, which leaped at right angles, but from a lesser height, into the same great chasm. We soon left these magnificent unnamed falls behind us, and on May 16th we reached Mumia's, and found Twining had arrived two days before us, and exactly two days later, as I have already mentioned, Pringle's division marched in from the south, and the whole expedition was once more reunited, and, moreover, at the prearranged time.

The result of our work was most gratifying, for, though we had each travelled nearly 250 miles by different routes, the position of Mumia's, as worked out by the two surveys, agreed within two miles. Here I may pay a tribute to the accuracy of Joseph Thomson's work, performed under much more difficult conditions, for we found that his previously-determined longitude of Mumia's differed from our own by only two minutes.

In Kavirondo we heard that Lugard had defeated the combination against him, and that the road to Uganda was now clear, though Williams was still fighting in certain districts in the neighbouring country of Usoga. Although freed from anxiety on this score, we found a new cause of uneasiness in the fact that small-pox was raging in Mumia's and the surrounding villages. Martin had left a number of small-pox patients behind in Kavirondo, the disease having as a consequence spread. Martin stoutly avers that the disease originated amongst some of the Soudanese whom Lugard had passed on to him for transport to the coast—indeed, that two men so handed over were at the time actually suffering from small-pox. However this may be, Martin's caravan was much afflicted by the disease; the natives of this district of Kavirondo died in hundreds, and the survey expedition, in spite of its precautions, was not fated to escape scatheless.

Kavirondo and Usoga have been so often described that I need not dwell on these countries or their inhabitants. Kavirondo is highly cultivated, open, and apparently well adapted for wheat; its inhabitants appear to be true negroes, and their language approximates to that spoken by certain Soudanese tribes on the hill. Usoga is still more fertile, and more cultivated, abounding with timber, and inhabited by a Bantu tribe, closely akin to the Waganda. In neither country is there any paramount chief, both being divided into a number of petty districts. Usoga is tributary to Uganda; but the Waganda, in spite of several expeditions, have failed to obtain any hold of Kavirondo, although in ancient times a small Bantu colony appears to have established itself on the shore of Berkeley Bay.

At Mumia's the survey expedition was divided into three parties. The larger, under my command, with Pringle and Foaker, was to visit Uganda; Twining, with about 100 men, was to complete the railway survey, and find a terminal station and harbour; while Austin remained at Mumia's to purchase food, and generally prepare for the return journey to the coast. The first two parties marched together to Berkeley Bay, through rich country, and then separated. Twining, on completing his task, relieved Austin, who made an excursion towards Elgon, while the main body of the caravan proceeded to Uganda. Usoga was rapidly traversed, the Nile crossed, and the capital of Uganda reached towards the middle of June. Captain Williams, R.A., Lugard's second in command, came out to meet us, and conducted us to the latter's office, where we were introduced to the Company's administrator in Uganda.

Our camping-ground was far from good, owing to the heavy rain having made it distinctly marshy; but we made it comparatively comfortable, and were glad to rest after the weary marches over the succession of unbridged swampy streams that at this period disgraced the main road between the Nile and Kampala.

While at Mengo we went to see King Mwanga, who had only recently been reinstated at his capital, and paid visits to the two mission-stations, where we were hospitably received. But our impressions of the capital of Uganda were by no means enthusiastic. This may have been partly caused by the fact that it had not yet recovered from the destruction caused by the recent civil war, of which the traces were still much *en évidence*.

Having handed over the mail and ammunition to the Company's authorities, we were anxious to get back to our work, but stayed a week to give Lugard and the other Europeans an opportunity of answering their home letters. Before the end of the week Lugard announced his intention of returning to the coast with us, as by so doing he need not withdraw any rifles from Uganda, where there were none too many. He was anxious to return to England, to lay before the Directors and the public generally his version of the recent events in Uganda, as he feared the Roman Catholic mission was sending home misleading information.

CHAPTER VI.

LUGARD'S CHRISTIAN WAR.

ALTHOUGH before we reached Uganda the actual fighting was well over, it was only while we were at Kampala that the final negotiations which led to the new partitions of the country between the Protestants, Roman Catholics and Mohammedans were actually completed. It may not be out of place to give a short description of this civil war—one of the most important and far-reaching in its consequences that has ever occurred in Uganda. I say this advisedly, for it was directly owing to this contest that the proclamation of the British Protectorate over the country was hastened. The struggle between the Christian parties, and the rôle played therein by the officers of the Imperial British East Africa Company, brought the question of Uganda prominently before the European public, in a way which campaigns against the Mohammedans or neighbouring peoples could never have done.

At the same time, I feel that, as far as possible, I must confine myself to the purely military aspect of the conflict, and refrain from discussing, except in a general way, the events which led up to it. I limit myself in this manner because, being the officer deputed by Government to report on the causes of the war, much of the information I acquired is necessarily confidential.

As soon as the combined Christian party had ousted the Mohammedans in the war of 1889, friction between the Roman Catholics and Protestants became evident. The former, with the King at their head, were the more numerous, and undoubtedly aimed at securing supreme political power; had they been successful, they would certainly have gradually crushed Protestantism out of the country. But though Uganda was at this time divided between these two factions, the bulk of inhabitants were really heathen; a few, indeed, actually acknowledged themselves such, and were called Futabangi, or bang-smokers; but the majority were content to follow in name the religious persuasions of their immediate chief.

When the Mohammedans had been driven out, and the Christians entered into possession and power, the two sects were not allowed different provinces, but were mixed up all over the country, and a complicated arrangement was made, by which a sub-chief of one sect had a superior chief of the other placed over him. However well-meant this might have originally been, it did not take into account Waganda nature, and led, on both sides, to constant oppression and friction.

So high had the ill-feeling run that, in 1890, when Mr. Jackson visited Uganda in the interests of the Imperial British East Africa Company, the Protestants seriously contemplated retiring to Usoga, and it was entirely owing to him that they were prevented from carrying out this idea. When Captain Lugard arrived, at the end of the same year, the parties were greatly estranged, and we have only to read his book to see with what difficulty he succeeded in averting civil war in the spring of 1891. On one occasion at least, it was owing to his determined attitude, supported by his colleague, Captain Williams, that an outbreak was prevented. Lugard, by great tact and firmness, succeeded to some extent in lessening the antagonism between the rival parties, and in April,

1891, led a combined army against the hostile Mohammedans. Shortly after the close of this successful campaign he proceeded to Kavallis in search of Emin Pasha's Soudanese, who had been left behind in Equatoria by Stanley. During his long absence, Williams, with a force far too weak for the work it had to do, successfully held command at Kampala.

The Christian parties, freed from immediate fear of their belligerent Mohammedan kinsmen, again took to quarrelling bitterly amongst themselves. In July, 1891, and again in the autumn of the same year, hostilities in the provinces actually did take place, but Williams, by a splendid display of judgment and firmness, succeeded in preventing these isolated outbreaks from resulting in a general conflagration. No one can imagine what he underwent during those trying months; he had constantly to be on the *qui vive*, and had again and again to turn out at night, and personally quell incipient disturbances. In fact, there can be no doubt that, during this period, the civil war was averted solely by the powerful moral influence which Williams had succeeded in obtaining over the natives.

At the end of 1891 Lugard returned to Uganda, having by his brilliant expedition to Kavallis completely effected the result at which he aimed. He again resumed charge, and, from various circumstances, had an enormous amount of work on his hands. Meanwhile, the friction between the two Christian parties continued, and mutual thefts of guns became of frequent occurrence. The last of these gave rise to the incident which bore such an important part in precipitating the crisis.

A Roman Catholic, whose gun had been stolen by one of the Protestants, and who could obtain no redress from the Katikiro, whose faction shortly before had suffered a similar loss, made a plot to steal a gun from a Protestant. The plot was successful, and the Catholic took refuge in his own enclosure with the stolen property. A few indignant Protestants armed themselves, with the intention of recovering the gun, and forced their way into the Catholic's premises. They were fired on, and one of their number fell dead. The Protestants returned the fire and withdrew, leaving the corpse on the ground.

Feeling ran high over this sad occurrence, and Lugard visited the King to secure justice, but was treated with scant courtesy. Being tired and ill, he shortly returned to the fort, leaving to represent him Dualla, his Somali interpreter. The King tried the case, and decided that, according to Uganda law, the Protestant, by forcibly entering the Catholic's private enclosure with arms in his hands, had put himself in the wrong, while the Catholic was acquitted and suffered no punishment whatever.

This decision created the most intense and painful excitement amongst the Protestants, and Lugard, who did not consider that justice had been done, wrote to the King protesting against his decision. His envoy, Dualla, reported that he was treated with gross disrespect, and that insulting messages were sent to Lugard himself. The latter remained firm, and demanded that the Catholic should be handed over to him for re-trial, and, to show the Catholics that he was in earnest, issued some forty muzzle-loading guns to the Protestants, who were the weaker party at the capital. This had at first a good effect, but the Catholics soon resumed their hostile attitude, and on the evening of January 23rd their war-drums resounded through Mengo. This in itself did not necessarily mean fighting, as many times before and since has the capital been startled by the boom of the war-drums, without any conflict following. This time, however, it looked as if they meant business.

On the morning of January 24th the Catholics assembled in force, and during the morning a Protestant was shot, it is said while stealing potatoes. Lugard demanded that the Catholic who had fired the shot should be handed over to him, and the King sent him a prisoner, who all agreed was not the guilty man. Both parties were now drawn up as for battle, and Lugard saw that a conflict was imminent. He accordingly issued some 300 muskets and 150 sniders to the Protestants, with strict injunctions that, should a struggle ensue, the Roman Catholic priests and their mission-station must be scrupulously respected. The Protestant missionaries had already taken refuge in the fort, to which Lugard's porters had previously conveyed some of their property. The Catholic mission had declined to accept a similar offer of asylum, but asked instead for a small guard, a request that Lugard felt bound to refuse, as he did not wish to scatter his garrison.

Negotiations were still continuing with the King and Catholic chiefs, when a few shots were fired, and the battle of Mengo commenced, and at once became general.

Before narrating the actual incidents of the fight, it is well to understand the relative positions of the combatants. The Roman Catholics, the stronger party, occupied a line from Rubaga Hill to the King's Hill, on a front of about 1,600 yards, but with their main force concentrated on the King's Hill, about 1,200 yards from Kampala Fort. The Protestants occupied an almost parallel line, about 900 yards long, with their left resting on Kampala, and their right flank on Namirembe. Namirembe and Rubaga were both peaks on the same range, while, roughly speaking, the King's Hill and Kampala were dominant points, on parallel spurs, running eastward from them. Comparatively open ground extended from Kampala to Namirembe, but the rest of the country was more or less covered with enclosures and banana plantations. The Roman Catholics, who did not apparently anticipate any active action on the part of the fort, intended to drive back the Protestant left, and, in this way cutting them off from Kampala, hoped to easily defeat them.

The first result of the action was that the Protestant right wing captured the hill of Rubaga without much difficulty, and set fire to the Roman Catholic mission buildings. The fathers were in great danger of their lives, and their Housa doctor and some of their immediate retainers who opposed the attack fell fighting. In the meantime the Protestant left attacked the King's Hill, but were repulsed with heavy loss, and considerable numbers retired to their original position; then the Catholics, pressing forward, threatened to break in between them and the fort.

Lugard had the Maxims ready in Kampala—one in the south-west angle of the fort, the other in the eastern outwork, and, seeing the determined advance of the Catholics, opened fire from both. The older Maxim, in the outwork, broke down almost at once, but the fire from the other checked the advance of the Catholics. Lugard seized the opportunity to launch at the King's Hill a force of Soudanese, under Williams, and this counter-attack, being well timed and energetically executed, was too much for the Catholics, who, being also pressed on their left, fled after a brief resistance. Williams, who had personally more than one narrow escape, led his men without a check to the key of the enemy's position.

The King and a large number of chiefs made their way to Bulingugwe Island, while the Catholic army dispersed. Their quarter of the capital was soon in a blaze, and it was some time before the utmost efforts of Lugard and Williams could restore order.

As soon as the battle had been decided, help was sent to Rubaga, and the Roman Catholic priests were brought for safety to Kampala, a guard being placed over their remaining property. Scarcely any of their effects had been burned, as their fireproof store had fortunately escaped destruction. The Fathers themselves were treated at Kampala with the utmost hospitality. As the day closed the smoking embers of Mengo were easily visible from the fort, which was crowded with refugees and wounded.

After this signal victory, Lugard at once opened negotiations with the King and Catholic chiefs, who had made Bulingugwe Island their rallying-place. At first these peace proposals, which practically amounted to reinstating the hostile factions in all their former dignities and offices, seemed likely to succeed; but after Monseigneur Hirth and his priests proceeded to Bulingugwe the Catholic chiefs became more self-reliant. Meanwhile Lugard feared that the hostile Mohammedans, who were still a power on the north-west frontier, would invade the country, so he could not afford to dally indefinitely with a vacillating King. Accordingly, on January 29 he sent an ultimatum, offering a choice between accepting his terms, and peace, or refusing them, and war. The reply amounted to an insult, the Roman Catholics making counter-proposals which Lugard and the Protestants could not possibly accept.

This same day the Roman Catholics attacked the property of a Protestant chief on the mainland, with a view to capturing and destroying the few canoes which his party could depend on. Had they succeeded in this attempt, their position on Bulingugwe would have been almost inaccessible, as they would then have had possession of all the canoes, while the Company's steel boat was far away at the south of the lake. They succeeded in burning some buildings and doing other damage, but about fifteen Protestant canoes belonging to Kome escaped their grasp.

Lugard, confronted with a hostile rising which had meanwhile taken place in Chagwe, with a formidable Catholic concentration in Buddu, and with the probability of a

CAMP ON THE VICTORIA NYANZA.

Mohammedan invasion, had no course open to him but to
capture this stronghold. Accordingly, on January 30th the
attack took place. Williams, with a number of Soudanese
and a Maxim, was to proceed to Munyunyu, which is separated
from the island by a narrow channel, and from that point
cover the landing of the rest of the force on Bulingugwe.
The assaulting-party was composed of Waganda, strengthened
by Dualla with a few Swahilis, and had orders to cross the
channel in the fifteen canoes which they still possessed,
issuing from Guba, a short distance up the bay. As the
island was only some 500 or 600 yards from the mainland,
Williams could easily effect his part of the proceedings,
provided the landing took place on the north shore of the
island.

Bulingugwe is a small island, not over a square mile in
area, and commands the southern portion of Murchison
Bay. On the north, towards the mainland, it has some
open spaces, on which the King and Catholics had built
their camp, but the remainder of the island is more or less
densely wooded. A hilly ridge, rising to a height of perhaps
150 to 200 feet, runs from east to west, and slopes gradually
down to the north, but more steeply to the southern shore,
which is rocky, with deep water close to land. The bulk of
the Catholic canoes were on the southern side, where they
could neither be seen nor injured by fire from the mainland.

The covering and assaulting parties separated about a mile
and a half from Kampala, Williams, with the former, taking
the direct road to Munyunyu, while the latter took a more
easterly route to Guba. On arriving at Munyunyu, Williams
had a fine view of the Catholic camp, and saw that the priests
had not proceeded to Sese, as they had promised to do, but
had established themselves close to the northern shore.
Hardly had he noted this, when he was fired on from the
island. Almost at the same time the assaulting canoes were

sighted clearing the eastern point of Munyunyu Bay, and steering for the corresponding extremity of Bulingugwe. This was a foolish departure from the prearranged and well-considered plan, as under these circumstances the configuration of the coast rendered it impossible for Williams to co-operate.

The result did not long remain in doubt. After a brisk skirmish, Williams saw, to his disgust, the Protestant canoes retiring towards Guba. This repulse was apparently due to Dualla, who deviated from the course to pursue a hostile canoe, and was followed by the rest of the attacking-party.

The Protestants, however, rallied and returned to the attack, and this time it was well managed. The canoes coasted the mainland till opposite the centre of the north shore of Bulingugwe, and then dashed across. Williams covered this passage with the fire of a Maxim, and they landed with practically no opposition. The Catholics were not, however, to be so easily defeated. A strong party formed in the east of the island, and made a vigorous and well-carried-out counter-attack on the Protestants, who were huddled up near the landing-place. This counter-attack would very likely have been successful but for the fact that it was exposed to enfilade fire from the Maxim, which proved too much for the enemy, and defeated this their last effort.

A wild panic seems to have followed. The Catholics rushed to their canoes. A few had been beached near the western end of the island, and these were first launched. Their crews appeared to contemplate landing on Williams' flank, so he opened fire on them, sinking several canoes, and driving the remainder out to sea, on which he ceased firing.

The bulk of the boats, however, were on the southern shore of the island, sheltered from fire by the intervening hill, and to this place the panic-stricken crowd hurried. All scenes of great terror are very painful to behold, and this one was no exception to the rule. Hundreds were fighting to secure places in canoes already full; many of the fragile vessels were upset, others were broken on the rocks, and it is estimated that several hundreds of the fugitives perished in the water. The vaunted impregnable Bulingugwe was now in the hands of the victors. A large number of women and children were captured and sent to Kampala; Lugard offered them asylum near the fort, but they preferred to live with their Protestant kinsfolk. The Catholic loss did not exceed 100 killed and wounded, although perhaps three times this number were drowned in the panic-stricken rush for canoes.

All the Catholic missionaries, with the exception of Monseigneur Hirth, who had fled with the King, and two others who had previously proceeded to Sese, were on the island, where they had a most unpleasant experience. When Williams opened fire with the Maxim, he had been careful to fire clear of the priests' camp, but the whistling of bullets, though at a distance, sounded to them unpleasantly close. At first the Fathers lay down in their camp, and had they remained thus they would no doubt have been spared much of the treatment they subsequently suffered at the hands of the Protestant Waganda; but they decided to make a bolt for the southern shore of the island, where they would be out of fire. Fortunately, they got safely away, although in the forest the risk they ran of stray shots was much greater than if they had remained quietly in their camp. The Protestants who discovered them apparently deprived them of all articles of clothing that could readily be detached, and treated them with scant ceremony, just short of actual violence. Finally they were taken to Williams, and their troubles were at an end. The whole of the mission camp was, however, looted, and Lugard and Williams found it difficult to recover any of the property thus lost.

The second fight had resulted in another victory for Lugard and the Protestants; but, unfortunately, the King and leading

Catholic chiefs had escaped in canoes, and thus the victory did not decide the campaign. In fact, Lugard's position was one of great anxiety and responsibility. On the west he was cut off from communication with his Unyoro forts, and with the small garrison of forty-five Soudanese he had established at Luwambu, in the north of Buddu. In Buddu itself was a large party of Protestants, with several gentlemen of the Church Missionary Society; their position had caused him some uneasiness, until he heard they were retiring on Ankoli, where he knew they would be safe.

The position of Bagge, who, with the steel boat, was soon due from German territory, was also grave, as the Catholics commanded the western waters of the lake by their hold on Sese. To the east things were nearly as bad; the Catholic province of Chagwe was in revolt, and it was with the greatest difficulty, and after severe fighting, that a strong party of the Company's men, who had gone to Usoga for food, were able to return to Kampala. The Wavuma prevented any water communication with Usoga, and so Reddie, with his eighty rifles at Wakoli's, and Martin's large caravan, which was awaiting Lugard's mail in Usoga, were both out of touch with Mengo. Over all hung the threatening cloud of hostile Mohammedans, who, with or without Kabarega's help, might soon be expected to invade Uganda. A gloomy state of matters, truly; but Lugard proved equal to the occasion.

On March 1st Molondo returned to the capital, after defeating the Futabangi in Chagwe. The Catholic chief of the province was, however, assembling his forces between Mengo and Usoga, so the defeat of the Futabangi did not in itself open the road.

On March 2nd Lugard despatched twenty-nine of his best men in canoes to relieve his small post in the north of Buddu. This little band, after overcoming some opposition, reached the fort at Luwambu, to find it evacuated.

The same day Lugard heard that the Chief of Chagwe, with

his men, was making a détour, to avoid the capital and rejoin his fellow-religionists in Buddu. Lugard promptly saw that this concentration must be prevented, and on March 3rd sent Molondo (Kakanguru) with a few hundred men to intercept the Chagwe force. Most disquieting reports were also received at Kampala from the missionaries in Buddu. It appeared that they had altered their original idea of retiring into Ankoli, and had determined to make for Mengo, taking a somewhat circuitous route to avoid the Roman Catholic forces assembling in the north of Buddu. They had been followed, and a rear-guard action had taken place, in which the Roman Catholics were beaten off with loss; but the Protestants had almost exhausted their ammunition. The missionaries urged that assistance should be sent at once. It thus appeared that the Protestants from Buddu and the Roman Catholics from Chagwe were both making détours north of the capital, and that, should Molondo not intercept the latter force, a collision between them was imminent.

Lugard at once decided to send a detachment to assist the Protestants and their missionaries, but at first none of the Protestant chiefs in the capital would venture to leave it. At last, only after Lugard himself had got ready to march alone, they agreed to lead out a relieving-party, and started on March 4th. Molondo's successful attack on the Roman Catholics of Chagwe, however, decreased the danger to the missionaries, who, with the Protestants from Buddu, marched safely into the capital on March 8th. Some men from Luwambu accompanied them; but it was not till the 9th and 10th that the whole of the garrison turned up. Ferag, who was in command of this fort, reported that he had marched to Msaka, the Church Missionary Society mission-station in Buddu, only to find it abandoned. He was heavily attacked by the Catholics, but had beaten them off, and, though separated from his rear guard, he managed to make his way to Kampala without much more resistance; next day his rear guard arrived independently. The situation was still further cleared by Bagge's safe arrival on the 15th of the same month. He had encountered no little danger amongst the Sese Islands, and had been greatly befriended by the German officers at Bukoba.

On March 15th an expedition was despatched, under Williams, to expel the Catholics from Sese, while at the same time a feint was made by land against Buddu, so as to distract the attention of the enemy. Williams had under his command two Europeans and a Maxim, eighty of the Company's men, and 600 Waganda musketeers. This expedition was conveyed in the steel boat and in canoes. They first sailed to the island of Kome, whose Protestant chief had supplied most of the canoes, and then steered for the northern coast of Sese, where the Waganda were landed. This operation was not effected without some opposition, but under the fire of Williams' Maxim the Waganda canoes dashed into the shore, and the Island of Sese was captured after little resistance. Williams at once sent a guard to the Roman Catholic mission-station, but it was discovered to have been looted and destroyed by the islanders. Williams now circumnavigated the island, and was thus the first to ascertain its true shape, and the fact that, instead of a large triangular island as shown on the older maps, it consisted of one large island and an archipelago of smaller ones. The true configuration and distribution of the islands was not, however, mapped till I visited the group in 1893.

The expeditionary force, after leaving a garrison in Sese, returned to the capital, while Williams sailed south to visit the Germans on some political matters. About this time news reached Mengo that Kabarega had attacked the Unyoro forts, and had been repulsed by the Soudanese garrison. Lugard was thus victorious along the whole line.

Negotiations with the King and the Roman Catholics now commenced, with the result that, on March 30th, the former returned to Mengo, and on April 5, 1892, a treaty of peace was signed with the Roman Catholic party.

During these events Reddie, with his eighty rifles in Usoga, and Martin, with his large caravan, though they made certain tentative efforts to open communication with Lugard, had been deterred from any real attempt by the alarming news of the state of Chagwe, and of the reverses the Company had sustained in Uganda. Martin, after waiting some time in Usoga and Kavirondo, in both of which places his caravan suffered severely from small-pox, marched for Mombasa. At Lake Naivasha, about 400 miles from the coast, he met the railway survey caravan, as already related, and informed us of Lugard's supposed critical position.

This is the bald outline of the Christian War of 1892, and those who wish for fuller details can find them in Captain Lugard's book, 'The Rise of our East African Empire.'

Before the close of the war, Lugard had made overtures to the Mohammedans, with the result that they were brought back into Uganda. The final redistribution of territory allotted six provinces to the victorious Protestants, one to the defeated Catholics, and three to the repatriated Mohammedans. This distribution caused great discontent amongst the Roman Catholics, while it raised fresh hopes of political ascendency in the hearts of the Mohammedans, hopes which led to the Mohammedan rebellion of 1893, regarding which I shall have more to say hereafter.

CHAPTER VII.

UGANDA TO KIBWEZI.

WHEN we were about to return to Mombasa, Captain Lugard asked me to conduct him and his caravan to the coast, as he was anxious to return as quickly as possible in order to represent the cause of Uganda at home. To this I agreed, but when, although we were in no sense under his orders, he also asked me to detail an officer and 100 men to remain for duty in Uganda, I was obliged to refuse. The officer I could not spare, and it would have been a breach of contract with my men, seeing they had been specifically enlisted for the survey expedition, to have thus summarily extended their period of service. However, I did the best I could. We handed over some rifles, a good deal of ammunition, and what provisions and trade goods we were able to spare, to the Company's authorities. I also succeeded in getting a few Swahilis to volunteer to remain in Uganda, and thus allow some time-expired men to return to the coast. Then, after our seven days' halt at Mengo, the combined caravan faced coastwards, and resumed the march through the weary succession of swamps that seemed so marked a feature in Mwanga's kingdom.

The Nile was reached in due course, and now it was found that a number of Waganda women were accompanying Lugard's men to the coast. These women Lugard ordered to remain behind, and as they appeared to acquiesce quietly, he got into a canoe and pushed off. The women, however, made an excited rush into the water, seized the canoe, and crowded into it, with the result that it was at once swamped. Fortunately, the water was still shallow, and no great damage was done. But the incident was sufficient to alarm the ferrymen, who paddled every canoe out into mid-stream, and refused us a passage unless Lugard sent their female compatriots back to the capital. After some delay this was done, and the crossing accomplished. Next day we halted, partly because Lugard, Pringle, and Foaker were all ill, and partly to allow a missionary, Mr. Smith, who was also bound for Usoga, to catch up our caravan.

The march was then resumed, and soon we were camped in the Company's enclosure at Wakoli's, and warmly welcomed by that friendly old chief. From this point a couple of mail-men were despatched to Mumia's to inform Twining of our largely increased numbers, in order that he might lay in additional supplies of food. On leaving Wakoli's the chief accompanied us some distance, and, after many good wishes for our safe arrival at Mombasa, turned back on what proved his last journey. For near his capital, while actually talking to Smith, who had come out to meet him, one of the mission porters shot him through the body. The assassin was instantly torn to pieces by Wakoli's infuriated followers, and Smith would undoubtedly have shared the same fate had not the mortally-wounded heathen chief restrained his men and taken Smith under his protection. The whole of the Waganda who formed the mission caravan were, however, speared, and Smith, for his greater security, was imprisoned in Wakoli's house.

For several days the wounded chief lingered on, and then died, enjoining his people, with almost his last breath, to protect Smith and remain as heretofore—friends with the

Europeans. Smith had now for some days a very anxious time, and, indeed, was in peril of his life until Williams, himself scarcely recovered from a bad attack of fever, hastened to Usoga and rescued him from his dangerous position. Wakoli's death was a great loss to the Company and to his own country, for he was a far-seeing and capable man, who, while the firm friend of the Europeans, was at the same time consolidating under his rule several of the surrounding petty chieftainships to their great advantage. It was not, however, until months after it happened that we heard the story of Wakoli's sad death.

On the borders of Usoga one of Lugard's mail-men turned up to say that they had been attacked at Tunga's, and his comrade slain. Lugard was at once for war, and sent back instructions that a Wasoga contingent should immediately follow and co-operate with us. I represented to Lugard that, as the true facts of the case were not known, and Tunga had never before been actively hostile, the *casus belli* seemed somewhat weak, and I also deprecated the employment of savage Wasoga allies, as the survey expedition was quite strong enough to do any fighting that was necessary. I suggested that we should march through Tunga's country and find out from Mumia's whether the other mail-runner had turned up or not, as the so-called survivor was not, apparently, a character whose unsupported word could be implicitly relied on. Lugard saw the force of this reasoning, and, as it afterwards turned out, it was well that he did so, for we found that the murdered mail-man had reached Mumia's with his letters unmolested, and that his comrade's story of violent assault by Tunga was a specious tale to cover his own cowardice in deserting his bolder comrade.

But Lugard had raised a spirit that he could not now control. The Wasoga had long cast envious eyes on the fat flocks of Tunga, and eagerly prepared to swoop down on the spoil. Lugard's counter-orders were of no avail. A strong body of Wasoga followed our caravan, while we were informed that, more to the north, an equally numerous column was advancing against Tunga.

The Wasamia also had risen to support their Wasoga friends and secure a share of the plunder. Lugard issued strict orders that these various bodies of warriors should return peaceably to their homes, as no attack was to be made; but our savage allies had scented the prey, and were loath to turn away. I was on rear-guard duty that day with twelve Indians, and as the Wasoga would not listen to reason, or to the orders of their administrator, I drew up my men across the path and announced my intention of opening fire on them if they persisted in disobedience. For a few minutes things were at a dead-lock, and about 2,000 Wasoga were kept back by the twelve Indians, who behaved with perfect steadiness. Finally, the Wasoga turned regretfully back, and we hurried on to catch up our main body.

The other column, moving on our flank, got almost to the borders of Tunga's district, when Pringle, with the advance guard, stopped them. Lugard ordered them to retire, but they declined to do so. Pringle then asked Lugard if he wished these men turned back, and on getting an affirmative reply, extended his advance guard, fixed bayonets, and moved against our allies. Seeing that we were in earnest in supporting Lugard's repeated orders, they now retired. The Wasamia contingent also fell back, presenting a most extraordinary appearance, as their heads were decorated with samples of almost every conceivable product of the country. Tunga's people were shy, but not hostile, and on our arrival at Mumia's we found that this murderous attack on the mail-man was absolutely mythical.

At Mumia's we learned that abundance of food had been collected, but that our transport was in a bad way. Thanks to the incessant wet, sixty of our donkeys had died, and the survivors were mostly very weak. Small-pox had attacked the porters, and some thirty had either died or were too ill to work. Our carrying capacity was thus reduced by 150 loads, and instead of assisting Lugard by relieving him of fifty loads, as I had wished to do, I could not carry all my own. About thirty loads, including the Berthon boats, which had proved very useful and serviceable, were consequently deposited in store at Mumia's, and transport economized to the utmost. Even askaris and headmen were expected to carry loads of flour, a necessity which was cheerfully accepted by our men, who now had their faces set homewards. One way and another, I succeeded not only in providing for my own requirements, but in assisting Lugard by carrying twenty-nine loads of food for his followers. Indeed, but for these twenty-nine loads we should have been fairly comfortable.

The first few marches, short as they were, proved that our donkeys were terribly weak, and every day we had to send back porters from camp to bring on the loads and help the exhausted animals. In this connection Lugard paid me a very high compliment, coming as it did from a man of his wide experience in African travel. Considering the condition of the donkeys, he said it was quite impossible that we could reach Kikuyu at all, unless we first sent food ahead and formed an intermediate depot for provisions. However, in spite of these pessimistic prophecies, I determined to push on, as the alternative proposed by Lugard would have meant a month's delay, with its consequent large increase of expenditure. I thought that if we could keep the donkeys going for eighteen days, making short marches and daily sending back porters to assist them, we should accomplish so much of the distance that, by issuing the remaining ten days' rations to the men, we could march on rapidly and reach Kikuyu before our supplies gave out. Events proved I was right, although the

"OUR SUPPLY OF FOOD."

flooded state of the Morendat River, by compelling us to make a détour round Naivasha, ran us rather short.

On July 7th we started from Mumia's, and on the 12th reached the Guaso Masa. This river was in flood, so we marched up its left bank to where it is joined by the Etakatok. This larger tributary was in heavy flood, and necessitated a bridge, the construction of which was a matter of some difficulty, owing to the absence of large timber. We now regretted very much that we had been compelled to leave our Berthon boats behind, in order to help Lugard with his twenty-nine loads of flour.

However, we had to take things as they were, and soon all were busily at work. We got a tree felled nearly across, and two men crept along it, to secure it to the further bank; but the current proved too strong, and tree and men went sailing down the stream. The men got safely ashore, but the tallest tree in the neighbourhood was on its way to the Victoria Nyanza. Lugard's efforts seemed more likely to be successful at first, but a tree-trunk, felled farther up the stream, came down with a rush on his incipient bridge and carried all before it.

It was now evident that our work must be more systematic, and the first essential was to find a good site. Austin discovered an admirable one a little way up-stream, where the river was only about fifty feet wide; and here we set to work in earnest. The biggest timber we could get was about twenty-two feet in length, and, as the current was very rapid and the stream deep, I decided on building a cantilever bridge, somewhat after the Kashmir type. Pringle superintended the actual work on the bridge, while parties were told off to cut and prepare trees, and others made ropes from the bark of the wild fig-trees and from hides. We found it possible to construct short piled abutments from both banks, which reduced the central span to about forty feet, and by the time this was done darkness put an end to our labours for the day.

The following morning the work progressed rapidly, and by evening we had passed two-thirds of the caravan over the river. Next day the remainder crossed, and in the meantime Pringle pushed on a few miles, and set to work on a bridge across the Nolosegelli. This was comparatively easy, as trees could be found of sufficient length to span the stream, and, when strengthened by piles, they proved strong enough to support the roadway. It had originally been my intention to return from this point viâ Baringo, while Pringle marched back by the Guash Ngishu route; but, hampered as we were by Lugard's caravan, I decided to send Pringle and Austin with 100 men by the Baringo road, while I personally, with the remainder of the caravan, returned by the easier way which I had lately traversed.

Pringle and Austin accordingly left, to rejoin us at Kikuyu on August 9th. They had found it necessary to bridge several more streams, but had otherwise met with no particular difficulties on the well-known road they followed.

A day later Foaker and I also branched off towards the Nandi Hills, as I was anxious to examine the Guash Ngishu plains. We recrossed the Nolosegelli by a tree-bridge, and then pushed northward, camping just beyond a formidable swamp, amid pouring rain. Our second march led us over open grassland, all waterlogged by the incessant wet, and, to add to our discomfort, we could not get a stick of firewood to cook our food. The third day was even more trying, for we found that several streams barred our path. The first of these we were able to ford, but the second proved too deep, and after searching up and down, we found a place where the water-channel was narrow; here, in the total absence of timber, we built a trestle bridge with tent-poles and porters' staves lashed together. It was a flimsy structure, but it enabled us to cross after about four hours' delay.

We now pushed on cheerily towards some wood, which was

visible about seven miles ahead, with visions of a decent meal as a finish to the day's work. But it was not to be. About a couple of miles short of the wood was a still more formidable stream, far too wide for our light portable bridge. We turned wearily and ascended the stream, but at sunset had to camp as best we could, again without an atom of firewood. The whole place was under water from the rain, and our tents, and those of the porters, looked somewhat idiotic, perched as they were on ant-hills which rose above the surrounding marsh.

The fourth march brought us to woodland, and at the first convenient spot we halted and had a square meal. Next day we rejoined the main body of the caravan near the Walegeyon River. The donkeys had become feebler and feebler, and each day the porters, on arrival in camp, had to return a greater distance to bring in the loads. But, as far as this was concerned, our difficulties were now nearing an end, for the great ravine was only four days distant, and from that point we could reach Kikuyu in ten long marches. Lugard had been very successful with his rifle, and, in addition to other game, had bagged a lioness.

At Walegeyon camp fresh rations were issued, still further to relieve the exhausted donkeys, and we moved on towards the forest. Large numbers of Masai warriors were sighted, but they made a détour to avoid us, and passed rapidly, going in the direction of Ketosh.

The forest was passed without incident, and at our old camp on the edge of the Eldoma Ravine our last ten days' rations were issued, and all warned that we must now step out.

In two days we arrived at the Guaso Masa, which was in flood. Lugard's caravan was leading, and he pronounced the river impassable without a bridge. However, on going a short way down the stream, I was surprised to see one of my

7—2

Indians on the other side. It appeared that he had found the remains of an old bridge of Martin's, by which he had crossed. As Lugard had pitched his camp, he decided to stand fast, so the survey caravan passed the stream and camped on the other bank. I had intended to march several miles farther, as the next day's journey was a long and trying one; but, as Lugard was under my escort, and had already pitched his tents, we were obliged to camp near him.

The next march to Nakuro was, as I have said, a long one, and was rendered very difficult, as the grass was high and matted, and we lost the slender track. Ultimately, late in the evening, we had to encamp on the bank of a small stream, a few miles short of Nakuro. So exhausted were the men by this march, rendered unnecessarily long by our premature halt the day before, that several of them did not get in till well after sunset.

As we neared Lake Elmenteita next day, we saw large numbers of Masai kraals, and found they belonged to a victorious party, who had recently returned from the war-path. Though in large numbers, they were perfectly friendly, and the Lagonani informed me we need be under no apprehension at night, as he could answer for the good behaviour of his warriors.

It was on the eastern shores of Naivasha that Dualla nearly succeeded in embroiling us with the Masai. There were a number of zebra about, and Lugard had killed and wounded several. One of the latter had escaped and been run down, or found dead, by the Masai, who, according to native custom, proceeded to divide the spoil. This happened close to camp, and Dualla, with one or two men, went to claim a share. The Masai, however, made off with the whole of the flesh, and were boldly followed by Dualla, who nearly caught up the rearmost warrior, heavily laden with meat. The latter suddenly dropped his load, and, turning on Dualla, drew his sword. Alarmed at this development, his pursuer stepped back, trod on the tail of his overcoat, and fell flat on his back. In this undignified position Dualla fired at his adversary, but missed, and would have very shortly been disposed of, had one of our men not hurried to his assistance. The Masai disliked the odds, and disappeared in the bush, and Dualla returned to camp, very thankful for his escape.

Without further incident we reached the Morendat, only to find it so swollen by the recent rain that we had to make a détour round Naivasha. This delayed us two days, but on August 7th we reached Fort Smith, where we were welcomed by Mr. Purkiss, and made acquainted with events in Kikuyu. Here Lugard parted company with us, and pushed on for the coast.

We heard at Kikuyu that mail-runners, with despatches for me from Her Majesty's Government, had missed us on our way back. While we made a circuit round Naivasha, they went to the Morendat, and, finding the river unfordable, adopted the same course that we had, and so missed Pringle as well as myself. It was an unintentional game of hide-and-seek. Messengers were sent to the coast, conveying this intelligence to the Consul-General, and we resumed our survey coastwards.

We had intended to work outward from Kikuyu in three parties. One, under my personal command, was to follow down the valley of the Athi to where Twining had ceased work, while Pringle and Twining, after sending the sick and bulk of the impedimenta along the direct route from Machako's, were to command separate parties, and explore the Salt and Kiboko Rivers. A message had been sent to Dr. Moffat at Kibwezi, asking him to lay in food, and we depended on this being done, and on finding, as had been arranged, the commissariat depot at Tsavo stocked against our return. Austin and I, with fifty rifles, branched off just outside the

Kikuyu forest, and made for the Athi, with nineteen days' provisions. We expected to find no inhabitants along the route—least of all Masai; but, after travelling some five miles, we saw the Athi plains dotted with Masai kraals. Now, we were by no means sure of a friendly reception, as Purkiss had a few months before fought with this very tribe. On that occasion the Masai had raided Kikuyu in force, and Purkiss, with fifty men, had supported his fickle friends. The result was a smart engagement, in which the Masai lost heavily. Purkiss had captured a number of fine spears, and a few of these, which he had presented to us as a parting gift, Austin and I now had with us. As soon as we were seen, there was a great commotion in the Masai camps, and large numbers of Elmoran assembled and moved forward to meet us. We, too, advanced, until only a small reedy stream separated us from the spearmen. Once they were assured that we came in peace, they invited us to cross, and soon we were busy shaking hands all round. Suddenly they recognised some of the captured spears, but, to our surprise, they took it in good part. They frankly admitted that they had been badly beaten, and regarded it as the fortune of war, but they pronounced it a great shame for us to assist such a treacherous lot as the Wakikuyu. They pointed out that, though we had European agents who looked after the interests of the Wakamba and the Wakikuyu, we had so far dealt unfairly with the Masai, in not telling off a European to consider their vested interests in the raiding-grounds of East Africa. Altogether we had a very interesting discussion, and the Masai asked me to write to Mr. Ainsworth at Machako's, as they wished to make peace with the Wakamba. I wrote a letter, and handed it over to them, and after many good wishes we parted the best of friends. This letter was about three weeks later delivered to Mr. Purkiss, who kept and returned it to me as a curiosity. Our march to the Athi after this pleasant interruption was a long one, but we experienced the novel sensation of marching for miles through thousands of wildebeest. These animals were comparatively tame, and troops of them used to canter about within a hundred yards of us. Had we wished to do so, we might with ease have slain scores of them.

The subsequent march down the Athi was full of interest. For several days we followed the river bank in open grassland swarming with game; lions, leopards, and a solitary buffalo were seen, while the deeper pools of the river swarmed with hippopotami. In one small pool I counted forty-six heads. Waterbuck and mpalla also fell to our rifles, and the porters were in the best of spirits with the prospect of abundance of meat. Where the river makes its great bend towards the south-east, the country changed. Up to this time we were not sure that the so-called Upper Athi was not a tributary of the Tana, as, indeed, it had been shown on some of the more recent maps, but there was no longer room for doubt that it joined the Sabaki. The banks of the river now consisted of beautiful parkland, containing abundance of game of all sorts; but this did not last long, for the open glades soon gave place to jungle, which became thicker and thicker, until at last we were obliged to cut a path for ourselves. Progression was often very slow. We came across some Wakamba settlements, the inhabitants of which were all in the act of removing to the other side of the river. And it transpired that the Masai of Kapote had been raiding the valley of the Machako's River, and devastating that rich and flourishing district. We did not, however, encounter these warriors, and continued our work in bush that seemed to be always getting worse. Aloes, in almost impenetrable clumps, became frequent, and, however we might rejoice at the future wealth of valuable fibre thus displayed, we heartily wished the raw material elsewhere.

We discovered a great fall on the Athi, and soon after passed the broad mouth of the Keite River, and a little later attained the most advanced point reached by Twining on his expedition from Tsavo. There was no water visible in the broad bed of the Kiboko as we marched up it, but by digging we got a plentiful supply near our camp. Next day we continued to follow the course of the river, and came upon gradually increasing pools of water, which were, however, much fouled by game, and distinctly brackish to the taste. Along the edges of the pools was a deposit of salt, which our porters collected, but which, to judge from subsequent results, must have possessed powerful medicinal properties. As our provisions were now running short, Austin and I decided to follow an old native track east of the mountain of Bwinzau, and that appeared to run to Kibwezi. In several places we had to cut our way, as the path was little used, and, after one night without water, we reached Kibwezi on September 7th, to find that Pringle's party had arrived an hour before us, from the exploration of the Salt River. He had found it necessary to alter our plans after my departure with Austin, for on reaching Machako's he got a letter from Kibwezi to say that food was very scarce, owing to the failure of the second rains, and that no arrangements had been made for us at Tsavo. Foaker had accordingly been despatched to buy food at Ndi, Twining told off to transport food from Ulu to Kibwezi, and Pringle himself carried out the more important of the river surveys—viz., that along the Salt River.

He had met no Masai, but numbers of rhinoceros had afforded the caravan plenty of excitement. On one occasion, as Pringle was working at the rear of the column, with an askari about 100 yards behind him, a rhinoceros appeared, and, after its usual undecided tactics, charged the askari. The latter took no thought of the wind, but rushed along the path past Pringle, dropping his mat on the way. The rhinoceros stopped to investigate the mat, and, not finding much in that, charged Pringle, who had meanwhile exchanged his notebook for his eight-bore. There is a theory that you can always turn a charging rhinoceros if you reserve your fire. Pringle gave him one barrel at about fifty yards without apparent result, and fired his second at ten yards. But that rhinoceros was not one of the sort to turn, and, but for the fact that Pringle was a very active man, they would have changed rôles, and he would have constituted the bag. As it was, the wounded animal made off, and got clear away. On another occasion a rhinoceros charged the caravan, and began to play cup-and-ball with a bale, to the great amusement of Pringle and his followers. Judge of the former's disgust when he found it was his own bedding which had formed the bale, and had, moreover, acquired during the operations a variety of holes.

Pringle had to make some long marches, but had succeeded in making a certainty of the opinion we had already come to—that a practicable railway route could be got on to the Kapote Steppes, along the valley of the Salt River.

At Kibwezi we found a large caravan, bound for Uganda, under Martin. He had a duplicate of the despatches that had missed me at Naivasha, and these proved to be orders for me to return to Uganda, and report fully on the true causes of the recent troubles. This was rather a blow to me, as I was within twelve days' march of the coast, and had now to turn back, and retrace my steps for 600 miles. However, orders must be obeyed, and I prepared to hand over charge of the survey to Pringle. Fortunately, I had for some time past been drafting my report, and now, in five days' hard work, I ran through, with Pringle and Twining, the more technical chapters; I had already worked out the whole basis of the estimates, and the fieldwork plans were almost all up to date, so I could hand over to Pringle more than enough to enable him to edit my report on the lines I proposed. Of course, there was still a vast amount of office work to do before it and the estimates could be printed and the plans published; but this work Pringle carried out at home, in a way that secured for him the well-merited thanks of the authorities.

The hour of parting now came, and it was with heartfelt sorrow that I said good-bye to the gallant staff, who had so successfully backed me up from first to last. Never had an officer more loyal or more zealous comrades; and from beginning to end, in camp or on the march, in comfort or in hardships, in sickness or in health, we had pulled together. The short time in which the fieldwork had been accomplished —work which comprised the survey of over 2,700 miles of route—alone shows how ably I must have been supported, and with what zeal all had co-operated with me; and I think we ourselves shall all look back with unmingled pleasure on those months of work, hard and trying as they were, which we spent together on the preliminary survey of the Uganda railway.

On September 10, 1892, I turned my face up-country, and with forty porters and four Indians, who volunteered to accompany me, started on my return journey to Uganda. We marched hard to overtake Martin, who had already left Kibwezi. At Machako's I overtook his caravan, and went with him to Fort Smith, where I proposed to await further orders. Lord Salisbury had directed me to return to Uganda, but since then a change of Government had taken place at home, and Captain Lugard had returned to the coast, two things which might well cause a modification in my orders. I represented this to the Consul-General at Zanzibar, and informed him I would wait definite instructions at Kikuyu. If the orders were to proceed, I could go on with Martin's caravan, which had to wait there for Major Smith, who had been commissioned to relieve Captain Williams in Uganda;

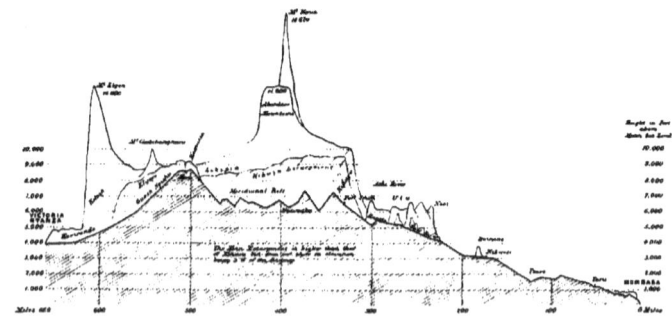

and if it proved no longer necessary for me to revisit Uganda, I could catch the next mail-steamer from Mombasa home.

On the borders of Kikuyu we met our old friends the Masai, who had been so amicable towards Austin and myself. They recognised me at once, and were astounded at the celerity with which I had travelled, as they concluded I had been to the coast and back. My reputation rose immensely, and I was pestered for medicine of various kinds, but chiefly of the sort that ensures success in cattle-raiding. Donkeys were brought to propitiate me, until Martin, who noticed that these attentions were becoming embarrassing, and saw the chance of getting a few donkeys cheap, walked off my admirers to his tent. Here he explained that great white Leibons did not care to perform in public, but that he had the very specific they wanted. Then a bottle of Eno's Fruit Salt—the efficacy of which in such cases he had learned on Joseph Thomson's expedition—was produced, and for effervescing draughts of Eno several donkeys were bartered away by the credulous Masai. The morality of the proceeding I do not attempt to defend, but Martin's excuse was that the Masai would have been hurt had we refused the gifts, or given them no medicine in return, while Eno could not but have a beneficial effect on their systems generally, and thus indirectly tend to increase their success on the war-path.

Having again returned to Kikuyu, this would appear a fitting time to introduce a connected account of the many disturbances that marked the foundation of our rule in that turbulent country.

CHAPTER VIII.

FIGHTING IN KIKUYU.

THE country of Kikuyu is singularly favoured both as regards soil and climate; but its inhabitants are not up to the same standard, and have caused more trouble than their numbers and fighting power should warrant. Both country and people have frequently been described by other travellers, so I need not enter into great detail with regard to either. The former is a long strip of elevated tableland on the eastern side of the great meridional rift, and though it is surrounded by a belt of splendid forest from three to twenty miles wide, the interior is open and well cultivated. The soil is exceptionally rich, and, as the plateau is furrowed by numerous little parallel streams flowing to the Athi and Tana Rivers, there is abundance of water. The long tapering spurs that separate the streams, when not under cultivation, are frequently covered by beautiful springy turf. The rainfall is about forty inches a year, and is divided into two rainy seasons, with occasional intermediate showers. The climate is bracing, and as the temperature falls at night to about 45° Fahr., heavy dew is of frequent occurrence. To give some little idea of the fertility of the soil, I may mention that about eighteen kinds of European vegetables grew luxuriantly in the Fort Smith garden. This garden was originally intended for the European officers, but its produce was so plentiful that twice a week the native garrison was allowed to help itself.

The Wakikuyu, or people of Kikuyu, are akin to the Wakamba, but have a different dialect, and affect Masai dress and ornaments. As they rely largely on forest fighting, their spears, though modelled on the Masai pattern, are shorter, and therefore handier in the bush, and for the same reason their shields are narrower. Each warrior carries a sime, or spatulate-shaped sword, in a leather sheath, and bears a bow and quiver of poisoned arrows. Their pluck is not excessive, and they do not venture to meet the Masai in the open, though they have frequently held their own in the forest belt, which, indeed, they retain for defensive purposes. The Wakikuyu are very excitable, treacherous, and addicted to drink. Their liquor is principally made by fermenting the juice of the sugar-cane, and each succeeding crop means a fresh drinking bout, which generally results in intertribal bloodshed. Since Europeans settled in Kikuyu, the tribesmen seem to consider that a little war against the fort is a fitting termination to the harvest carnival. Having got thoroughly drunk, they become aggressive, and the universal sentiment seems to be, ' Come, let us harry the foreigners.' After a little bloodshed on each side, during which the pombe-making is necessarily interrupted, the now sobered natives make a truce, and proclaim perpetual peace and friendship, which lasts till the next brew of their too seductive liquor.

As agriculturists the Wakikuyu are very enterprising, as is shown by the miles of potato plantations, which are far in excess of their own requirements. New clearings are daily being made with fire and axe in the surrounding forests. They have also a rude idea of irrigation, and lead little water-channels from the valleys on to the tops of the spurs. It must not be supposed that the sweet-potato and sugar-cane are the only produce of the country, for maize, various kinds of millet, beans, yams, bananas, tobacco, and oil-seeds, are also largely grown; bees, too, are cultivated, though not nearly to the same extent as in Ukambani. Their leather-work is inferior to that of the Masai, but their iron-work is good, and their tools are not so primitive as in certain other districts.

A Wakikuyu village, in the southern districts at all events, is almost invariably situated in a clump of forest, and every entrance is artificially strengthened by gates and pitfalls, while sharpened stakes and spikes are freely used in the surrounding grass. Inside are grouped the wooden huts of the natives, and round each hut is a circle of granaries built on the same lines, and looking like miniature dwellings. Cattle, goats, and sheep are abundant, and during peace are kept in the village; but let the war-cry once be raised, and all the live-stock is driven, by paths known only to the inhabitants, far into the neighbouring forest, there to remain until the invader is expelled or peace has been secured.

Almost all travellers have drawn attention to the curious fact that Masai women may visit Kikuyu without interference or danger, but my experience shows that this is not universal. During my visits to Kikuyu, we had many complaints from the Masai that the Wakikuyu were frequently breaking the unwritten law, that the womenkind were free to come and go, though the males of the two tribes were at war. The Wakikuyu warriors would have one believe that they raid the Masai, but I fear these raiding-parties rarely leave their favourite forest belt. It is true that a band of young braves, got up in their war-paint, often assemble and make it known to all and sundry that they mean to extirpate the Masai. Their bravery is loudly applauded, and is, moreover, fortified with copious draughts of pombe. Then, breathing gore and destruction, the heroes depart, and plunge into the forest *en route* for the nearest Masai kraal. As a rule, this is the extent of the raid, for the open plains appear to exercise a depressing influence on their spirits, and, though they may spear some unfortunate old man who may have approached the forest for firewood, they rarely arrive at conclusions with the Elmoran.

The early days of the Company's settlement in Kikuyu were days of defeat and discouragement. Various Europeans had visited the country, and all were loud in its praises, while there was an equally unanimous consensus of opinion that the inhabitants were about as treacherous as they could be. Joseph Thomson had visited the southern end of the tableland; Teleki, too, had traversed its southern districts; Jackson and Gedge had crossed Teleki's route, and returned by Thomson's, and all had experienced more or less fighting, after commencing with assurances from the natives of peace and friendship.

In 1890 the Company decided to form a station near Kikuyu, as a base of operations for caravans proceeding across Masailand, and Captain Lugard was entrusted with the task. The Company had suggested Ngongo Bagas as a suitable spot, but Lugard decided on a place called Dagoretti, as it was nearer the food-producing districts of Southern Kikuyu. He chose the site more from political than military considerations, as he considered that there would be less chance of friction with the natives if the fort was not actually located amongst their clearings. By this means he also hoped to be able to influence the Masai, who could hardly venture to visit a station in the midst of their hereditary enemies, although they might go to Dagoretti with safety. Once he had selected his site, he set to work with characteristic energy. The natives pretended to be delighted at his advent, and blood-brothership was made with a powerful chief called Wyaki; provisions were supplied, proffers of assistance freely promised, and everything seemed *couleur de rose*. Lugard considered the Wakikuyu the best-mannered savages in East Africa, and that his predecessors must have been mistaken as to their true character.

Dagoretti Fort was situated on a spur in the forest, and consisted of a strong stockade intended to enclose storehouses and buildings. Wood was plentiful, and work was pushed on apace. The surrounding jungle was cleared to give a good field of fire; but, unfortunately, the fort did not command its own water-supply. The path to the water was through jungle, and on the Kikuyu side the actual stream was dominated at close quarters by a bush-clad spur. The road to the cultivation also led through forest. Thus the fort, though strong against actual assault, was, from a military point of view, weak in situation. Meanwhile, before it was completed as Lugard had originally intended, orders arrived for an advance on Uganda. This required a strong force, and Lugard marched off, leaving Mr. George Wilson and some forty natives to hold the new station of Dagoretti. After-experience showed that this garrison was perilously weak.

Mr. Wilson was a very capable and energetic civilian, who had great influence over natives, whom he treated with the requisite admixture of firmness and patience. At first all went well. The Wakikuyu remained peaceable, and the Masai showed signs of cultivating the friendship of the new-comers. Then the scene changed in exactly the same way as previous travellers had related. The Wakikuyu became hostile, and Wyaki led off by murdering two of Wilson's porters who had visited his village to purchase food. The disadvantages of Fort Dagoretti were at once apparent. To bring in food, parties had to traverse the forest road, where they were exposed to the ambushes of the now hostile inhabitants, and even those who drew water were shot at from close quarters, and several of Wilson's weak garrison were disabled by arrow-wounds. Day by day matters became more unpromising; day by day the list of killed and wounded increased. Still, Wilson did not despair. He sent to the neighbouring fort at Machako's for an additional supply of ammunition, and for men if they could be spared. To his disgust, help was refused him. A Swahili trading caravan at Machako's offered to fight its way to Wilson's assistance, if supplied with ammunition, but the officer commanding refused to part with any. Still Wilson gallantly held out, but he saw that matters were fast becoming hopeless. Finally, when his ammunition was reduced to about five rounds per rifle, he abandoned the fort, and fought his way through the forest to Machako's. There he reorganized his force, and with fresh supplies returned to Dagoretti, to find nothing left of the fort or its valuable stores but some smoking remnants. Thus ended the Company's first attempt at locating a station in Kikuyu.

The position was, however, too important to abandon without a fresh effort, and in 1891 Captain Eric Smith, of the 1st Life Guards, assisted by a young probationer named Purkiss, set out for Kikuyu with a strong caravan, completely equipped in every respect. Smith did not halt on the outskirts of the cultivation, but boldly marched to Wyaki's village, and before that astonished potentate quite knew what was happening, Smith's camp was pitched in the centre of his village. Further negotiations were easy, and he acquired an excellent piece of ground a short distance from the village. He decided to build the new fort on a flat-topped spur, and as the country round was covered with hundreds of acres of sweet potatoes, with a small stream flowing in an open valley within easy reach, the new station could not be starved into surrender. Wood was a difficulty, but, as Smith had a strong caravan, large, well-armed working-parties proceeded daily to the forest to fell and bring in poles.

For months Smith and Purkiss toiled incessantly, and when we reached Kikuyu in March, 1892, the fort had only been recently completed. It was a formidable affair, oblong in shape, and surrounded by a ditch which was in itself a difficult obstacle; and this was still farther strengthened by a barbed-wire fence on the glacis. Flank defence was afforded by a bastion and two caponnieres, and the work itself was entered by two drawbridges. The fort was as complete inside as out. Brick quarters had been built, and comfortable barracks made for the native garrison. Commodious stores for grain and goods were erected, and in the centre of the square, surrounded by deep springy turf, a tall flagstaff flew the Company's ensign. The only two weak points were that the cattle-sheds were outside, near the main gate, and that near the north-east corner there was a little dead ground. Two days after our arrival in Fort Smith its founder left for England, and the command devolved on young Purkiss, who, with a garrison of 100 men, was to hold this important station. Purkiss was a capital fellow, who could turn his hand to anything. He had been a sailor, and had also had Cape experience, and proved a valuable acquisition for the Company.

During the construction of the fort there had been no trouble, as Smith still kept his camp in Wyaki's village, and that amiable old scoundrel was of course on his good behaviour. When the fort was complete and Smith moved into it, Wyaki's friendship began to cool, and by the time we arrived he had not been to see Smith for about a month, and was invariably not at home if the Europeans called on him. Rumours of intrigues with the Waguruguru, with whom Wyaki was related by marriage, were also rife, so Smith asked us to accompany him on a farewell visit to the native chief. We took ten Indians, dressed in their smart khaki uniform, and, as our visit was unexpected, we arrived at the village just as Wyaki was in the act of bolting. The old gentleman, though caught in the act, was equal to the occasion. He said he had just been called away on important business, but, as he had unfortunately been out on the last few occasions his dear friend the Commandant had called, he must let his business slide, and show us round his kraal. We thus entered in state, and were led to the royal enclosure, where stools were provided. At Smith's suggestion the Indians presented arms, much to the perturbation of our host, who assured us that, though much gratified by the spectacle, he could not dream of troubling the Indians to go through further evolutions. After a short visit we returned to the fort, escorted by Wyaki and his councillors.

Shortly afterwards Smith departed for the coast, and the railway survey continued its journey towards the lake. Purkiss, thus left alone, got on very well. He made friends with a neighbouring chief, Wandenge, whose district was about twelve miles from the fort, and started a bazaar at his village. Large quantities of food were cheaply procured and stored to await passing caravans, and small parties of from twelve to twenty men could travel backwards and forwards to Wandenge's village in safety.

But Smith's fears that trouble might arise from the Waguruguru were only too well founded. In the summer of 1892 this powerful section of the Wakikuyu attacked one of Purkiss' trading-parties some miles north of Wandenge's territory. Maktub, the Swahili headman, had only ten men with him, but made a gallant defence. It was, however, of no avail, and he and the greater portion of his little party were killed. This handicapped Purkiss greatly, as Maktub was his senior native officer, and, in the absence of European assistants at Fort Smith, a man of considerable importance. The Guruguru district was about fifteen miles away, and Purkiss could hardly go so far from the fort, and leave it in charge of a native subordinate. His apparent inaction encouraged the hostile faction, who were kept well informed of his dispositions by our old

8—2

friend Wyaki. Foraging-parties, mail-men, and all who strayed far from the fort, were harassed by the Wakikuyu, who openly talked of repeating on Fort Smith their success against Dagoretti.

Such was the state of affairs when the returning survey expedition, accompanied by Captain Lugard, arrived there about the beginning of August. Captain Lugard's caravan was not armed, and so Purkiss applied to me for assistance, which I felt bound to afford. Being pressed for time, Lugard took no part in the operations, but left almost at once for the coast. Purkiss was now warned by the few friendly chiefs, who had stood by him so far, that, unless he took action, a general rising against the Company's authority might be expected. He accordingly asked me to take military command of a punitive expedition against the Guruguru, and placed himself under my orders, offering to accompany me or take charge of the fort, as I thought best. As he represented the Company in Kikuyu, it was of course advisable for political reasons that he should accompany the expedition, and I deputed Twining and Sergeant Thomas to remain in the fort during our absence.

The Guruguru expedition was secretly organized, so that not even our own natives knew anything about it till they were formed up at midnight. Two friendly chiefs had remained in the fort all night, and now came forward as guides. The small force at our disposal was divided into five companies of about thirty men each. Purkiss commanded the leading company, which was followed by that under my personal command. Then came the baggage under Foaker, and Pringle's and Austin's companies brought up the rear. The night march was very trying, as the path was bad, and in many places wet and slippery. Numerous streams and ravines had to be negotiated, and the advance guard had to make frequent halts, to prevent the rear going astray in the darkness. Just as day was breaking, we entered the enemy's country, and had to move prepared for action. The Wakikuyu generally make a stand on the far side of a ravine, so, on reaching one of these obstacles, we had to be very careful. While the first company was crossing, it was covered by the second, by which it was rejoined as soon as it had crowned the opposite bank. Our opponents had thus no opportunity of exercising their usual tactics, and our advance was little delayed.

About 11 a.m. we were in the heart of the enemy's country, and looked about for a favourable camping-ground. A small village in a clearing on the summit of a spur seemed just the place we wanted, and here, accordingly, we settled down, strengthening our position as much as possible against a night attack. Meanwhile, the natives kept assuring us that they did not want to fight; that they would pay the fine imposed by Mr. Purkiss, and would return the arms taken from Maktub's party; but these protestations we knew were only to gain time, while they assembled a sufficient force to attack us. About 2 p.m., having from 800 to 1,000 men in position round the village, they ceased all talk of peace, and began to sing their war-songs. It was now evident that they meant mischief, and as I was not desirous of awaiting a night attack, I moved out with three companies along the spur, leaving Pringle in camp with his own and Austin's men. We had hardly reached an open space about 500 yards away, when the Waguruguru closed in on us from three sides. Their main body was to the south, across a small stream, and this charged towards us with shouts of defiance, while two smaller detachments bore down on our right flank and rear. Taking the main attack first, we poured in a few volleys, which checked their ardour, and then I turned the right company about, and led them against those of our assailants who were now approaching our rear. Their chief, who from a commanding tree-stump was directing the attack, fell dead at almost the first fire, and his followers hastily retreated. I then promptly wheeled my company to the left, and checked the advance of the Wakikuyu flank attack, which had approached within easy bowshot. A few of the enemy got into a patch of thick jungle and threatened to annoy us, but were soon cleared out by a volley or two. Meanwhile Purkiss and Foaker had continued a well-directed fire on the enemy's main attack, which compelled them to retire hastily. Having thus repulsed the onslaught, we resumed the offensive, rapidly crossed the stream, and while one company covered the movement, the others occupied the large village in which the main body of the enemy had assembled. A number of the hostile party attempted to form between us and camp, but were soon dispersed by Pringle, who had kept a sharp lookout for such a movement. The enemy were now fleeing on every side, and as they had been taught a sharp lesson, we contented ourselves with burning their village and returning to camp.

Immediately after our return envoys arrived with presents of goats and sheep and asked for peace. We told them that we had not yet received satisfaction for the attack on Maktub, and that the dead men's rifles must be returned to us before we could listen to overtures. Next day we continued our advance. Village after village was occupied and searched, and in some we found tokens, such as portions of the dead men's accoutrements, which clearly showed that the inhabitants had participated in the attack on Maktub. All this time the enemy hovered round at a distance, but did not venture near; only once, when their position was a very good one on the far side of a particularly difficult ravine, did they make a stand. They drew up and taunted us, inviting us to come on and share the fate of Maktub and his men, as they wanted more clothes and arms; but when our two leading companies accepted the challenge and advanced up the slope, their hearts failed them, and they retired rather hastily into some villages.

On gaining the high ground, we found ourselves on a great open clearing, surrounded by seven large villages, and, as soon as the main body came up, these were attacked. Pringle advanced on three strong kraals on the left, Austin took two in the centre, and Purkiss cleared the right flank. In no case did the enemy make more than a shadow of resistance, and soon seven pillars of smoke rising skyward announced to the countryside that the enemy's main stronghold had shared the fate of the other hostile encampments we had already destroyed. We now marched towards Wandenge's village, to the eastward, and on our way came across grim tokens of Maktub's last stand. The grass and bushes were trampled, and here and there lay the scattered skeletons of the little party, though not alone, for many of the enemy had shared their fate. Our porters were quick to recognise many of the skulls of dead comrades, owing to some peculiarities of the teeth. The sun had set when we reached Wandenge's, and, as it poured with rain, we had a somewhat cheerless night; but it was consoling to hear from the friendly old chief that the lesson read to the Guruguru would produce a salutary effect. We assured him that if it was not sufficient it would very soon be repeated.

The following day we returned to Fort Smith, to find all well, but that evening an event occurred which nearly cost poor Purkiss his life. Though we captured sheep and goats in the Guruguru district, we had been struck by the strange dearth of cattle. Now, Purkiss had a strong suspicion, which was confirmed by some of the prisoners, that Wyaki had sent runners to the enemy to warn them of our night march. Into this question he intended to inquire next day, and meanwhile went to his room, which was next the messroom in which we were having tea. To our surprise, Wyaki suddenly appeared on the scene. He looked in at the messroom window and passed on to Purkiss' room. In a few minutes we heard a tremendous row, and rushed out to see Purkiss and Wyaki emerge from the former's room, locked in a deadly struggle. Before we could reach the combatants, Purkiss snatched away Wyaki's sword, and gave him a violent blow on the head. We now dashed forwards and separated them, and in less time than it takes to tell the story Wyaki was bound and helpless. It was with great difficulty that we prevented Purkiss' infuriated followers from spearing his treacherous assailant on the spot. The news had by this time spread outside the fort, and we heard the alarm-cry echoing far and wide across the countryside, and the cattle being hastily driven off to the woods. However, the two friendly Kikuyu chiefs were still with us, and these we sent with the message that Wyaki should be tried for his offence next day, and that we did not intend to make a *casus belli* of his unsupported action. For several hours we heard nothing, and meanwhile all the sentries were doubled, and everything made ready to repulse an attack. About 11 p.m. our envoys returned to say that Wyaki's relatives had decided not to take up his quarrel, and that the country was settling down.

It appeared that Wyaki, who was rather drunk, went into Purkiss' room to taunt him with his failure to secure the cattle of Guruguru. Purkiss, seeing the state he was in, ordered him out of the house, and on Wyaki becoming still more insolent, pushed him towards the door. Wyaki at once drew his sword and attacked Purkiss, who was unarmed, and could not get to the weapons he had laid aside on entering his room. An unequal struggle now commenced, and Purkiss grappled with the Kikuyu chief, in an endeavour to deprive him of his sword. The rest of the struggle we had ourselves witnessed.

Wyaki was tried next day in the presence of seventeen of

his brother chiefs, to whom all the evidence was translated. Of the verdict there could be no doubt, nor had Wyaki any defence to make, except that he was drunk. So we decided to take him away with us to the coast, and deport him permanently from the country, where he had proved such a treacherous enemy, and the cause of so much bloodshed. This decision was far more lenient than the Kikuyu chiefs had expected, and they then and there made a treaty of friendship with Purkiss.

The survey expedition had now to wend its way coastward, as several days had been lost over the trouble in Kikuyu. A certain number of Wyaki's friends had gathered to see him off, and, as many were armed, we thought there might be futile attempts at rescue, so we warned the natives to refrain from such folly. One foolhardy individual attempted to incite an attack on us, but was at once knocked over, and literally sat on by several of his comrades. Wyaki's wound had been attended to, and he appeared none the worse for it. He was brought out chained, for greater security, to two of our own men. Ten Indians fell in round him and fixed bayonets. All being now ready, the caravan moved off, and was soon in the old camp outside the forest. Wyaki, however, never reached the coast, as he died at Kibwezi. It appeared that his skull had been slightly fractured by the sword-cut he received from Purkiss, and this caused complications, which killed him. Strange to say, poor Purkiss died at the same station a few years afterwards, on his way down from Uganda, and the graves of the two combatants lie close together.

In October of the same year I again found myself back at Fort Smith, where at this time quite a number of Europeans were assembled. Captain Nelson was now in charge, with Purkiss as second in command; Major Eric Smith, accompanied by James Martin and another European assistant, were halting *en route* to Uganda, and under this escort travelled

Herr Eugene Wolf. Mr. Hall also arrived from the coast with an experimental donkey caravan, or, rather, with the remains of it, for the season had been unfavourable in the coast regions, and drought had succeeded the exceptional rain which had marked the beginning of the year. Thus, quite a large force was encamped at Fort Smith; and as the people of Guruguru had submitted, paid their fines and returned the missing arms, there was every prospect of peace. But the unexpected often happens. A party of mail-men, under a headman named Suliman, left for the coast one morning; their leader stopped behind to receive some final instructions, and then hurried after his men, who were some hundred yards on their way. As he passed a stream, almost within rifle-shot of the fort, he was set upon by a party of drunken young braves and severely wounded—in fact, it is a wonder he was not killed, as the sime had sunk deep into his face, and almost completely severed his nose. The unfortunate man was promptly succoured and helped back into camp, when his wounds were dressed by Herr Wolf, who had some surgical skill.

Nelson at once sent out demanding the surrender of the perpetrators of this outrage; but their fellow-villagers returned a defiant message, and preferred war. I placed myself and my few men at the disposal of Major Smith, who, as Deputy-Administrator, was in supreme command. It was settled that, if the enemy did not accept the ultimatum that night, we should proceed against them in the morning. The natives elected for war, so three companies were despatched, under command of Captain Nelson, who retained personal control of one, while Purkiss and I led the others. A few miles brought us to the scene of the hostile village, and Nelson surrounded it. From three sides we rushed in, though rather hampered by the numerous poisoned stakes which were planted on all the approaches; but the enemy did not await the attack, and retired to the southward, where they were joined by numerous allies. After burning the village, Nelson led us against this new combination. To my company was allotted the task of capturing a large village that protected our enemies' left flank. On nearing this, I threw out two flanking-parties, and with the centre moved directly on the gateway. Several of my men were engulfed in cleverly-designed pits which guarded the approach; but the enemy, disconcerted by our flankers, hastily retired, after setting fire to their huts.

Nelson in the centre, and Purkiss on the left, had been equally successful, and the enemy fell back on the edge of the forest. Having occupied the spur, Nelson now ordered a further advance, but advised us on no account to allow ourselves to be drawn far into the dense wood. The move forward was hardly opposed, the enemy promptly retiring into the jungle. To give them an opportunity of fighting, my company pursued them for about a quarter of a mile, supported on the edge of the thicket by Nelson and Purkiss; but the tribesmen evidently did not mean to risk a stand-up engagement. So we returned to camp with a certain amount of spoil, after burning several villages and setting fire to the ripening fields of sugar-cane, which burned freely.

The tribesmen still refused peace, so before sunrise next day Purkiss and Hall were despatched to surprise a hostile gathering to the eastward. So successful were they, that, after a moderate skirmish, they drove away the enemy, and returned with several hundred goats and sheep. As Wyaki's kinsmen were mixed up in the business, Smith determined to destroy his village, which was a regular nest of bad characters. We could see from the fort that the village was occupied, and, as its approaches were rendered very difficult by barriers and stockades, we hoped the enemy would make a stand. The assault was organized in three columns. I had to pass the settlement to cut off the enemy's retreat. Purkiss was to attack the gate, while Smith's column was to cut its way with axes through the jungle on the right. Smith had planned the attack with some skill; but the result was marred by the impetuosity of the column commanded by Purkiss. For the complete success of the movement, it was necessary that I should be given a slight start; but when Purkiss' men saw me doubling forward along a small valley to gain the enemy's rear, they hastily charged the gate, and this necessitated a similar premature advance on the part of Smith's column to support Purkiss. Only a few shots were fired, and the enemy beat a precipitate retreat, whereupon Smith carried out the work of destruction very completely. The huts were dismantled, and the timber stacked near the fort as fuel. A broad clearing, over fifty yards wide, was also cut in the belt of forest surrounding the village, and this completely annulled the value of its really formidable gate defences. The tribesmen now submitted, and peace was again declared.

The cattle-sheds, as I mentioned before, were situated outside the fort, and as they formed an undoubted source of weakness, I was asked to design a defensible outwork to contain the live stock. This I did on the open spur north of the fort in the form of a detached ravelin, whose faces could be flanked from the main work, while its gorge was beyond accurate arrow-shot of the fort. This ravelin had a small guard-house at its salient, and a fire was every night lighted outside, which enabled the sentries on the parapet of the main work to see at once if any of the enemy were approaching. This work was rapidly completed by Purkiss, and proved of great value later on, when the Wakikuyu once more ventured on an appeal to arms, and attacked Fort Smith.

The gathering here now broke up. Smith led his large caravan towards Uganda, and was followed a fortnight later by my safari.

Shortly after this Nelson died from the effects of an illness contracted in the joint expedition that he and Ainsworth made against Kilungu. Purkiss was accordingly once more in command of Fort Smith, and all went well for a time.

But in the spring of 1893 the irrepressible Wakikuyu again commenced hostilities, and once more chose a most inauspicious moment—at least, for themselves. Martin, with a large caravan, had returned from Uganda, and was encamped at Fort Smith, when a couple of his men were killed within 200 yards of the fort. Instantly the excitable tribesmen were in a ferment, and fighting seemed imminent. Just then, however, the advanced portion of Sir Gerald Portal's caravan arrived on the scene, and Lieutenant Arthur and his Zanzibar troops proved a powerful reinforcement to the garrison. Several villages were attacked and destroyed, and peace was again proclaimed.

For a few months things proceeded quietly; then a still more formidable combination was made against the Company's authority. All the tribesmen who had been concerned in the previous disturbances appear to have made common cause against Purkiss. Fort Smith was regularly invested, and a night attack was made against the cattle ravelin, but was repulsed. Against the fort itself the tribesmen could make no headway. Purkiss now took the offensive, and, by a well-planned sortie, inflicted a severe defeat on the natives; but this was marred by the headlong zeal of some of his Swahili troops. About twenty of these, under a headman, pursued the discomfited enemy for several miles, and only stopped when their ammunition was exhausted. They then retired towards the fort, and were quickly surrounded by their cunning foes. Fixing bayonets, the Swahilis fought their way on, but would undoubtedly have been annihilated had not Purkiss, with fresh men, gone to their assistance. As it was, more than half of this rash detachment were killed, and this partial success put new vigour into the enemy's operations. The fort was closely invested by a circle of strong picquets, with large supports encamped in the surrounding villages, and Purkiss was harassed day and night. His ammunition was running low, when he decided on a fresh sortie. This was successful, and the enemy were temporarily driven back. The arrival of a fresh caravan under Hall still further improved matters, and after what was undoubtedly the most serious attack which Fort Smith had yet undergone, the now discouraged Wakikuyu once more sued for peace.

In the summer of 1893 Purkiss was ordered to Uganda, and Hall took charge of this African Castle Perilous. He cultivated friendly relations with the Masai, and soon had a colony of several hundred of these warriors encamped near the fort. He even succeeded in getting them to cultivate the land to a certain extent, and in case of need could always depend on a couple of hundred of their spearmen. The Wakikuyu, who viewed this newly-founded colony with disfavour, were soon again in arms, but Hall, supported by 200 Masai Elmoran, soon gave them a lesson, and again reduced them to peace. In this fighting a Portuguese clerk at Fort Smith greatly distinguished himself.

Such was the state of matters in Kikuyu when I passed through on my way to the coast in the spring of 1894.

These turbulent tribesmen are not likely to keep quiet until a few additional forts are located in their country, as the damage done to their villages can be rapidly repaired, and their cattle, their chief care, are generally driven off before the commencement of hostilities to asylums in the forest. A few smaller stations, so placed as to block the approaches to these, would probably go a long way towards rendering the tribes in the neighbourhood of Fort Smith more desirous of lasting peace. To reduce Kikuyu to order is certainly worth doing, as the country will, on the advent of the railway, prove a rich and valuable possession.

CHAPTER IX.

RETURN TO UGANDA, AND SHORT ACCOUNT OF THE COUNTRY.

THE long-expected orders came at last, but, *embarras de richesse*, there were two contradictory ones. According to one, I must return to Uganda; according to the other, to the coast; and both were telegrams received at Mombasa within a few hours of each other. I was apparently justified in doing as I pleased; so, as the more recent of these almost simultaneous messages was the one recalling me to Mombasa, I divided my few remaining stores amongst the other Europeans, and with a glad heart continued my way coastwards.

In five marches I had accomplished about 100 miles, when I met Bishop Tucker's caravan bound for Uganda. The Bishop told me that still more recent orders had been sent from Mombasa, but that the small party of runners to whom they had been entrusted had been surprised and cut up by Masai at Kenani, and that the mails, and with them the despatches for me, had been lost. On my announcing my intention of continuing my journey to the coast until I heard something definite, he showed me a letter he had received from Mr. Berkeley, which, amongst other things, said that fresh orders had been received from Lord Rosebery directing me to proceed to Uganda, as originally intended.

It thus appeared that once more I must retrace my steps,

and I felt I was getting distinctly weary of oscillating backwards and forwards between Kibwezi and Kikuyu. People at home had but a vague idea of the difficulties of communication in the interior of Africa, and could not have anticipated that the little delay in making up their minds meant for me an unnecessary walk of five hundred weary miles.

From Bishop Tucker I heard the details of the Masai outrage that had recently occurred on the Kiboko River, where a native trading caravan was attacked and dispersed only a few weeks before. It appeared that a number of Elmoran on the upper waters of the Kiboko, seeing a small caravan, with a large number of cattle, sheep and goats, encamped on the road, attacked them at night. The traders had built a thorn boma, but kept as usual an indifferent watch, and were completely taken by surprise when the Masai warriors, headed by their Lagonani, bounded over the flimsy fence. The Swahilis made a poor resistance, but a small party of Wagiriama, who accompanied them, fought and died like men in defence of their flocks. Two Government mail-men also gave a good account of themselves, and succeeded in saving the mail-bag. The Masai, however, got off with the loot, and the wounded survivors of the caravan made their way with difficulty to Kibwezi, to spread consternation in that peaceful mission-station by rumours of a Masai advance.

Bishop Tucker was very anxious that I should accompany his caravan to Uganda, and I would have been glad of the society of himself and his talented staff, but I feared lest the Roman Catholic missionaries of Uganda should make capital out of such a combination. It seemed advisable that I should shun even the appearance of bias, that might have resulted from six weeks' travelling in company with their rivals of the Church Missionary Society.

So I started alone, without stores or provisions, and with

a discontented lot of time-expired men, who naturally objected to my change of destination. Though I did not quite know how we should get on from there, I pledged my word to my porters that, once we reached Machako's, they would be at liberty to march for the coast; fortunately, I had a better reputation for fair-dealing than some of my predecessors, or my men would have deserted then and there. At Machako's I raised a few new men to see me as far as Fort Smith, and hoped to get some more at Kikuyu, with whose help I could make my way onwards. Mr. Ainsworth kindly furnished me with some provisions, of which by this time I was nearly destitute.

At Machako's, however, I was overtaken by a small caravan which Mr. Berkeley had thoughtfully sent after me, rightly considering that the recent orders and counter-orders might have resulted in leaving me without porters or supplies. In charge of this caravan came Mohammed bin Khalfan, who had been with me on the railway survey, and amongst his porters and askaris were many old friends. We now pushed on more confidently.

On this occasion, travelling as I was with under fifty men, I had splendid sport. Near the rocky hill of Ulukenia I came on four lions, but they had already seen me, and, on my attempting a stalk, they rapidly made off. As we neared the Stony Athi I was somewhat weary and footsore, as I had been making long marches and the weather was hot. I was travelling along a little path that led by the side of a rocky nullah-bed, thinking that the line of trees which marked our prospective camping-ground, on the banks of the Athi, was not so very far off, and enjoying in anticipation a well-merited rest under their grateful shade, when I was roused from my dreams by an appalling roar at my side. Hastily turning, I saw a magnificent old lion, who had been roused from his slumbers under a solitary bush about forty yards off, and whose temper seemed distinctly violent. I was unarmed, but my gun-bearer, Belali Stanley, was close behind me, and passed me the ·500 rifle. By this time the lion, who had been roaring steadily, made slowly off, frequently glancing over his shoulder to emit another protest at the rude way in which we had spoiled his rest.

Dropping on one knee, I fired when he was perhaps sixty yards distant, but, though my intentions were of the best, I hit him too far back. The wounded animal turned with a savage roar and charged directly at us; but his hind-quarters were partially paralyzed by the first shot, and, while he was still forty yards from us, I stopped him with my second barrel. He dropped and lay quivering, but, harmless as he looked, we approached cautiously, in extended order, with our rifles at the ready. However, he did not require another shot, as my second bullet had penetrated his brain.

All feeling of fatigue vanished with my success, as I looked down on that splendid form, with its grisly gray mane, and realized that my first lion lay at my feet. My porters were delighted, and much chaff was bandied about at the expense of the inanimate body, before which a few minutes before they would have fled like antelopes. Lion flesh is not eatable, but as I had killed a hartebeest and a zebra the same day, there was high festival in camp that night.

The following day I got further sport, and wounded, but lost, a leopard. I had been stalking gazelle, when I became aware of a leopard watching the movements of the herd from an anthill. After a careful stalk, I got to within 180 yards, but beyond that point there was a total absence of cover of any kind. As a regular gale was blowing across the range, my target, the leopard, was difficult to hit. Three times I sighted and fired, but on each occasion failed to make the proper allowance for the wind. The fourth time I was successful, and the leopard leaped into the air, and then made off, evidently hard hit. We pursued, but, wounded as he was, he kept ahead of us, and as we topped one undulation in the ground he would be just disappearing over the next. It was now past sunset, and after we had followed him for two miles, he vanished into a great expanse of reeds, when we reluctantly gave up the pursuit.

My luck was now in the ascendant, as next march, in a clearing in the forest, I came on a herd of warthog. They retired into a clump of bush, and there was no help for it but to follow. My gun-bearer and I went in as quietly as we could, when suddenly the hog rose up all around us, and with much grunting crashed away through the jungle. One flashed past me, giving me a snap-shot, which was successful. Thus in three short days I had added two new trophies to my previous list.

After one day's halt at Fort Smith, where Nelson and Purkiss loaded me with good things, I started with a portion of the Bishop's caravan in order to form a food depot at Naivasha. We reached the lake in five marches, and built a strong boma at its north-eastern angle, close to the water. As there were a good many Masai about, and the Bishop's men had only sixty rifles, of which forty were to remain to guard the food depot, I halted a day, and escorted the bulk of the mission caravan past the Masai. That night we had an alarm. Two shots were heard, and the camp sprang to arms with shouts that the Masai were on us. After a careful search, I came to the conclusion that some prowling hyæna had caused the commotion. Possibly the thrilling night experiences at the same place of a more recent traveller may have arisen from the same insignificant cause.

At the Gilgil camp there were more Masai, a few of whom visited us, and, after inquiring tenderly for Pringle and Austin, demanded hongo. This I refused as usual, and they went away in disgust. Towards evening we had another visit, no doubt to see how the land lay. Suspecting this, I had put on double sentries, and, small as our camp was, we made a fair show. After our visitors left, I waited till it became quite dark, and then reduced the sentries to the normal number.

We saw no more of the Masai on this journey, and, as we mustered only about forty rifles, we were not sorry. We continued to rapidly traverse their splendid grazing-grounds, where often the plain was carpeted with white clover, and where the drought, that periodically causes such anxiety in Australia, need never be feared. It was certainly a desirable country; and one could not help wondering what it would be like when the advent of the railway had made European colonization feasible. Wood there was in plenty on both sides of the meridional trough, and some of it valuable wood withal. Streams were also abundant, and everywhere stretched fertile country waiting for inhabitants, and ready to yield a rich harvest as a reward for labour. It would be pleasant to linger over this portion of the journey, and recount the many little episodes of these happy hunting-grounds which cling to the memory, but time will not permit.

In the forest of Mau, to our great surprise, we again met human beings. As we had just finished pitching camp on a small open space which sloped down to a marshy valley, we became aware of a group of warriors observing our movements from the far side of the swamp. As they were several hundred yards away, it was impossible to tell whether they were Masai or Wanandi, or even to form any idea of their numbers. Leaving orders to construct a hasty boma, I set off with half a dozen men to reconnoitre the strangers, and, if possible, have speech with them; but, though they kept their ground until we could see that they were of the warriors of Nandi, they vanished into the forest as we approached more nearly.

We could see from their trail that they could not have

A TYPICAL CAMP.

mustered more than twenty spears, and that they were marching in the direction of Kamasia. No one had imagined before this that a route existed between this point and the Nandi country, and it would have been most interesting to follow back the well-marked path; but my caravan was too weak to attempt such an adventure. In the forest we found signs that Martin's donkeys had suffered, and discovered more than one bundle of wire hidden away in the bush. As we could not carry it on, I left a letter on a cleft stick for Bishop Tucker's caravan, which was following, in case they might have some transport to spare. Bishop Tucker has described the interest caused by their finding in these uninhabited regions this extemporized post-office.

We pressed on, hoping to overtake Martin, who had left Kikuyu some thirteen days before us, as his camping-grounds showed he could not be very far ahead. At the three hills of Nandi I bagged a splendid water-buck; and next day, amidst the fig-trees on the banks of the Guaso Masa, a record reed-buck fell to my rifle. Soon Kavirondo was reached, and we learned that Martin was hardly a week ahead.

At Mumia's I made arrangements for food for the return journey, as I did not expect to remain long in Uganda, and hoped, if Smith would give me some time-expired men, to make an expedition back through Nandi. The headman here told me he had sent on the Berthon boat and gear to the Nzoia, but I found, on reaching the river, that the rope on which we worked the flying-bridge was missing. As my men were duffers at rowing, I had to scull the whole caravan across, somewhat to the detriment of my hands. Tunga's was a waste, thanks to a recent raid by Grant, but in two days we reached the hospitable banana groves of Usoga.

Six days more brought us to the Nile, and, to our agreeable surprise, we found that most of the Uganda swamps on the main road had been bridged by Williams. As we marched for Mengo, we could everywhere see signs of increased prosperity, though the friendly inhabitants were evidently distrustful of the future, owing to the uncertain attitude of their Mohammedan compatriots. At Mengo I was warmly welcomed by my old friends in Smith's caravan, which had arrived three days before us, and by Williams, who had during his six months' rule worked wonders in Uganda. The capital had been rebuilt and extended, and everywhere new plantations and gardens had sprung up. Little did I know when I entered Kampala that I was fated to remain in Uganda for nearly a year and a half.

Uganda is an ancient kingdom, whose present King claims an unbroken descent of thirty generations from the illustrious Kintu. Round this original founder cling numerous mythical legends, of which, perhaps, the most interesting was related to me by Mr. Ashe.

Kintu was a favourite of heaven, and received frequent invitations to feast at the court of its king. On such occasions he was never allowed to return empty-handed to earth, and each gift that he received was of value to mankind. It was, however, a rigid rule that he must never revisit the heavenly court unless by express invitation, and must never turn back for anything he might have forgotten.

On one of these occasions Kintu was presented with a head of Indian corn, which was not yet known on earth, but the value of which he fully realized. Unfortunately, he partook too freely of the nectar of the gods, and on awaking next morning forgot about the gift, and set out on his return earthwards without it. Suddenly remembering his valuable present, he presumed on his friendship with the king of heaven, and retraced his steps in order to secure for mankind this new and wonderful grain. Brought before his divine host, he was reminded of his breach of the single rule that regulated his visits, and could only plead as excuse his appreciation of the latest mark of divine favour, the fruit of which he desired his people to enjoy. The king of heaven could not allow his misconduct to pass altogether scatheless, so he detailed one of his retainers to accompany Kintu, as a perpetual warning to mankind of the consequences of disobedience. That retainer's name was Death.

Though this be the legend of a heathen people, it is strange how it inculcates the same moral as is shown in the story of the fall of our first parents—viz., that disobedience brought death into the world.

Kintu was supposed to have come from a distant region, and settled in what is now the province of Butambala, with his wife, a goat, a dog, and the banana and tobacco plants. From this small beginning arose a mighty kingdom. Whatever else he may have been, he must have been a man of character and organization, for he welded into a single state the districts that now form Butambala, Butunzi, and part of Busuju. In due course he died, and was buried in Butambala, where his tomb is now to be seen.

King after king succeeded him, and gradually the original State extended its borders, and embraced under one central government the additional provinces of Busiro, Mawakota, and Kyadondo, and these six provinces constituted old Uganda. Little by little the kingdom grew in strength, and absorbed or dispossessed the weak and divided Bantu chieftainships which surrounded it, gradually spreading over all the neighbouring hill country. Singo was absorbed, Chagwe conquered, and part of Bulamwezi was added to Kyadondo. Buddu's turn came: Bulamwezi was further extended at the expense of Unyoro, and Uganda finally emerged as we know it, a strong, consolidated kingdom, divided into ten provinces.

It was not destined to rest even here, for gradually the armies of the Kings of Uganda spread terror into the surrounding countries. Under the immediate predecessors of

Suna, under this great King himself, and under his greater son Mtesa, the sway of Uganda had been much extended. Usoga was conquered, and its twenty chieftainships parcelled out amongst the nobility of Uganda. Unyoro became tributary, so much so that Kabarega was formally installed as King by Mtesa's envoy. Koki, too, that small but interesting Wahuma State, was glad to rank as a dependency of its powerful neighbour, and the country of the Baziba, right to the south of the Victoria Nyanza, acknowledged the rule of the Uganda kings. The neighbouring kingdom of Ankole was only too happy to be on friendly terms with them, and the Wakedi and Wakavirando with difficulty retained their independence. The Sese Islands were reduced to submission, and only the hardy islanders of Uvuma could afford to despise the prowess of the Waganda warriors. With an actual kingdom of 10,000 square miles, the Kings of Uganda had extended their rule over nearly three times this area.

As may be supposed, this comparatively ancient African kingdom had developed a regular code of court etiquette, and of civil and military administration. The King was assisted in the government by two great chiefs—the Katikiro, who combined the offices of prime minister and chief judge, and the Kimbugwe, who was practically the head of the royal household. The ten great provincial chiefs, all of whom, except the Kangao of Bulamwezi, had duplicate titles, together with a few non-territorial chiefs, such as the Mujasi, or head of the King's askari, and the Gabunga, or chief of the canoes, formed the great council of state, though on certain occasions a number of lesser chiefs were also consulted.

In addition to the King, two other personages were entitled to the royal appellation of Kabaka, but in their cases the dignity was more honorary than political. They were the King's mother, the Namasole, and one of his sisters, the Rubuga. These royal ladies were endowed with extensive estates, scattered through the provinces, and held little courts of their own, with their own Katikiro and other officials. A curious etiquette ruled that both his royal relatives might not visit the King together, as there was not room in the palace for two such great ladies at the same time. A similar rule came into play when the King appointed a commander-in-chief for a military expedition, as this honoured official, after he had taken the necessary oath, and been clothed with his new dignity, was considered to possess the royal powers. He had, accordingly, to at once leave the capital, and make any further arrangements that might be necessary from his camp beyond its outskirts, for there could not be two kings in Mengo.

The provincial chiefs, and, indeed, with few exceptions all the Uganda chiefs, held their titles, not by hereditary right, but at the King's pleasure, and so one often saw the strange spectacle of a chief degraded to a peasant, and a peasant elevated to a chief. Each chieftainship carried with it certain estates, which did not belong to the individual, but to the title, and thus, if a chief were superseded, his lands passed to his successor. The peasants, being attached to the soil, changed their allegiance, as a matter of course, to the new chieftain, and thus the chance of friction was obviated.

A curious rule, which was in force even up to a year or two ago, laid down the unwritten law that a great provincial chief must have his residence separated from the capital by an unbridged swamp. This was no doubt a survival from more ancient reigns, when the chief of the province wanted timely warning of the approach of the royal executioners, so as to give him an opportunity for flight. However practical and useful a rule this may have been in former times, it was rather absurd, in 1892, to see a broad and well-made road lead from the capital to a swamp, and after this obstacle, across which no attempt at a bridge had been made, continue as well constructed as before to the headquarters of the provincial potentate. Prejudice dies slowly, even nearer home, and the Uganda chiefs are only now beginning to realize that a departure from this ancient custom means no real loss of dignity.

Under each provincial chief are a number of districts which go to form the province; though the majority of these are directly under him in so far that he can appoint their rulers, a certain number are under the King's patronage, and occupied by King's men. The properties of the Namasole and Rubuga are also practically independent of the head of the province. In civil matters the royal estates and districts deal direct with the capital, while the provincial chief governs and levies the taxes of only those districts which are in his own gift; on the other hand, in war-time the whole mobilized force of the province is under his banner and follows his drum.

It will thus be seen that the older Kings of Uganda, by retaining directly in their own hands certain districts in each province, held in check the power of their great nobles, and lessened the chance of their acquiring a dangerous ascendancy in the State. The Katikiro and other high officials also had country estates, which were not under the rule of the provincial chieftains except in time of war, and then only for purposes of mobilization.

While the various chiefs had judicial powers according to their degree, the supreme court sat at the capital under the Katikiro. In recent years it was quite homelike to see this great official at work. In a lower room of his two-storied house he held his court. A carpet was spread before his table, which was neatly furnished with paper, ink, pens, blotting-pad, and all the necessary adjuncts for his work. Along one side of the room squatted a number of youthful clerks, who were busy copying his drafts or recording his decisions. Seated at his table, the Katikiro was a shrewd man of business, and he had much need to be so, for his court was crowded for long hours each day with suitors and officials; and not only had he to give judgment, but to manage the ordinary work of administration. Visits to the King or to the Commissioner, and conferences with his brother chiefs, took up part of his time, and, altogether, his position was no sinecure. Though so sternly business-like during the day, in the evenings he unbent, and was generally to be found sitting in his inclosure in a neatly-built veranda, solacing himself after the cares of office by playing on the Uganda lyre.

Court etiquette demanded that the provincial chiefs should pass part of the year in personal attendance on their sovereign at Mengo, as well as that they should be present at great councils of state. The result of this was that each had extensive quarters and gardens in the capital.

The royal house was kept up partly by taxation, and partly by obligatory labour. The taxes were collected from the peasantry, and each chief, as they passed upward, deducted his own recognised percentage. There was one very sensible rule, to the effect that, in case of military service, those who went to fight were exempt from taxation, while those who stayed at home in peace paid a double share. Usoga and Koki likewise contributed largely to the royal treasury in ivory, cattle, sheep, goats, and cowrie-shells; tribute was also levied in the form of hoes and bark cloth.

The obligation to labour was enforced only on the people of Uganda itself. Not only had the royal gardens to be cultivated when necessary, and roads kept up throughout the country, but large numbers of workmen were annually brought to the capital to refence the royal inclosure, and repair or renew the palace buildings. This corvée labour was a distinct nuisance, and very unpopular, and I afterwards tried to institute payment for all work in Government service. In this I was partially successful, and I believe my successor, Colonel (now Sir Henry) Colvile, continued the same system.

Sir Gerald Portal, our predecessor, in spite of his Egyptian training, had enforced the corvée system, and caused, in consequence, a certain amount of dissatisfaction, as, however ready the peasantry may be to build and work for their King in accordance with historical custom, they naturally demurred to working in a similar way for Europeans, with their many new-fangled ideas. Ultimately we may hope to see this forced labour altogether abolished, and the method of payment for work universal throughout the country, coupled, of course, with a just and regular system of taxation.

In cases of disputes in distant parts of the country, the King and council appoint two chiefs as commissioners, and these may either be delegated to settle the point themselves, or simply to collect evidence, and thus enable the matter to be adjudicated on at the capital. Similarly, in travelling throughout the provinces, it was always better to secure a King's Mubaka, who saw that food was provided, and civility shown to the traveller whom he had been deputed to assist.

Down even to Sir Gerald Portal's time it was the custom that all Government caravans should be fed for nothing when making a journey in the provinces. When these caravans were few and intermittent, this did not matter much, but later, when much more travelling was necessary, it became a positive hardship to the peasantry along the main route, and the abolition of this vexatious impost was one of the reforms carried out when the Government replaced the Company in Uganda.

The organization for war was based on a feudal system, and was very complete. Every principal chief had his own standard and drum-call, as well as a place of assembly for the men of his district. When the King's war-drum sounded the call to arms at Mengo, each district was bound, under heavy penalties, to pass on the signal, and so within twenty-four hours the whole country was aroused. The warriors, fully armed, at once assembled round their village headman, and, under him, hastened to join their district chief. The latter, acting under the orders of his superior, the head of the province, either joined the latter's standard or hurried independently to the seat of war, as he might be directed. So well was this system worked out that within a few hours of the call to arms thousands of fighting men could be assembled in the capital. The King had also a separate body of askari, a portion of whom formed a small standing bodyguard at Mengo, while most were settled on the King's estates throughout the country. The former acted under the leadership of the Mujasi; the latter joined the forces of the provincial chieftains.

The Waganda in olden times fought with shield and spear, and had made themselves feared by all. Two spears were carried, and, on charging the foe, one was used as a missile, while the other was reserved for combat at close quarters. But when I was in Uganda the spear had been to a great extent replaced by the musket and rifle, somewhat to the detriment of their fighting powers, for the transition had been too recent to allow of the Waganda adopting tactics suited to the new weapon. They still acted as if armed with the spear alone, and, rushing to close quarters, fired at short range, but with little idea of aim. The now empty musket had to be recharged, and for this purpose the foremost warriors retired, and thus the impetuosity of the attack was lost. Had they retained a stabbing spear, and after the fusillade at close quarters pressed home with this, the attack would have been much more formidable. As it was, they could not get the full value out of the musket, for which they had discarded the old weapon they knew so well how to handle. Not that I wish to infer that spearmen did not still figure in the Waganda line of battle. Far from it; a Waganda army generally mustered three spears for one musket, but the spearmen stood as onlookers until the musketeers had decided the fight, and then only rushed forward to take part in the pursuit.

Though available for this, and in rare cases for the attack, they were mainly used for transport, commissariat and scouting work. Thus, while the musketeers marched ready for action, about twice their number of spearmen carried the baggage and supplies for the force, while a separate division scattered over the country foraging, and incidentally acquiring information.

On arrival in camp the transport deposited their loads, and set to work to build huts for the army, and this they accomplished in a marvellously short space of time, so that by evening a new and imposing city of grass huts would have sprung up. As the expedition carried provisions for only one or two days, foraging was an important duty, and the men detailed for it covered an immense extent of country in collecting supplies for themselves and their comrades. In the immediate presence of the enemy they were protected by musketeers, and naturally could not stray so far from support, so that if two opposing forces got into touch a decision had to be rapidly brought about, or both might expect to be on short commons.

The Waganda in battle array bore some resemblance to the formation adopted by the Highlanders of Scotland. They were drawn up in a number of parallel columns, each headed by its chief, and the front rank of which contained the best armed men, while behind them followed the spearmen. The attack was most impetuous, but, as they did not understand the use of supports or reserves, anything more than a temporary check was likely to involve the retreat of the whole force, until they had time to reform, which sometimes did not happen until they had travelled many miles from the battlefield. On the other hand, their pursuit after a victory was well carried out, and the discomfited enemy was in most cases given no opportunity of rallying.

The effect that education and the influence of the missionaries have had in this intelligent and powerful people is almost incredible. Only twenty years ago writing was unknown, and the bulk of the population were absolute heathens. Now every chief considers it a disgrace not to be able to read and write, and much of the official work is carried out by correspondence. I get letters from my old friends among the chiefs of Uganda every few months asking after my welfare, and these letters are not only well and clearly written, but are dated in English fashion.

Much has been said in disparagement of the missionary work in Uganda, of the interference of the missionaries in politics, and of the bloodshed which has resulted from the Christian war; but had these critics enjoyed my opportunities of seeing the immense results of the hard and unremitting work of these devoted men, often in danger, always in more or less discomfort, I think they would themselves admit that, much as we may regret the bitter sectarian differences that have distracted the country, the good done far outweighs the evil.

Instead of a savage heathen kingdom, where a man's life was rated at the price of an ox, and a woman was an article of barter, and where justice went to the highest bidder, the Uganda of to-day is a well-ordered State, steadily improving in the arts of civilization and culture, where no man can lose his property or his life at the arbitrary will of the great, or without a fair and open trial. This alone is no small thing to have achieved, and a large share in its accomplishment is undoubtedly due to the patient toil of the Christian missionaries, who have adhered steadfastly to their self-imposed task through the stormy times of war and through the dark days of persecution.

That they sometimes meddled in politics is true; but, even with the best of intentions, how could it be otherwise? It must be remembered that the missionaries had been at work in Uganda long before the advent of the East Africa Company, and had gradually become the counsellors of their people, not only in religious matters, but, in the absence of other Europeans, in political and everyday affairs as well. Their followers, having got into the habit of consulting their religious teachers on the ordinary questions of daily life, could not at once see that this practice must suddenly cease because a Company's Administrator, new to the country and its customs, had taken up his residence at the capital. Nor can we altogether blame the missionaries if they sometimes gave advice on matters that might have better been referred to Kampala. Be that as it may, they have done splendid work in the past, and long may they continue to do so in the future.

CHAPTER X.

WAR AGAINST THE WAVUMA.

I DO not propose to enter into an account of my work in connection with the inquiry into the cause of the civil war in Uganda. Suffice it to say that the Company's representative, Captain Williams, gave me every facility in my work, and that Sir Gerald Portal, through whom my report was forwarded to the Home Government, completely approved of my conduct of the investigation and the means I had taken to establish the truth. I think I may fairly claim that my report, which Sir Gerald Portal went through most carefully before it was sent home, influenced him to a great extent in his recommendation that a British Protectorate should be established over Uganda.

In January, 1893, this distasteful task was nearing completion, when Williams asked me to accompany him on an expedition against the Wavuma, whose chiefs had left him no option but war.

The Wavuma occupy a group of islands in the Victoria Lake, which lie off the coast of Usoga and the eastern province of Uganda. The whole group and its inhabitants are named after the largest of their islands, Uvuma, which has an area of about 170 square miles, and is divided into two districts, each under an independent chief. Those next in importance are Usiri and Ugaya, each of which constitutes a separate chieftainship. These districts, though independent in peace, are capable of combination against a common foe, and, indeed, to this, as well as to the silver streak which separates them from the mainland, do they owe their freedom.

Most of the islands contain high hills in the interior, rising 500 to 600 feet above the level of the lake, with bare grassy uplands, which afford such excellent pasture that the cattle of the Wavuma are justly celebrated. The slopes of the hills are broken by a multitude of densely-wooded ravines, and the more level ground on the shore of the lake is also well timbered. Nestling among the trees, and almost entirely invisible from the water, are numerous little villages, surrounded by excellent gardens and plantations, for the Wavuma are not only fishermen, but agriculturists. In their fields are grown great quantities of millet, maize, and sweet-potatoes, while the ubiquitous banana is not wanting, though it does not form such an important food staple as among the neighbouring mainland tribes. Great granaries are constructed, which resemble nothing so much as villages of miniature huts picturesquely situated on sheltered hillsides, and in these the surplus grain is stored.

The numerous bays and isolated rocks and shoals that surround the islands afford an extensive fishing-ground, and the population cure various kinds of fish, after a rude but effective method, and drive a brisk trade with Uganda and Usoga. The fishing is conducted in various ways, but mainly by baskets resembling lobster-pots, and by an erection of cane and reeds that acts as the more civilized stake-nets do at home.

The Wavuma build their own canoes on the same general lines as those of the Wasese; but, as they allow a greater proportion of length to beam, their canoes are, on the whole, swifter and more graceful. In the management of them they have no equals on the lake, and, as they are practised swimmers from childhood, they do not hesitate to face

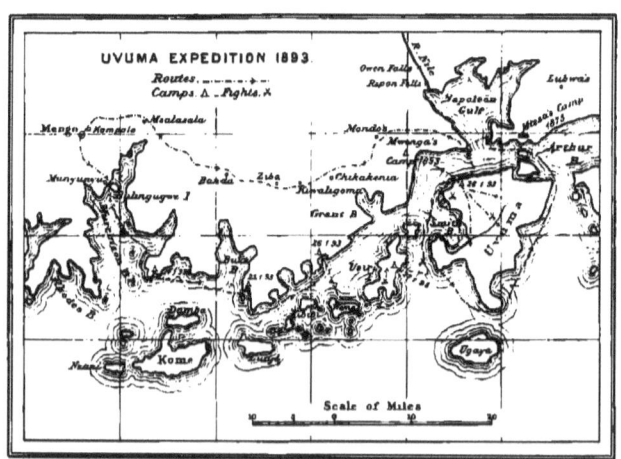

storms that compel the more timid paddlers of the western islands to make for shelter. The people of Uganda believe wonderful stories of the Wavuma dexterity in the water, and think them capable of diving and capturing fish in their native element. They are also credited with approaching a hostile canoe under water, and destroying it with the short knives they always carry. Their method of procedure is supposed to be the simple and effective one of cutting the sewing which secures the planking.

The Wavuma make excellent cordage from the fibre of a species of aloe, and this, as well as their pottery, which is ornamented with geometrical designs, is much valued on the mainland.

These islands, in company with all the numerous others that lie in the northern waters of the immense Victoria Lake, have a great future before them, as coffee grows luxuriantly in a semi-wild state on them. If native accounts are to be believed, a branch, cut from the parent bush and planted in a suitable spot, will grow and produce a crop within two years. This is quite possible when we consider the favourable distribution of the rainfall and the magnificent soil, which is of great depth. Not only do they have two well-marked rainy seasons, with numerous intermediate showers, but even in the short dry periods all the vegetation is abundantly nourished by the heavy dews which arise from the lake. The actual rainfall amounts to about fifty inches per annum, but this does not in itself give sufficient idea of the moisture of the air. The temperature is not oppressively hot in the daytime, and the nights are cool all the year round. The railway survey took home samples of native-grown and native-cured coffee, and these samples were found to contain two separate varieties. The mixture in this rough condition was quoted at 75s. per cwt.

The Wavuma are a Bantu tribe, who in language and

customs are almost identical with the inhabitants of Usoga. There can be little doubt that the Wavuma and Wasoga formed the most eastern wave of Bantu conquest in the regions north of the lake, as the Wakedi and Waelgumi, north of Usoga, and the Wakavirondo, to the east, are more akin to the Nubian tribes of the Soudan. A small colony of Bantu origin has, indeed, settled on the islands and shores of Berkeley Bay, but has apparently made little further progress inland. The Wavuma and Wasoga ought thus to have been a race of hardy frontiersmen, and we find that about the beginning of the century the Wasoga spearmen were greatly feared, while the Wavuma have retained their reputation up to the present time. The Wavuma do not appear to have that curious mixture of Wahuma blood which prevails in Uganda, and it is possible that these later conquerors from the north-east failed to obtain a footing in the islands.

We first hear of a conflict between Uganda and Uvuma about the beginning of the present century, when the former country, then raised to a high pitch of strength and organization under their warrior King, Kamania, overran Usoga, and attempted to annex the Wavuma Islands. Kamania met with a certain amount of success, but did not subdue the islanders, and was not unwilling to make an honourable peace.

Suna, the son and successor of Kamania, followed in his footsteps, and, after a bloody war, completely subdued Usoga. He also attacked Uvuma, but without much success, although the islanders were deprived of some of their smaller islands to the westward. From this time, rather short of the middle of the present century, the Wavuma began to be regarded as a separate people. The cruelties and wholesale massacres that marked Suna's reduction of Usoga drove many of the inhabitants of that country to take refuge in the islands, and Uvuma thus gained in strength by the very misfortunes of its neighbour.

Safe in their island fastnesses, they became a veritable thorn in the side of Uganda. No Waganda canoes could venture by lake to Usoga, and the hardy island warriors, not content with simply blocking this valuable route, raided the people of the western islands which acknowledge the sway of Uganda, and carried their depredations to Sese, and even to the coast of Buddu. From the wooded coves of Uvuma swift canoes would dart out when least expected, and land bands of warriors on the mainland coast. Villages were burned and sacked, women and children made captive, and the victors, laden with spoil, would once more be safe on the lake before sufficient force could be organized to oppose them. The relations which existed at this time between Uganda and Uvuma resembled those which prevailed in the time of Queen Elizabeth between the great empire of Spain and England. The comparatively great power of Uganda was powerless against the hardy islanders, who held the command of the lake, and rendered its waters unsafe to the canoes and trade of their enemies.

In 1875 Mtesa, then King of Uganda, resolved to finally subjugate the Wavuma, and with this object he summoned a mighty fleet of 230 war-canoes, and a still mightier army, whose numbers were estimated by Stanley at 150,000 fighting men. This formidable combination was, by August of the same year, assembled at Nakarongo Point in Usoga, opposite the small Uvuma Island of Nzira, which was Mtesa's first objective. The Wavuma, for their part, made preparations to defend their country, and mustered an almost equally powerful fleet, though their warriors could not have numbered a fifth of Mtesa's force. Not only did they labour under the disadvantage of inferior numbers, but they were not as well armed as their powerful rivals, for Mtesa had a large number of musketeers, and even possessed four small howitzers, while the Wavuma had no missile more formidable than the sling. Stanley the great traveller, was with Mtesa, and it is to his book that we are indebted for an account of this interesting campaign.

Mtesa had hardly settled in camp, when the Wavuma, on the occasion of a review of the Uganda fleet, gave him a taste of their mettle. One hundred canoes boldly attacked his imposing fleet, and after a brilliant skirmish, in which they showed their superior manœuvring power, retired with fourteen prizes. The Waganda were so discouraged that Mtesa appealed to Stanley for advice. He suggested that a causeway should be built to the island, and for several days the Waganda worked enthusiastically at this novel idea. But their zeal soon waned, and the work progressed but slowly.

On September 14th Mtesa decided to hazard another sea-fight. The Waganda advanced boldly, and opened a heavy musketry fire on the island. Their opponents did not sit tamely under this, but made a furious attack with about 200 canoes, which were concealed amongst the reeds. The combat was brief, and soon the Waganda retired hastily towards their own shore, hotly followed by the enemy, whose pursuit was only abandoned when they came under a heavy fire from the howitzers and musketeers drawn up on the half-finished causeway. This combat was indecisive, but the moral superiority rested with the Wavuma, who remained masters of the channel.

Mtesa, furious at his want of success, issued orders for a fresh attempt, which took place four days later. The Waganda fleet, led by many of Mtesa's best and bravest chiefs, advanced stoutly to the island, and opened a heavy fire on the Wavuma drawn up to receive them, and on their canoes which lay by the water's edge. Again the island warriors manned their boats, and, making a rapid and vigorous attack on Mtesa's fleet, forced it back to the causeway, from which, however, a murderous fire was poured upon them, shattering a dozen of their vessels. Under cover of this welcome fire, the Waganda fleet re-formed, and moved forward once more, and the Wavuma, having lost heavily in killed and wounded, sullenly fell back. Twice again Mtesa ordered a repetition of these attacks, with similar results; but the Waganda did not pursue their advantage and land on the enemy's soil, and so had to content themselves with a somewhat barren victory.

A few days later another doubtful battle was fought, and on September 22nd occurred the last engagement of the campaign, which resulted in a decisive victory for the Wavuma. Against the 213 Waganda canoes, the islanders mustered a force of 203. They did not oppose the advance of the former, and only when the Waganda were within musket-shot of the island did the Wavuma make their usual impetuous attack. But the Waganda fleet was scattered before it, and driven, in confusion and with great loss, to within range of fire from the mainland of Usoga. This victory left the Wavuma undisputed masters of the lake, and Mtesa feared to risk another encounter. Stanley's aid was again evoked, and his book describes by what means he succeeded in inducing the unconquered islanders to go through the form of submission. A few tusks of ivory and two young girls were paid to Mtesa as tribute, and peace with honour was secured. The result of this war, nominally a victory for Uganda, was really in favour of the Wavuma, whose prestige was enormously increased, and who still remained the masters of the lake.

No further attempt was made against them until 1893, when Captain Williams found it necessary to humble their arrogant pride. A new generation had grown up in the islands since the war of 1875, who remembered only the glorious and successful resistance their country had offered to the whole might of Uganda, led by its greatest King. In common with the surrounding nations, they looked with contempt on the incapable ruler who had succeeded the great Mtesa, and who had in a few short years divided and weakened his glorious heritage. Their raids on the coast of

Chagwe had produced the result that a belt of fertile country near the coast contained hardly any inhabitants, and that many Waganda women had been carried off into captivity. It was also known that they prosecuted an intermittent slave trade with Arabs in German territory, and that they blocked, to the Company's caravans, the short and economical lake route between Kavirondo and Uganda. Finally they brought themselves into direct conflict with the Company's agents, and brought about the campaign of 1893.

Captain Williams, the Company's representative in Uganda at this time, had entered into negotiations with Uvuma, in an endeavour to open the lake route to the Company's trade. For more than a month he tried to bring them to terms by pacific means, partly through Lubwa, and partly by his own agents. But the Wavuma would not listen to reason, and finally sent him an absolute defiance, saying that they had defeated Mtesa and Stanley, and did not fear Mwanga and Williams. Seeing that peaceful efforts were of no avail, Williams accepted the challenge and prepared for war. These preparations took time, as practically the whole of the Waganda war-fleet had to be assembled, an operation requiring nearly three weeks. The force he intended to employ consisted of 100 Soudanese soldiers, 2,000 Waganda guns, and about 3,000 spearmen, supported by two Maxims. This considerable body of men was to be transported in two boats and 250 canoes, the crews of which farther increased his numbers by 5,000 men, and brought the grand total under his command to 10,000. To help him in managing this array, he had as assistants Major Smith and myself. Kakanguru, who as Molondo had done so well in the late civil war, was appointed Mugabe by the King, and through him Williams made the necessary arrangements for the mobilization of the native contingent.

This was supplied almost entirely by the Protestants, for

the Roman Catholics stood aloof, and of the Mohammedans only two petty chiefs, with about forty men, took part in the expedition. The Waganda entered on the campaign with somewhat mixed feelings, as, though very anxious to conquer the islanders, they were by no means certain of success, and there can be little doubt the terms of the Wavuma challenge exercised a depressing effect.

Williams had other causes for anxiety, as it was possible that the Mohammedan faction, who had lately been giving considerable trouble, might seize the opportunity afforded by his absence with such a large force, and endeavour to depose Mwanga, and install his uncle Mbogo on the throne. To guard against this, Williams brought Mbogo and the young Prince, the son of Karema, into the fort, where they were to remain under a guard until his return. He also left Grant, with 200 soldiers, at the capital, and instructed the Katikiro to draw in men from the provinces in readiness for emergencies.

The mere suspicion of a Mohammedan rising was sufficient to throw Mwanga into a state of alarm, and he suddenly announced his intention of moving into camp on the shores of Chagwe, with the avowed object of watching the progress of the operations against Uvuma. His real reason was probably the desire to put as great a distance between himself and his turbulent Mohammedan subjects as possible.

On January 22, 1893, the fleet was assembled in Murchison Bay, and on the following day the expedition left the capital for Munyunyu. The spectacle, as viewed from the fort, was one of wild excitement. At short intervals bands of Waganda, headed by their chiefs, with their banners displayed, rushed past *en route* for the lake. The roar of the drums, the flutter of standards, the shouts of the warriors as they brandished their guns and spears, which flashed in the sunlight, made a scene of noisy but vivid life and movement.

Every hill and vantage-ground was crowded with spectators, and the whole capital wore a garb of unwonted excitement.

At last all was settled, and Williams and I marched to Munyunyu, where Smith had already preceded us, and pitched camp at no great distance from the water's edge, in readiness for the embarkation on the morrow. It was a beautiful moonlight night, and the shores of the lake were dotted with groups of twinkling fires, which marked the numerous camps of Wasese paddlers and Waganda warriors. In front rose the dark wooded island of Bulingugwe, rising gloomily from the still, moonlit waters of the lake, while from the reeds and papyrus that rustled on the shore rose strange noises, and the deep bellowing of the hippopotami, who for this night had to forego their customary raids on the neighbouring plantations.

Early on the morning of the 24th the embarkation commenced, but it proved a somewhat lengthy business. Williams himself, as general of the whole force, embarked in the Company's steel boat, with a Maxim and a crew of about thirty men. Smith, as second in command, took Stokes' sailing-boat, with a similar armament and crew. The remainder of the Soudanese were accommodated in four large canoes, while the Swahilis and baggage occupied about a dozen smaller craft. With sail and oar and paddle this little flotilla got under weigh, and well out into Murchison Bay, when the wind fell and an absolute calm followed.

The view was now one of great beauty. The two boats, with their attendant canoes, pushed onward, breaking the glassy surface of the lake into long lines of ripples. On every side little groups of canoes could be seen emerging from the indented coastline and hastening to concentrate on the main body. On three sides fine bold hills raised their grass-covered summits above the dense mass of forest and vegetation that clothed the shores of the bay, while little columns of blue smoke, rising from amidst the trees, marked the numerous settlements that studded its coast. Far to the south stretched a horizon of open water, above which, like a long, low cloud, rose the dim outline of the ridge of Nzaze Island. In the middle distance there stood boldly up a small conical islet, thickly clad with trees, on which, in the days of Mtesa, prisoners used to be confined, to die a lingering death from starvation, or a rapid one in the jaws of the crocodiles which haunted its rocky margin.

By the time we rounded the eastern headland, and cleared the bay, we had been joined by the rest of the fleet, so Williams encamped for the night amongst some luxuriant banana groves that encircled a little inlet. Here until a late hour we were busy in the work of organization, in which Williams was indefatigable.

On the 25th the sun rose in a cloudless sky, and there was hardly a breath of air, but while the morning was still cool the embarkation began. As Stokes' boat, though good under sail, was heavy to row, Williams directed Smith, in whose boat I served, to push ahead quickly. We soon dropped the fleet, and towards the afternoon neared the island of Diamaluni, where Smith anchored, in two fathoms of water, to wait for Williams. The Waganda fleet soon hove in sight, and presented a most imposing appearance; indeed, at first we took it for a low wooded island beyond the horizon, rendered visible by refraction; but soon we could make out the steel boat, and it was seen that the fleet was rapidly approaching. As they swept past us, racing for the halting-place on the Chagwe headland about a mile distant, the scene baffles description. The foam flew from five thousand paddles, which flashed in the sunshine, as the graceful war-canoes glided swiftly through the water. Each displayed the banner of its chief, and the shrill cry of the paddlers as they encouraged each other rose loud above the din of the war-drums and the bray of the horns, making a babel of barbaric sound. With the camping-place in sight, the Wasese redoubled their exertions, and the great canoes fairly leaped through the water as they raced to gain the strand. When all had passed, we got up our anchor, and followed more slowly, and found that Williams had selected an ideal halting-place. A little sheltered bay, with a beach of lovely white sand, lay under the shadow of a lofty ridge, whose base was, as usual, clad with magnificent forest. Here, on a narrow strip of springy turf that separated the strand from the forest, our tents were pitched.

Next day the fleet started together, and, soon rounding Bukunja Point, bore down the channel which leads to Uvuma, between the bluff headlands of Chagwe and the line of little islands that lies beyond. A sea-breeze sprang up, and the boats hoisted sail. Now the superior sailing qualities of Stokes' yawl became evident, for the steel whale-boat, with its single lug, began to drop behind. We shortened sail the better to keep station, and, under an increasing breeze, skirted the rocky coastline, with its numerous landlocked harbours. With the rapidity noticeable on this great freshwater lake, a sea sprang up which, though of little moment to the boats, compelled the Waganda canoes to break their formation and closely hug the shore. All day we steered to the north-east, until the beautiful but deserted islands of Kibibi and Wema lay on our starboard beam, and the first of the enemy's islands, Usiri, was but a few miles distant. Then, turning to port, we encamped for the night in another exquisite bay. A few of the enemy's war-canoes had reconnoitred our fleet, and even now lay to in the mid-channel; but as evening was coming on they were seen to draw off, and make for the wooded islets of Usiri, our first objective on the morrow.

Everyone anticipated a fight next day, so Williams un-

UVUMA FROM USIRI.

folded his plan of operations. We were to advance in line with one of the boats on each flank; if under sail, the fleet was to dress on, and take its time from, the slower-sailing steel boat, but if under oar, Smith's boat became the directing flank. A few simple flag signals were also agreed on, as the great length of the line, about half a mile, and the din of the Waganda horns and drums, made it impracticable to rely on bugle-calls.

On the morning of January 27th everyone was early astir, and by 7.15 a.m. the fleet was under weigh. Williams at once headed for the uninhabited island of Wema, in order that the canoes might be sheltered from the sea-breeze should it blow as strong as yesterday. Under the lee of this island he signalled 'Left wheel,' and the great line swung round in wonderful order on Smith's boat, which hove to until the operation was completed. We now faced the western end of Usiri, and rapidly neared it, when several of the enemy's war-canoes were observed retiring through the channel which separated their island from Wema. Again, at Williams' signal, our fleet swung round to the right and bore down this channel in pursuit. At its southern end the channel was divided by an isolated rock, on whose summit grew a few gnarled and twisted trees, and soon we perceived that the enemy had led us among dangerous shoals. The rapid pursuit had to be abandoned, and we slowly felt our way southward amidst sunken rocks and ridges. Williams got through in the steel boat, but we were not so fortunate, as we grounded once and touched several times. Even the canoes, which drew but little water, got through with difficulty, and not without mishaps. Indeed, but for the fact that the strong sea-breeze had dropped, and the water become comparatively calm, we must have lost a number of them on the sharp, jagged rocks that lurked on every side just beneath the surface.

Once clear of this dangerous channel into which the enemy had so artfully led us, we had to halt to re-form, and then stood east along the southern shore of Usiri in three squadrons. Williams led the advance, Smith followed in support, while a third squadron kept close inshore on our left. Suddenly the latter was seen to alter its course and make for land, and soon we could see white-coated streams of Waganda ascending the steep side of the island; not unopposed, however, for muskets began to speak on all sides. The rapidly-advancing puffs of smoke showed that the enemy were being driven back, and soon dense masses of smoke from burning villages marked the victorious course of the Waganda, while the distant reports of guns and rifles showed that the enemy still offered a stubborn resistance. Meanwhile, the two remaining squadrons kept eastward along the coast on the lookout for a hostile fleet. But the Wavuma omitted to take advantage of what would have been a grand opportunity. Had they massed their canoes under shelter of Usiri, and attacked our fleet as it filed slowly out of the rocky channel, they would have stood a good chance of doing us immense damage, for we could not have brought our whole force to bear on the point attacked. Had they even attacked Williams with the advanced squadron while the landing on Usiri was in progress, they would have stood a fair chance, as we, with the rear squadron, were too far behind to use our muskets, and could hardly have brought our Maxim to bear without danger of hitting friendly canoes. But fortune favoured us, as the Wavuma had not sufficient force at hand to take advantage of their opportunity, having assembled their war-fleet more to the eastward.

That night we encamped on Usiri, which had not been finally subdued until near sunset. But Williams' work was not yet complete, as a large number of captives, mostly women and children, had been taken. These Williams went over in detail, and discovered that sixty or seventy were Waganda, who had been carried off into slavery. The rest of the captives were escorted clear of the camp and liberated, to their great surprise. One of the island chiefs was also amongst the prisoners, and, on his agreeing to pay a fine and abandon the hostile coalition, he, too, was liberated, and allowed to retain the flocks and herds we had secured on his territory. This chief was loyal to his agreement, and at a later period the wise and lenient treatment he received at the hands of Williams proved sound policy, for, after the defeat of the enemy's fleet, it led to the collapse of the Uvuma coalition and the bloodless surrender of Ugaya.

Several of the prisoners had been taken as they swam out into the lake, and an incident concerning one of these is worth relating. As we pulled in towards the landing-place, and were still the greater part of a mile from shore, we saw an old man floating in the water, apparently in a state of great exhaustion. Williams humanely ordered one of our canoes to pick him up; so one of those containing Soudanese paddled close to him, and a burly soldier leaned over to help him into the canoe. Suddenly the old man, who had appeared to be so exhausted, drew a knife he carried in his girdle, and stabbed his would-be rescuer in the shoulder. A Msese boatman smote him on the head with a paddle and half stunned him, and the savage old fellow was dragged into the canoe and taken ashore. His surprise was unmistakable when he was liberated with the other prisoners.

All the afternoon a squadron of thirty or forty Wavuma canoes had watched our movements from the east, and, though the Waganda were greatly gratified at their capture of Usiri, we Europeans knew that ultimate success depended on the result of the naval fight, for, until we obtained the undisputed mastery of the lake, the occupation of a small island meant nothing.

The morning of January 28th, which was to decide the naval supremacy of the lake, dawned clear and bright. At 7 a.m. the embarkation began, but it was not till an hour later that our line of battle commenced to move to the north-east, where some of the enemy's canoes were visible. About eight miles distant the long, undulating line of the hills of Uvuma lay stretched on the horizon, while about half-way was what appeared to be a small wooded island, though in reality it was the great boot-shaped peninsula forming so marked a feature on the western shore of the principal island. Some miles to the south-east lay the hostile island of Ugaya, whose inhabitants were reported to be the bravest and most fearless of the brave Wavuma.

As we approached more closely to the wooded promontory, a party of about thirty Wavuma war-canoes were made out paddling southward. Williams, on the right of our line, opened fire with his Maxim at about 2,000 yards, and a few minutes later Smith directed me to bring into action the second Maxim. The distance was too great to enable us to clearly make out what was the actual effect of this long-range fire, but the Wavuma canoes quickened their speed, and soon passed out of range to the south, not, however, until one canoe was abandoned. The promontory was, I have already said, shaped like a boot, and Williams wheeled to the right and approached the heel, behind which, from a sheltered bay, another squadron of the enemy had sallied out and joined the first. The combined force of about seventy canoes kept just out of range, so he wheeled about and faced northwards. This operation was carried out none too soon, for another body of the enemy, also divided into two squadrons of thirty to forty canoes each, had, while we were occupied to the south, left the shelter of the toe of the promontory, and were now paddling rapidly down on us, as we slowly advanced to meet them. They had chosen their time well, as a strong breeze had sprung up from the north and raised a nasty sea, which caused us much inconvenience. Our original opponents, who had apparently been waiting for this attack, now advanced against our rear, but were rather too far away to secure that simultaneous assault which they had no doubt intended.

Against the more dangerous enemy in our front our attention was mainly directed, for they were now rapidly advancing against our flanks, still in two squadrons. At 1,500 yards Williams' Maxim opened fire, and a little later Smith, too, gave the word, and I blazed away. The waves were so high that good shooting was out of the question, as one moment the gun pointed to the sky, and the next into the nearest wave. It was waste of ammunition to fire more than four or five shots at a time, as the motion of the boats brought the sights once more on the enemy. The daring of the latter was magnificent, for here were seventy canoes charging a fleet of 250, though under the fire of two Maxims to which they could not reply. Time after time I had to lower my back-sight as the range decreased. We could see the bullets tearing the water into foam round and amongst the hostile canoes that were racing down on us, but they did not appear to falter in their charge. It almost seemed as if they would make good their attack and get home on us, when a hand-to-hand fight would have followed and given time for our enemy in rear to also join in the fray. No one could say how the Waganda would behave in such a case. I redoubled my fire, and the now shorter range made it more telling. At last, to our great relief, the squadron opposed to us hesitated, halted, and fled. We had now time to look to the other flank. Williams was busily and effectively occupied with his Maxim, but the enemy's right-hand squadron still pressed on. Suddenly he ceased fire. His Maxim had jammed. Hurriedly we swung our Maxim over and poured its fire into the flank of his assailants, who were rapidly closing. This long-range fire was far from effective, but soon, to our joy, we saw the smoke curling from the bows of the steel boat, as Williams, having repaired his gun, reopened fire. His range being short, his fire was now very destructive, and under the cross-fire of both Maxims the enemy, who were only a few hundred yards away, faltered, and turned to flee.

The guns still continued as hot a fire as possible to prevent their rallying, while a great shout from the Waganda fleet, drowning the rattle of the guns, proclaimed our victory. The enemy in rear, hearing this shout of triumph, turned and withdrew, and the apparently deserted promontory on our flank suddenly teemed with life, as spearmen and slingers sprang from every bush and clump of grass, and hurried to the shore to oppose our landing. It was a most literal rendering of Scott's scene in 'The Lady of the Lake':

> 'On right, on left, above, below,
> Sprung up at once the lurking foe.
> That whistle garrison'd the glen
> At once with full five hundred men,
> As if the yawning hill to heaven
> A subterranean host had given'

—only their numbers were not to be counted in hundreds, but rather by thousands. Crowding to the shore, they formed a great mass of spears, while their slingers, perched on every point of vantage, began to rain missiles on the nearest canoes.

It was no part of Williams' programme to land here, so he pushed forward in pursuit of the beaten squadrons of the enemy. The pursuit was conducted in good order, as we did not know that still intact squadrons of the enemy might not be lurking in hidden creeks to take advantage of any confusion. The dense bodies of the enemy on shore followed parallel to us, but, beyond a few musket-shots directed against their more daring slingers, they were not molested. To have turned the Maxims on them would have been sheer massacre. One of the slingers was a man of splendid courage. He took up his station on a jutting rocky headland, and hurled stone after stone amongst the canoes as they passed. Again and again the bullets whistled past him, but he heeded them not, and as we passed out of range we could not help feeling pleased that our daring enemy had escaped unhurt.

We could see that the enemy's canoes in front of us were baling hard and were somewhat crippled, but Williams kept his force in hand until we rounded the toe of the boot and saw that they had no more squadrons in reserve. Then he gave the signal for a general pursuit, and this caused, perhaps, the most exciting scene, of its kind, that will ever be witnessed on the Victoria Lake. The water was now like glass, as the wind had dropped as suddenly as it had risen. Four miles ahead of us lay the mainland of Uvuma, for which the enemy's canoes were making with a start of about 2,000 yards. Suddenly, on Williams' signal, the Waganda canoes quickened to racing speed, and, fast as we had been travelling before, appeared to leap forward and leave the boats standing still. The largest and swiftest canoes flew to the front, and soon the scene baffled description.

Far ahead the Wavuma strained every nerve and muscle to gain the friendly shore, while behind raced the Waganda, determined to cut them off. The surface of the lake, a moment before so smooth and unruffled, was cut into long furrows by the darting prows, while thousands of paddles dashed the water into foam. The Waganda warriors cheered, the boatmen yelled in unison, and, with streaming pennants and the deep roar of the war-drums, the Waganda fleet rapidly lessened the distance between them and the enemy. But the Wavuma were now nearing their island, and the race appeared even. We, though left far behind, could see what was happening. The enemy divided into two squadrons, and, while one of them disappeared round the north-west point of Uvuma, the other was driven into a small bay, closely pressed by superior numbers. Surely they must be captured, for now their pursuers have passed the entrance and urge their canoes more rapidly, in the certain hope of success. But no! the Wavuma wheel speedily to the right, and, by an inner channel which was invisible from the outside, gain the open water once more, and the chase continues; but some there were who, less fortunate, were driven ashore. Soon the Waganda were seen to land and stream up the hillsides, driving the enemy before them with a brisk fire of musketry. Meanwhile, a large squadron of the Waganda fleet had held straight on after those of the enemy who had rounded the point of Uvuma, and it was not till late that we heard of their success in capturing forty of the enemy's canoes. But few prisoners were made, for the islanders had taken to the water and gained the shore before the Waganda closed with them.

While these events were happening in front, Smith had commenced a long-range fire on some of the enemy who appeared in the south; but this skirmish was soon broken off, and we hurried on to rejoin Williams and the fleet in front. A large canoe of Lagumba's took us in tow, and, with its assistance and the sturdy efforts of our own rowers, we were soon off the spot where Williams had elected to camp.

We heard that the landing had been but feebly opposed, as the Wavuma had concentrated their main strength on the peninsula, and could not get round in time to offer an effectual resistance. Our side had thus secured a great deal of booty, and the camp resounded with the lowing of herds and bleating of flocks. Our loss had not been heavy, although towards evening a good many wounded men arrived to have their hurts attended to.

Having thus decisively beaten the enemy's fleet, and

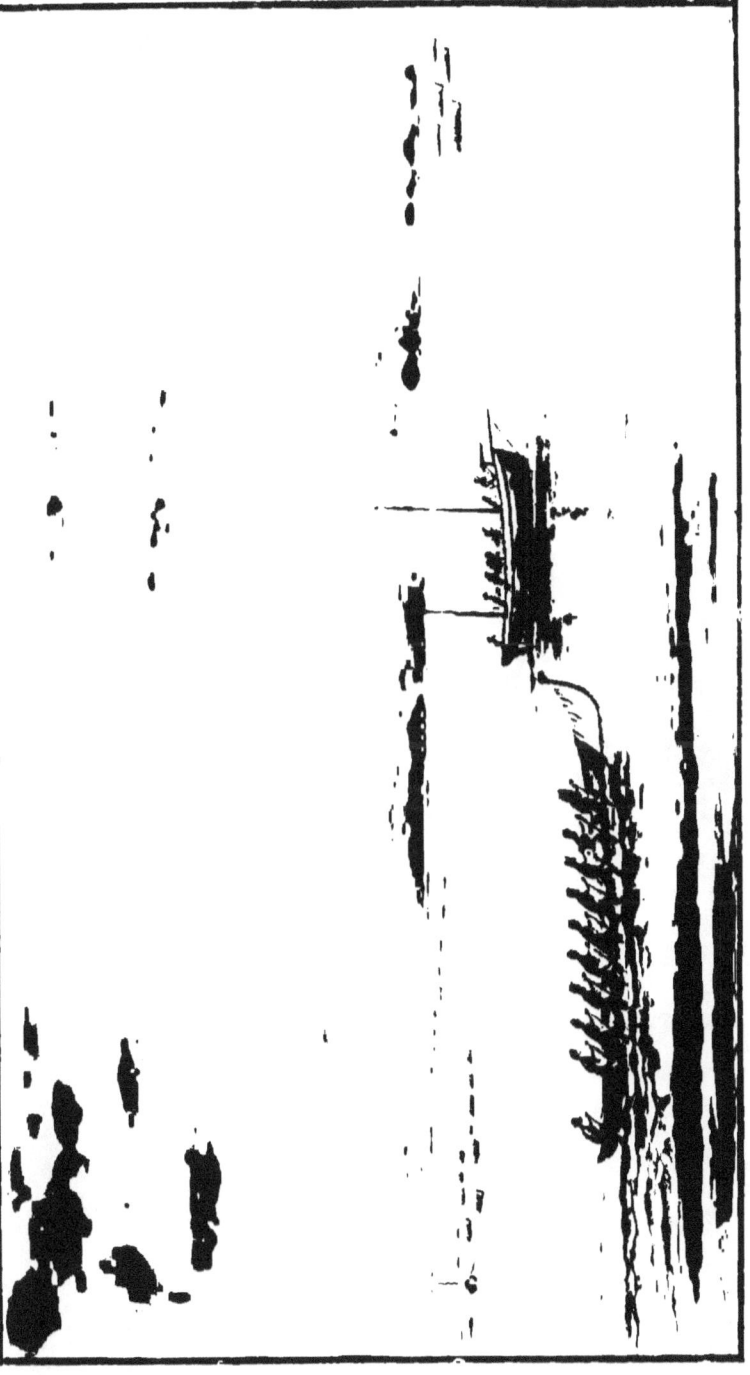

PURSUIT OF ENEMY'S FLEET.

effected a landing on the heretofore impregnable Uvuma, Williams was not disposed to grant the enemy breathing-time, as he rightly considered that, by pressing them whilst still discouraged by their reverses, they would be likely to submit the sooner. Accordingly, strong columns of Waganda were despatched inland, while the boats, with a few canoes, took the sea with the intention of engaging and dispersing any combination of the enemy's fleet. The camp was not left unguarded, as the Soudanese and a strong Waganda force under Kakanguru remained stationary.

The enemy would not venture on another naval engagement, having lost the day before about fifty canoes, either captured or disabled, and early in the afternoon our flotilla returned to its moorings. But the land columns were more or less stoutly opposed, and once suffered a decided reverse. The Sekiwala, one of the principal district chiefs of Singo, had pressed far inland, and overcome no little resistance, when he found his ammunition was running short. He accordingly gave the signal for retreat, which put fresh courage into the enemy. His column, as it retired, was repeatedly attacked, and the chief himself was killed while making a gallant stand against the now daring foe. This produced the usual result, and the Waganda retired in disorder into our camp. The Mujasi was at once despatched with a strong column to drive back the enemy, and after a brisk engagement routed them, and recovered the bodies of Sekiwala and those who had stood and fallen with him. This closed the operations of the day.

The amount of booty in camp was now very great, and the Waganda, somewhat discouraged by the resistance they had encountered that day, were anxious for a brief halt, in order to ship to the Uganda mainland the cattle, goats and sheep which they had captured. Williams suggested that this could best be done in the calm moonlight night, but the great dislike the Waganda have to night operations proved an insuperable objection.

The shipment of cattle commenced next day, and caused no little excitement. The King had, as I have said, camped on the mainland of Uganda to watch the operations, and now wrote to Williams, to say that he heard he was giving himself much unnecessary trouble about the division of the spoil, so he (the King) would relieve him of this troublesome task. The chiefs were much exercised over this message, as they knew that if Mwanga once got the cattle into his clutches their shares would be small indeed. Feeling ran high, and Williams was obliged to visit the King and adjust matters.

The Wavuma coalition began to collapse on January 30th, on which date the chief of North Uvuma submitted, and agreed to pay a fine. Further looting was consequently forbidden, and after the value of the fine had been deducted in kind, the balance of the cattle, sheep and goats was returned to the repentant chief. The chief of Ugaya also submitted, and paid the first instalment of his fine, so that this left the chief of Southern Uvuma alone in his hostility.

The same day there arrived a contingent of 100 war-canoes, belonging to the Usoga chieftain Lubwa, but, as their services were not required, they were thanked and sent home.

At this period I found it necessary to return to the capital, as Mr. Gedge, the *Times* correspondent, who had just reached Uganda, said he had important letters for me from Sir Gerald Portal. It turned out that these letters contained orders that I must await Sir Gerald's arrival, and assist him in Uganda.

Williams now proceeded against the chief of Southern Uvuma, who, though not daring to risk a naval engagement, offered a certain amount of resistance on land. This was, however, quickly crushed, Williams himself leading a charge of Soudanese against the enemy. Beaten and discomfited, the enemy swam out to some rocks and shoals, where they prepared to sell their lives dearly. The Waganda opened fire on them, but Williams and Smith stopped this, and persuaded the last hostile body of Wavuma to surrender. This closed the campaign, and Williams, after circumnavigating the island, returned to the capital on February 10th, having left Smith at Lubwa's to receive the remainder of the fines, which the Wavuma loyally paid.

Not only had Williams distinguished himself by the organization of the campaign and in its execution, but the terms of peace he concluded with the islanders were a model of forethought. He decided that the gallant Wavuma should remain free and independent as heretofore, under their own chiefs, the friends of the Company, but in no sense vassals of Uganda. A contrary decision would have caused a bitter feeling that it would have taken generations to erase, but the terms imposed by Williams rendered the Wavuma our friends almost as soon as peace was declared.

In June, 1893, when I was Acting-Commissioner of Uganda, the Wavuma chiefs paid me a visit at Kampala. I confirmed the decision of Williams, that the Wavuma were not tributary to Uganda, but independent under their own chiefs. They volunteered to place themselves under Lubwa as permanent head, but this course I discouraged, as Lubwa was, in virtue of his chieftainship in Usoga, a vassal of Uganda. They also offered to hire canoes to the Government for the lake route from Kavirondo to Port Alice, but rightly pointed out that they could not at once do this, as so many of their canoes had been destroyed during the recent war that it would take some time to replace them. The interview was in every way satisfactory, and, after the chiefs had received some small presents, they returned to their island districts the friends of the British.

Shortly afterwards Dr. Moffat travelled to Kavirondo by boat, and passed the Wavuma Islands without the least trouble, and in November, 1893, the Wavuma sent a contingent of their canoes to take part in a great review that Lubwa held in my honour, on the occasion of my visiting his district. Captains Gibb and Thruston travelled from Kavirondo to Murchison Bay by canoe, and camped one night on one of the Wavuma Islands, where they were received in friendship.

Such results would not have been possible but for the humane way in which Captain Williams carried out his campaign, and the generous treatment he extended to the brave tribe he conquered.

CHAPTER XI.

SIR GERALD PORTAL'S WORK.

I HAVE in the last chapter mentioned that Mr. Gedge had arrived in Uganda with letters which materially affected my own plans; but more important still was the news that an Imperial Commissioner was on his way from the coast with a brilliant and talented staff to settle the vexed question as to whether Uganda should be retained or not. The Imperial British East Africa Company had so far incurred a considerable annual loss in sustaining British interests in the country, and now they had definitely decided to withdraw. The question was, Should the British Government take their place?

Uganda had lately been much before the European public, on account of the events of the recent civil war, and the extraordinary reports of those events sent home by the White Fathers of Algiers, the Roman Catholic mission in Uganda. Into the truth of these reports it was my duty to inquire. But Sir Gerald Portal, the Imperial Commissioner, had to take up a much wider field, the question of the extension of the British Protectorate over these regions.

Before going into these matters, it may be well to glance at the state of the country at this time. Just before his departure for the coast in June, 1892, Captain Lugard had concluded arrangements with the Roman Catholic and

Mohammedan parties in Uganda, arrangements which had resulted in a repartition of the country, which he fondly imagined would result in permanent peace. But his departure at the close of these settlements naturally prevented his seeing how this new division of Uganda would work in practice. A famous Scotch poet has said,

> 'The best laid schemes o' mice and men
> Gang aft a-gley,'

and this more or less accurately describes the development of events.

Before the Christian war of 1892, Lugard had three parties of Waganda to consider: the Roman Catholics, who formed the majority in the country; the Protestants, who constituted a formidable minority in Uganda; and the Mohammedan party, who had been expelled by the Christians, and who, aided and abetted by Kabarega of Unyoro, had systematically raided its borders. The Mohammedans were weaker than either of the two Christian parties, and were hostile to both; indeed, Lugard had himself led an expedition against them the previous year. After the civil war of 1892 he had still these factions to consider, but the Protestants and Roman Catholics had changed places in regard to numbers, as Mwanga had altered his creed, and drawn a number of nominal Catholics with him. The Protestants had stood by Lugard, the Catholics had opposed him, and the Mohammedans had attempted to induce Selim Bey's Soudanese to aid them in reconquering Uganda for Islam. Now, before the war the country was divided pretty equally between the two Christian parties, while the Mohammedans were out in the cold in Unyoro, where their strength was fast dwindling away, and had decreased by quite half since 1889.

After the war Lugard's repartition of Uganda gave the Protestants six of the ten provinces, the Catholics one, and the Mohammedans three. It is true that the three provinces allotted to the Mohammedans were small, and did not equal in total area the territory given to the Catholics; but, considering the relative numbers of the different sects, the distribution of the land was very unequal. The best authorities gave the total population of Uganda at this time as about 400,000, which, for an area of 10,000 square miles, would give an average of 40 per mile. But the average density of population per square mile for each sect must have been more nearly as follows: Protestants 35, Roman Catholics 60 to 70, and Mohammedans 15 to 20.

The political power of the three sects was still more unequal, as the Mohammedans, who perhaps mustered one-fifth the number of the Roman Catholics, were given three times the representative power of the latter in the councils of the State. Need it be wondered at that the Roman Catholic party confined themselves in sullen isolation to their own province, and considered themselves harshly dealt with, when they saw not only their victors, the Protestants, aggrandized at their expense, but even the common enemy, the Mohammedans, preferred before them? Need it be wondered at that the Mohammedans, who a few short months before had been a fast-dwindling power, whose adherents were deserting them, plucked up fresh heart, and, installed in the original provinces of the illustrious Kintu, dreamed of one day repeating history and extending their rule over the whole country? Already they had made a great step forward, and, though forming hardly one-twentieth of the population of Uganda, had secured a good quarter of the political power in the councils of the land.

The actual distribution of these three sects favoured the ambitions of the Mohammedans, for their provinces formed a concentrated block that more or less separated the Christian parties. The Catholics had been allotted the great southern province of Buddu, conterminous with the German territory on the one hand, and on the other with the Mohammedans, along the greater portion of their northern border. The East of Uganda was Protestant, from whose main territory two weak branches, the province of Mawakota and the great Singo district of Bwekula, stretched southwards on either side of the concentrated Mohammedan power. The latter, thanks to the desertion of their peasantry, had not enough hands to till their plantations, many of which were falling into ruin, but their proportion of well-armed men was considerable. They had already, since Lugard's departure, attempted to induce the Roman Catholics to join them in war against the Protestants, and, failing in this, had assiduously cultivated friendly relations with Selim Bey and his Soudanese soldiery, in view of the possible withdrawal of the Company's agents from Uganda. They had fallen into their old habits, and had even started a slave-market at one of the Unyoro forts, which they supplied by raiding the neighbouring States.

Nor had they confined their depredations to regions lying outside Uganda itself, for frequent dacoities and disturbances had taken place within its borders, and so bold had they waxed that in the winter of 1892-93 another civil war had nearly taken place. After a more than usually daring dacoity, Williams sent them an ultimatum, demanding the surrender of the guilty within a limited period. This resulted in a temporary lull; but the Mohammedans did not fulfil their promises, and, but for the hint from Selim Bey that his Soudanese troops might object to fight against their co-religionists, Williams might have proceeded to military operations against them.

Such is a brief statement of the condition of the parties in the spring of 1893. The Protestants, the predominant party, held the east and north, but had rather fought shy of settling in Mawakota and Bwekula, and, indeed, had more land than they could possibly develop. The Roman Catholics were more crowded in Buddu, where they had suffered greatly from an epidemic of the bubonic plague. They were discontented, and held themselves aloof, though they adhered strictly and loyally to the letter of their treaty with Lugard, and declined to unite with the Mohammedans in redressing their grievances by force of arms. The Mohammedans, turbulent and ambitious, showed no signs of fulfilling their engagements and settling down as loyal subjects of Mwanga, but rather dreamed of a day when, in conjunction with the Soudanese, they might hope to see the whole of Uganda once more under the rule of Islam, and under a Mohammedan King.

Long before the appointment of an Imperial Commissioner, Williams had seen that Lugard's settlement could not be a permanent one, and had opened negotiations with the Christian parties, with a view to extending the Roman Catholic territory. At one time these promised well, but, from reasons into which it is unnecessary to enter, the negotiations had broken down. This was a great blow to Williams, who saw that the future prosperity of the country necessitated a reconciliation between the Christian sects; but his labour was not entirely in vain, as he had more than paved the way for Sir Gerald Portal.

There is still one more question that cannot be left out of account in considering the state of these regions at this time : the question of the Soudanese. Lugard had in 1891 found a large number of these, numbering some 8,000 to 9,000, if their slaves and followers be taken into account, at Kavalli's, and had established them in a chain of forts running north and south across South-west Unyoro. The southern forts had shortly afterwards been abandoned, and the line wheeled to the left, so that they now lay nearly east and west between Uganda and Toru. These Soudanese were not in the Company's pay, for Lugard had not the wherewithal to pay them.

They were not even entirely in the Company's service, as they had only agreed to garrison the forts pending orders from Egypt regarding their ultimate disposal. On some of the forts, indeed, they flew the Egyptian flag. They were under no proper European supervision, but were left to the care of their native officers.

This great mass of people had to be fed, and the Company's resources in Uganda were unequal to supplying trade goods in sufficient quantity to purchase rations for them, so Lugard had given them leave to feed themselves by raiding Southern Unyoro. So liberally had they interpreted this permission that by the spring of 1893 they had laid waste and devastated some 1,500 square miles of territory, and it was with the greatest difficulty that the Company's small caravans, which periodically visited the Salt Lake, could obtain food while marching past the forts. Not only had the Soudanese laid waste Kabarega's provinces for two days' march to the north, but they had been equally successful in converting the province of Kyaka and the greater portion of Kitakwanda, south of the line of the forts, into a desolation. They had also interfered in Toru, and even began to create or depose chiefs according to their pleasure. Terrible stories of the atrocities committed by these unresponsible garrisons reached Uganda, and though, as usual, they fortunately proved to be grossly exaggerated, enough remained to show that, under the care of such protectors, Southern Unyoro was in an unhappy condition.

Such was the position of affairs when Sir Gerald Portal arrived and commenced work in March, 1893.

Short reflection showed that it would be impossible to abandon Uganda. Had we retired and left the Soudanese behind us, they would have made common cause with the Mohammedans, and Christianity and civilization would have been crushed out of the land. Had we withdrawn the

Soudanese, a task which would have taken months of preparation, and necessitated immense food-depots on the road to the coast, civil war in Uganda would have inevitably followed on our departure, and whichever party emerged as victors, the weakened country could not have held its own against foreign aggressors. Moreover, the moral effects of our withdrawal would have affected territories other than our own, and might well have caused international complications.

Having determined on retaining Uganda, Sir Gerald Portal had now to deal with the three great questions of the hour: the Soudanese, Catholic, and Mohammedan problems. The first of these was vital to our retention of Uganda, while the second was almost a European affair, and Sir Gerald devoted himself with characteristic energy to their solution.

Lugard had before his departure raised a company from Selim Bey's Soudanese, and to this Williams had subsequently added another. They had answered well, and formed, with the original company of Egyptian Soudanese, the garrison of 300 soldiers which Williams considered the irreducible minimum at the capital. Sir Gerald Portal decided on extending the successful experiment, and sent Major Owen and Captain Portal to the Unyoro forts to raise an additional 400 men, hoping that with this number of disciplined troops it would be possible to reduce their 6,000 followers to something like order. As Williams was now about to depart for the coast, and take his company of Egyptian Soudanese with him, Owen was directed to send into Uganda a strong company of the new recruits he was commissioned to enlist. This raised the question as to the sufficiency of the remainder to garrison the Unyoro forts, and Selim Bey pointed out that he had with difficulty held his own with the full garrisons, and that to reduce them, and at the same time retain the forts, was to invite disaster.

Sir Gerald Portal was himself strongly in favour of abandoning Toru, the Salt Lake, which had not proved a commercial success, and the whole of South Unyoro, and only after repeated representations from Williams, Owen, and myself, did he agree to modify his original intentions, and retain all except the most northerly of the four forts.

Owen was ordered to concentrate his main strength on the two forts nearest to Uganda, and hold the western fort as a detached post maintaining, and to a certain extent protecting, Toru. Being given a certain amount of latitude, Owen abandoned this fort, and constructed a new one in Toru itself, to protect that country and guard his food-supply, for, thanks to the devastation wrought by the Soudanese in the past, there was little food obtainable near the two eastern forts. Of the work done by Owen, Raymond Portal, and Grant in South Unyoro I shall have more to say later.

Having thus set in train the solution of the Soudanese question, Sir Gerald Portal devoted himself to the more troublesome one of a settlement of the Roman Catholic grievances. A full account of his success is given in his book, so I need not enter into details. Suffice it to say that the Roman Catholics were allowed an extension of territory, consisting of the province of Mawakota, the district of Bwekula, and the large island of Sese. In addition to this, they were granted a narrow strip of country between Mawakota and Mengo as a Catholic road, and a redistribution of plantations was made at the capital to enable their representative chiefs to reside at the Court when required to do so. This transfer of territory somewhat altered the relative density of population, and brought the Protestants somewhat above the average, while the Catholics were nearly right.

Two of the great questions had thus been satisfactorily settled, but the Mohammedan problem remained untouched. This turbulent party demanded an increase of territory likewise, though they had already much more than they knew what do do with. Their minimum demands were for the whole of the wealthy province of Busiro, and they prevailed on Selim Bey to support their claims.* At the same time they commenced a series of outrages at the capital, and during Sir Gerald Portal's short stay more murders or attempts at murder took place at Mengo than had occurred during many months. Sir Gerald Portal leniently rebuked the Bey, and sternly refused the Mohammedan demands; but his time was so much occupied with, to his mind, more important affairs than the attitude of this numerically weak faction, that he rather underestimated their powers of mischief. Other events had also happened to still further distract his attention, for his brother, Captain Raymond Portal, had become seriously ill in Unyoro, and lay in a critical state at Kampala. This gallant soldier died, and the shock to his brother, who was himself weak from the effects of fever, almost prostrated him. Preparations for departure to Mombasa were pushed rapidly on, and Sir Gerald had no time to devote to the clamours of the Mohammedans.

The day before his departure he held a farewell durbar, at which he told the Mohammedans their demands could not be granted, and urged them to cease their disorderly conduct, and settle down as peaceful and law-abiding subjects. To his surprise, the Mohammedan chiefs, in full durbar before the King and his council, threatened open rebellion if their terms were not granted. Had Sir Gerald been the firm and decided

* Selim Bey had hoped that his services under the Company would secure his pardon by the Egyptian Government, and permission to return to Egypt. But in the spring of 1893 news was received that the recommendations of the Company's officials had been of no avail, and that Egypt had refused to pardon his mutiny against Emin Pasha. From that time Selim Bey seemed to think that the British had failed to support his claim, and he became discontented and sullen in his attitude towards them.

man he was when he entered Uganda, he might even then, at the eleventh hour, have quelled the incipient rebellion by arresting the would-be rebel leaders; but, shaken by his brother's sad and unexpected death, and weakened by repeated attacks of fever, he hesitated over such decisive action on the eve of his departure, and the opportunity was lost. He contented himself with cautioning the Mohammedan chiefs, and ordering me to arrest and deport them, should they give trouble after his departure.

Next day he left for the coast, and the mantle of authority fell on my shoulders. The rebellion, threatened before his departure, soon came to a head, and the first three months of my work in Uganda were occupied in crushing the last and most formidable bid for power attempted by the followers of Islam.

Before giving an account of the rebellion and its suppression, it may be interesting to trace the rise of Mohammedanism in Uganda, and to chronicle shortly the struggle between the followers of the Cross and the Crescent, which ultimately resulted in this becoming a Christian country.

CHAPTER XII.

FIRST CONTEST BETWEEN CHRISTIANS AND MOHAMMEDANS.

AT what date Mohammedanism, which was afterwards to play such an important though sinister part in the history of Uganda, made its first appearance in that country is uncertain. The Arab and Swahili traders of the coast were enterprising, if somewhat unscrupulous, men, and long before the advent of Europeans had already penetrated far into the interior of Africa. It is certain that in the days of Mtesa, who ascended the throne of Uganda in 1860, the propagation of Islam had already commenced.

Mtesa was a capable and far-seeing man who, recognising how much the cultivation of friendly relations with the Swahili traders would increase the prosperity of his kingdom, encouraged them to settle in his dominions. Some years later Mohammedanism acquired a further stimulus by the King himself adopting it, and there can be little doubt that many courtiers followed his example. Uganda suited the Swahilis and Arabs, as the numerous external wars resulted in a large number of captives being for sale, and the country was also rich in ivory. An Arab colony was founded, and its first effects were not altogether baneful, as new wants and new ideas were introduced, and a slight step forward made in general advancement, for the Arabs represented to the Waganda a more advanced stage of civilization than they themselves possessed.

In 1862 the first Europeans reached Uganda in the persons of the distinguished travellers Speke and Grant; but it was not till fifteen years later, on the occasion of Stanley's visit to Mtesa, that the question of Christian missions was mooted. Stanley saw a great deal of the King, and gained considerable influence over him, with the result that, when he finally left the country, he carried an invitation to Christian missionaries to settle in Uganda, where they were promised a hearty welcome. In reply to this invitation, the pioneers of the Church Missionary Society arrived in 1877. One of these devoted men, Smith, was shortly afterwards murdered at Ukerewe, an island at the south of the Victoria Lake, and the other, Wilson, carried on the work single-handed until, in the autumn of 1878, he was joined by 'Mackay of Uganda.'

Mtesa welcomed the missionaries, and allowed free religious discussion, but their advent was looked upon with jealous suspicion by the Arabs, who, not unnaturally, feared that the spread of Christian influence would tell against their lucrative trade in slaves. From this time began the conflict between Islam and Christianity. No doubt the latter would have gained ground more rapidly than it did but for an event which happened in 1879. In February of that year two representatives of the Roman Catholic Missionary Society—the White Fathers of Algiers—arrived in Uganda, and took up an attitude of bitter antagonism towards the Church Missionary Society. This, too, was to cause much bloodshed and disaster at a later period, but its immediate result was to raise doubt in the minds of many who might have embraced the doctrines of Christianity. This division of the Christians was the opportunity of the Mohammedans, and it is practically certain that the propaganda of this religion was now zealously extended. Henceforth these three rival bodies of missionaries pushed their various doctrines, and while each was jealous of the other, all three gained converts. But at this time the faith of Islam was undoubtedly the most popular.

Such was the state of Uganda when, in the autumn of 1884, the great Mtesa died, and was succeeded by his son Mwanga. He had not long assumed the royal title, when it became apparent that a change of attitude towards the missionaries might be expected. Soon this change came, and Mwanga displayed a spirit of 'marked hostility' towards the native Christians, 'which deepened into a barbarous persecution.' Various external circumstances also tended to make him suspicious of Europeans and European influence. News reached Uganda that Germany had assumed a Protectorate at the coast, and that the territory of the Sultan of Zanzibar had been greatly curtailed by the European Powers. A white man had also reached Kavirondo through Masailand. There was an old superstition that Uganda would ultimately be conquered from the east, through 'the back-door of the Masai,' and Mwanga became seriously alarmed. The Arabs made the most of these circumstances in their own interests, and it must be remembered that they had not now to deal with a shrewd, self-reliant man like Mtesa, but with a narrow-minded coward.

Mwanga's attitude towards the missionaries and their converts became worse and worse, when news suddenly arrived that a Protestant Bishop—the brave Hannington—had reached Kavirondo, and was marching through Usoga to Uganda. The King had all his foolish fears aroused, and sent orders that Hannington was to be arrested and slain. This cruel order was duly carried out by Lubwa, who, after holding them for a week in captivity, massacred the Bishop and all his followers in cold blood. This took place in the autumn of 1885, and the King, having thus committed himself and being fairly under the influence of the Mohammedan or Arab party, commenced a cruel persecution of the native Christians.

In May, 1886, a barbarous massacre of converts took place. Day after day they were seized, and slain or mutilated. Several hundred were burned alive, not tied to stakes, as used to be the custom in Europe, but confined in cages. Others were cut to pieces with knives and the sharp fragments of cane splinters. The missionaries themselves were daily in danger of their lives. But this fierce persecution did not prevent the spread of Christianity, and, though a few weak spirits fell away, most held fast to their new faith, and many who had hitherto wavered came boldly forward and courted martyrdom.

The missionaries were refused admittance at court, their servants were driven away, and their houses watched. For a native to be found on their premises was as good as a death-warrant, for he was sure to be led off to execution or to torture. Finally Mackay and Ashe reluctantly decided it would be best to quit Uganda for a season, not from fear for themselves, but in order that they might avert suspicion from their remaining followers. Mwanga allowed Ashe to leave, but he retained Mackay on account of his mechanical skill. In July, 1887, Mackay at last left the country, where he was replaced by Gordon, and died at the south of the lake, after fourteen years of energetic missionary work in Uganda, work which is still gratefully remembered by the people of the country.

Mwanga, having thus played into the hands of the Arabs, now feared that they and the Mohammedan party were becoming too powerful in the land, so he began to intrigue against them in turn, and finally placed himself at the head of the heathen faction, still far the strongest in the country, and began a renewed persecution of Mohammedan and Christian alike. He aimed at the ultimate extinction of both, and thus drove these two antagonistic factions to act in concert. Much as the Waganda reverenced their King, such tyranny was not to be borne, and the united Mohammedans and Christians in September, 1888, deposed Mwanga and placed his brother Kiwewa on the throne. Mwanga fled with only a few pages and women, and after several escapes reached the south of the lake. Here he placed himself in the hands of the Arabs, who fleeced him unmercifully, while Mackay, to whom he appealed for help, turned a deaf ear to his entreaties. He then applied to the Roman Catholics, by whom he was received and enrolled as a catechumen.

After this bloodless revolution affairs in Uganda at first promised well. Kiwewa was of the royal blood of Kintu, the son of the late Mtesa, and the common people accepted him as King without demur. The Mohammedan and Christian chiefs seized practically all the power, and divided the principal chieftainships and offices amongst themselves, while Kiwewa ratified these new appointments and proclaimed a fresh era of toleration. This was, however, only a deceptive lull which preceded another storm.

The Mohammedan party were dissatisfied with the share of power which they had secured, and, though outwardly on the most friendly terms with their Christian comrades, formed a bold and comprehensive plot with the Arabs to sweep away the Christian faction altogether, and bring the whole realm under the banner of Islam. The plan was well contrived and successfully carried out by the assassination of the large majority of the Christian chiefs as they left the King's durbar one day in October, 1888, even the missionaries being at the same time arrested. The Christians throughout Uganda were paralyzed, and, as their recognised leaders had fallen, they fled in dismay.

By this one bold, unscrupulous blow the Mohammedans had swept all before them, and stood undisputed masters of the country. They did not, however, massacre the missionaries, though some advised even this step, but, after robbing them of all their possessions, put them on board the mission-boat and bade them sail away. Though a few faithful servants had stood by them, resolved to share their exile, the outlook was far from bright. They were adrift on the great lake without camp equipage, without arms, without stores to purchase food, and with a journey of over 200 miles before them. They were persistently dogged by misfortune, for they had not gone far, when their boat was stove in and all were thrown into the water. Some of the party could swim, and the boat was got ashore to be repaired as best they could. This shipwreck had occurred on an island, the inhabitants of which gave them food and otherwise assisted them. Again they put out to sea, and so, through danger and difficulty, Roman Catholic priest and Protestant missionary and native convert acting in kindly concert, they reached the south of the lake, where they found rest and safety.

Meanwhile, a second revolution had taken place in Uganda, and Kiwewa had been deposed in favour of his brother Karema. The Mohammedans desired Kiwewa to embrace their religion, with all its rites and ceremonies; but he declined, and slew with his own hands two of the great chiefs who worried him most. This sealed his fate. It was no part of the Mohammedan programme that the result of their successful plot should place a heathen on the throne to reign over them, so, having ascertained that Karema was willing to meet their wishes, they deposed Kiwewa and placed his brother on the throne. Thus the year 1888 closed with the Mohammedan party triumphant in Uganda, and the Christians scattered exiles, without leaders, or organization, or plans for the future.

A few Christian chiefs with their followers had fled to Ankole, where they were granted asylum. Gradually more and more of their brethren made their way to the same haven, until in March, 1889, a thousand were assembled there. Others had fled to the south of the lake, and communication was kept up between these two main divisions through a friendly Baziba chief, whose district lay in the south of Buddu. The Christian exiles in Ankole sent letters to the south of the lake asking their missionaries' advice as to proposals which had been suggested for reconquering Uganda, but before an answer could be obtained war had already commenced.

I have already mentioned that a Baziba chief of Buddu, Mukotanyi by name, befriended the Christians and gave them canoes by which they communicated with their pastors and comrades at the south of the lake. This had come to the ears of Karema and his chiefs, and an army was sent to punish Mukotanyi and close the road that led through the south of Buddu. When the Christians in Ankole heard of this, they determined to assist Mukotanyi, for, as they rightly said, if they lost the road to the lake they would be absolutely isolated. Marching rapidly, the Christian force intercepted the Mohammedan army, and a fierce battle took place, in which the latter was completely routed and the leader wounded. This occurred in April, 1889. News of the victory was at once sent to Mwanga, who was invited to place himself at the head of the united Christian exiles and make an effort to regain his throne. Meanwhile, the small Christian army, flushed with success, advanced northwards through Buddu and approached the Katonga River.

Karema, enraged at his first defeat, sent a large army against them under his Katikiro. The Christians crossed the Katonga, and the two forces met in battle on the line of hills that overlook the great plain through which the river flows in many swampy channels. The battle was fierce and well contested. The Christians, led by Nyoni Ntono and other chiefs, made a bold attack and broke the array of the Mohammedans, who began to give ground. The Christians fought with redoubled vigour, and seemed in a fair way to inflict a second defeat on their hated enemy, when, unfortunately, their leader, Nyoni Ntono, fell. This turned the tables: the Christians faltered, and, being in turn hard pressed by the Mohammedans, retired in disorder from the field, and recrossed the Katonga with a loss of about eight chiefs and sixty men killed, and many wounded.

The Mohammedans had suffered more severely, and did not pursue, but retired on the capital. They thus sacrificed the results of their victory, for, had they made a vigorous pursuit, the Christians must have lost still more heavily in crossing the swampy channels of the Katonga, and would have been utterly demoralized. As it was, they rapidly reorganized their forces and prepared to resume the struggle.

In May, 1889, Mwanga himself took the field, having landed at Damo, a little north of the Kagera River, whither he had been transported in Mr. Stokes' boat. The Christians rallied in considerable numbers round his standard, until he was at the head of an army of about 1,100 guns and 3,000 spears; but, unfortunately, they had not time to secure a proper organization before a fresh Mohammedan army was upon them, and they had to join battle. It appears that Karema, when the Mohammedans returned to the capital after the victory on the Katonga River, was dissatisfied with the lack of energy they had displayed, and degraded their general. A new leader was appointed and despatched with about 2,000 guns and 5,000 spears to follow up the success which had already been gained, and prevent a fresh effort on the part of the Christians. This army reached Buddu to find Mwanga installed at Damo with a formidable force. The battle that took place was fiercely contested, but there were dissensions amongst the Christian chiefs, and in consequence they did not fight as well as at Katonga. The result was a decisive victory for the Mohammedans, who killed the opposing general and dispersed his forces, while Mwanga, with 200 men, escaped to the island of Sese. This defeat was a sad blow to the Chris-

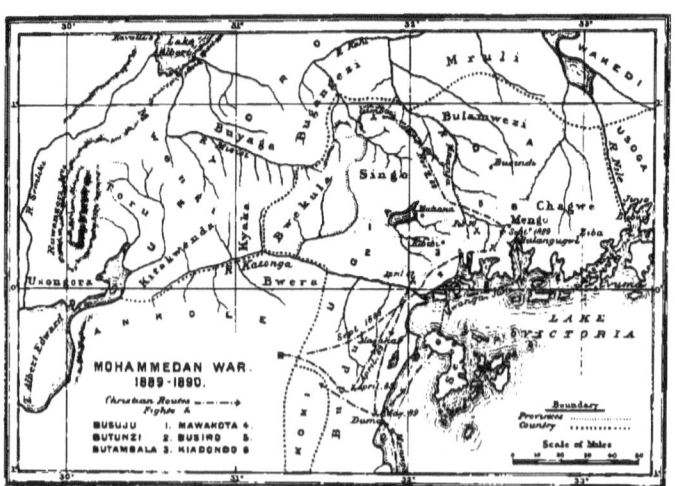

tian hopes, and they practically abandoned their hold in Buddu, and retired once more to Ankole.

In spite of their recent defeats at the Katonga River and at Damo, the Christian cause was gaining strength. The exiles were again rapidly reorganized in Buddu, while the inhabitants of the Sese Islands declared for Mwanga, and, by placing all their canoes at his service, gave him the mastery of the lake. Karema, who had killed all his relations, in case any of them should join the movement against himself, had already made his rule unpopular by sternly forcing Mohammedanism on his heathen followers, and thus caused many of them to flock to Mwanga's banner. By June of the same year the latter was strong enough to resume the offensive, and travelled eastwards with a powerful fleet, devastating the districts near the shore. He then transferred his headquarters to the island of Bulingugwe, only about seven miles from his former capital, and from this central position he harassed the enemy by almost daily skirmishes. These skirmishes not only served to annoy Karema, but proved of great use in training the Christian force, and the frequent successes which were gained brought still more recruits to the Christian standard.

About this time Mwanga, whose chiefs were now sanguine of ultimate success, wrote to invite the missionaries to join him at Bulingugwe, an invitation which was accepted by Protestants and Roman Catholics alike. He also wrote to the European expedition, under Messrs. Jackson and Gedge, which had just arrived in Kavirondo, in the interests of the Imperial British East Africa Company.

Meanwhile, the Christians who had retired to Ankole after their disastrous defeat at Damo in May were not idle. A young Protestant chief, Apollo by name, who had already given proof of his skill and courage, was appointed general, and, ably supported by others, devoted himself to raising and organizing a fresh army in Mwanga's cause. The admirable strategic position of Bulingugwe, secured by the other division of the Christian forces, rendered this operation a safe one, for Karema could not afford to detach an army to a distance of 100 miles to interfere with Apollo's plans while a daring enemy lay established within seven miles of his capital.

Bulingugwe was practically impregnable, as the Mohammedans had few canoes, and could not venture on an assault, and although the island itself produced no food, yet Mwanga, having command of the Sese fleet, could easily feed the considerable force he was gradually collecting. Situated about two-thirds of the way along Murchison Bay, the island was also well placed to afford a base for offensive movements against the coast, for this bay contains many minor inlets and a coastline of over fifty miles. Then, the Christians could swoop down on any point they pleased, while it was very difficult for the Mohammedans to move bodies of men sufficiently rapidly from one point on the bay to another in order to forestall a landing. Thanks to Stokes, who remained the firm friend of Mwanga and the Christian party, arms and ammunition could be obtained from the south of the lake, while the Mohammedans and Arabs were practically denied this advantage, and had to trust to their own resources.

When the month of September approached, the Christians felt strong enough to assume the offensive and make a fresh effort to recover their land. Apollo had assembled a force of 1,200 guns and about 3,000 spears, and reoccupied Buddu, while at Bulingugwe the Christians had mustered of fighting men 1,000 guns and a similar number of spears. Karema had concentrated at the capital an opposing army of about 3,000 guns and 4,000 spears.

In September, 1889, Apollo advanced from Buddu on the capital. The division of the Christian forces, which up to this time had proved of advantage to them, in so far as it restricted Karema to a defensive attitude, now proved a positive source of danger, for the Mohammedan army stood concentrated on inner lines, and could act against the divided forces of the enemy. But Karema was not a great enough general to fully grasp his advantage. Had he launched the bulk of his army against Apollo's division, he could undoubtedly have crushed him, and by so doing have added to his prestige and influence, while the danger to his capital during the temporary absence of this expeditionary force would have been slight. Mwanga was essentially a cautious opponent, who would have been most unlikely to make a dash on the capital, and even had he done so, and captured it, he must have at once fled to his island fastness on the return of the Mohammedan army after the defeat of Apollo. But Karema took half-measures, and despatched only a portion of his force to oppose Apollo's advance, and this resulted in an action in which the Christians gained a victory.

Apollo was now within two days' march of Mengo, when Karema detached fresh forces to drive him back. The Mohammedans were stronger than the Christians, and after a fierce fight the latter were compelled to retreat with loss. But here again the fear of an attack on their capital paralyzed the victorious army of Karema, and prevented their turning the victory on the field of battle into a decisive success by a vigorous pursuit. Instead, they fell back to cover Mengo, and thus allowed Apollo to rally his beaten division and send for help to Bulingugwe. The Christians there at once sent reinforcements to their hard-pressed comrades, but as Apollo had retired to a fresh position, they were unable to effect a junction, and returned to the island. This was surely Karema's opportunity, but once more he failed to grasp it. Mwanga again despatched a force to Apollo's assistance, and on this occasion a junction was effected, and Apollo resumed his advance on the capital with about 2,000 guns and a large number of spearmen.

On October 4, 1889, his army reached the Nalukorongo River, which flows on the outskirts of Mengo in a swampy bed, through plains much overgrown with papyrus. Here he halted his troops, with a view to delivering a decisive assault on the capital next day. The Mohammedans, however, made a determined attack with their whole force, and a stubborn battle was fought. Apollo, although his men were weary after the day's march and completely outnumbered, handled them with such skill and courage that, when darkness put a stop to the fighting, the Mohammedans had failed to make any impression on his position. What was the loss on either side is uncertain, but much blood had been shed before Karema's army fell back across the river, and left the Christians to bivouac on the field of battle.

Next morning Apollo took the offensive, and another bloody battle was fought. The Mohammedans, dispirited by their want of success the previous day, were everywhere beaten, and, though their Arab allies fought stubbornly in defence of their settlement at Natete, the Christian army carried all before them. Karema saw that the day was lost, and fled to the north-west, towards Singo, with the remnants of his discomfited following, hard pressed by their victorious opponents. For two days the retreating Mohammedans were followed and given no time to rally, and only when they had crossed the Maanja and entered the wilds of Singo did Apollo call back his victorious troops.

The Christians had not only captured the capital and driven the enemy to the borders of the country, but had secured an immense amount of spoil, amongst which was reckoned 700 tusks of ivory. The result of this victory was that, on October 11, 1889, exactly a year after the Christians had been expelled, Mwanga re-entered the capital of his country in triumph.

Now followed a short breathing-space, during which the

Christians took fresh measures to consolidate their position.
The chieftainships and great offices of state were impartially
distributed between the followers of the two sects, and Apollo
was appointed Katikiro, as a reward for his victorious
campaign. The peasants of the country flocked to Mwanga's
faction, and on every side were rejoicings at the return of
their former King, whose evil deeds in the past were forgotten,
while their recurrence was guarded against by what amounted
to a new constitution, which placed much more of the authority
in the hands of the council.

The Christians were not long allowed to rest in peace after
their labours, for Karema, too, had not been idle. Making
his headquarters in the frontier districts of Singo, and aided
by Kabarega of Unyoro, he had rapidly rallied a formidable
following, and commenced to raid the country that had
declared for his successful rival. Apollo decided that fresh
operations were necessary, and placed himself at the head
of a new army, which advanced towards Singo in November,
1889. His route was apparently that followed by Lugard two
years later, in his expedition against the same enemy. After
a few small skirmishes, Apollo came on Karema's army at
Vumba, about 110 miles from Mengo.

Vumba is situated on one of the numerous minor offshoots
from the great plateau wall of North-west Uganda. Rugged
and bolder than the hills of Uganda proper, this great back-
bone of mountains, which looks far over the plains of the
Kafu into Unyoro, extends in an irregular line running north-
west and south-east, and attaining an altitude of from 5,000
to 6,000 feet above the sea. The country, too, is different
from that more to the south, the grass being shorter, the trees
smaller and more scattered, and the numerous streams less
swampy, because more rapid.

From Buru, the culminating point of this great mountain
region, in which rise the headquarters of many different

systems of drainage, one can see far over Unyoro to beyond where Kabarega's capital nestles amongst the hills which rise out of the great Kafu plains. In clear weather one can even make out in the hazy distance the hills of Kavalli's, on the western shores of Lake Albert. From the main range of mountains many spurs run to the north-east, to lose themselves after a few miles in the rolling plains of the Kafu and Maanja Rivers. On one of these spurs lies the village of Vumba.

Karema's position was well chosen, for, while his men could obtain excellent cover amongst the many boulders and crags that crowned the summit of the spur, they had an open field of fire across its grassy slopes to their immediate front. Facing the Mohammedan position lay the almost parallel but lower range, from which rose the double peaks of the hill of Kiboga, and between lay a wooded valley about one and a half miles wide. Through this valley flowed a small stream, which took its rise in a swampy hollow covering the right wing of Karema's army. Behind him lay the fertile districts of Kiganda, Mwebia, Tuwembazi, and Ntuti, from which he could draw supplies for his forces. His line of retreat, in case of reverse, was open to Unyoro.

The Christian forces advanced to Kiboga, and encamped in the fertile plantations which marked the headquarters of the chief of Buniga, and thus the two armies occupied parallel positions about two miles apart. The strength of the Mohammedan position was at once apparent. To attack its right meant a long détour round the swampy hollow, thus laying open the main road to Uganda; to envelop its left necessitated an advance through the jungle of the Maanja plains, with the probability, in case of reverse, of being driven back on that impassable river. Nothing remained to be done but a direct attack on the position, and this Apollo elected to attempt. Drawing up his troops in the customary formation of a line of small columns, headed by the chiefs, he advanced against Vumba, and delivered a determined assault against a stubborn enemy, well sheltered amongst the rocks and boulders.

The details of this great fight are unfortunately uncertain, but Christian chiefs have told me it was a victory for their arms. On the other hand, letters written from Uganda at this time talk of it as a reverse, if not a defeat. The truth of the matter appears to be that the Christians did indeed, with terrible loss, carry Karema's position, but their further efforts were paralyzed by their general, the gallant Katikiro, falling wounded. This caused dismay and hesitation amongst his men, and gave Karema an opportunity to rally. The Christians then retreated, having lost, as they themselves admit, perhaps 600 men in the battle. Being pressed by the Mohammedans, the retreat became most disorderly. Fugitives soon reached the capital with most alarming accounts of the reverse, and once more Mwanga hurriedly took refuge on the island of Bulingugwe, to which he was accompanied by the missionaries and many of his chiefs.

This occurred about the end of November, 1889, and it was not till over two months later that the Christians regained the ascendancy. Karema apparently advanced and occupied Mengo, but made his headquarters somewhat more to the west in the fertile district of Brussi, in Busiro. Accounts of what occurred between November, 1889, and February, 1890, when Mwanga was reinstated in Mengo, are somewhat uncertain. The Christians did not lose heart, and laid in fresh ammunition, as their supplies had run rather low after the recent fighting. Then it would seem a great battle was fought near Brussi, in which the Mohammedans were decisively beaten and driven once more to Singo.

It is difficult to get the Waganda to tell the story of these events in consecutive order, but the foregoing would appear to be the bare facts. A young Christian chief showed me the battlefield, a little west of the range extending from the hills of Buddu to the twin grassy peaks of Namagoma. From his account, the battle was one of the most hotly contested during the war, and it was not till 800 Mohammedans lay on the field that they fled across the swampy Namaya River and again took refuge on the borders of Unyoro. About this time Karema died of small-pox, and his uncle, Mbogo, succeeded him as head of the now weakened Mohammedan party. Mwanga re-entered his capital in February, 1890, and a brief period of comparative peace followed.

It was indeed high time that war should cease, for the country was completely exhausted. For nearly two seasons but little cultivation had been undertaken, and many plantations were overgrown with jungle, while others had been destroyed. An area of 3,000 square miles was practically deserted through fear of Mohammedan raids. Only the hilly portions of Bulamwezi were occupied, the great plains which form the northern part of that province being abandoned to game. The same thing occurred in Singo, where the rule of the Makwenda, as paramount chief, was practically limited to a few districts east of Lake Isolt; the rest of this great province, which embraced within its limits over a fifth of Uganda, was deserted, and the rapid deterioration of its untended plantations was further accelerated by the depredations of vast herds of elephants. No one would inhabit the western portions of Busuju and Butunzi, and but few cared to dwell in the north-western districts of Buddu or its tributary Bwera.

In the days of Mtesa, the population of Uganda had been estimated to amount to 1,000,000, but it was now greatly reduced, not only by actual losses in war and by the secession of the Mohammedan faction, but also because great numbers of the peasants had fled from the country and transferred their allegiance to chiefs where life and property were more secure. It is doubtful if 600,000 souls remained in the country, and even these were to be still further reduced by famine and pestilence, for food was very scarce, and before the new crops could be reaped large numbers of the people had died of starvation or been reduced to living on roots and the wild products of the jungle. Then, as so often happens, pestilence followed in the footsteps of famine, and counted its victims by thousands. A virulent form of bubonic plague decimated the country, and threatened to reduce Uganda to little more than an empty name.

Since the days of this war there has appeared more than one book dealing with Uganda. The authors have done justice to their own services to the country and the cause of civilization, but they have largely overlooked the grim struggle which the native Christians, without European leaders, and without the support of regular troops, waged against the Mohammedan and Arab influence, although the successful issue of this struggle laid the foundation of future developments and the spread of British authority in the Lake Regions. Had the party of Islam been the victors, and turned Uganda into a despotic Mohammedan State, there can be little doubt that the progress of civilization would have been retarded for years, even had the country not fallen under the sway of the Mahdi.

I have endeavoured, however imperfectly, to give a connected description of this war, with its many hard-fought fights. It has been a matter of some difficulty to reconcile the often confused and contradictory accounts of the various operations, as related to me by the native chiefs, and that I have succeeded in some measure is due to the kindness of the Church Missionary Society, who placed at my disposal various letters bearing on these events, which enabled me to piece together the information I had myself acquired during my stay in Uganda.

CHAPTER XIII.

SECOND MOHAMMEDAN WAR (LUGARD'S).

THE position in Uganda in April, 1890, when it was visited by the Imperial British East Africa Company's expedition under Jackson and Gedge, was very much the same as described at the end of the last chapter. The Mohammedans had settled in Bugangezi, in Unyoro, with the sanction and approval of Kabarega, and, having thus acquired a secure base for their raids, they had devastated, or caused to be abandoned, nearly a third of Uganda. They could get arms and powder from Arab sympathizers in what is now German territory, by a road passing through Koki and the border of Ankole, and hence through the Unyoro province of Kyaka, which lay immediately to the south of Bugangezi. Their raids were getting bolder and bolder, and reaching farther and farther, and, though invariably ultimately defeated, they caused great disquietude and considerable material loss in the country. Cultivation was backward; the roads, formerly one of the triumphs of the kingdom, were falling out of repair; and famine and pestilence were abroad in the land.

In addition to external troubles, internal friction arose. When the common danger, which had united the Christian sects against the faction of Karema, had been lessened by the victory of the allies, the two Christian parties had taken to quarrelling between themselves. Headed by a Roman

Catholic King, his co-religionists were gradually gaining ground, and wanted to secure supreme political authority. The Protestants naturally objected strongly, and insisted on adhering to the political distribution of power which was made when the Mohammedans were driven out. So bitter did the feeling between these quondam friends become, that, on more than one occasion, hostilities were only averted by the fear of the still powerful Mohammedan party, who, on the first outbreak of civil war, would without fail step in and recover their lost ground.

So intense, however, had the ill feeling become, that, while Jackson and Gedge were in the country, the Protestant party seriously contemplated migrating in a body to Usoga, and setting up an independent kingdom. They were packing up their effects, and collecting their adherents to this end, and at first Jackson approved of the movement. The Roman Catholic missionaries, to whom there can be little doubt a good deal of the friction that gave rise to the Protestant proposal was due, now came forward and urged him to prevent the Protestant withdrawal. They pointed out, with truth, that the Roman Catholics alone could not hope to resist the Mohammedan party, and that the result of a Protestant migration to Usoga would mean that Uganda would at once fall back into the hands of Karema's faction, and that a powerful Mohammedan State would take the place of what promised to be a Christian kingdom. Jackson, somewhat against Gedge's advice, adopted these views, and stopped the migration of the Protestants to Usoga, an operation they could only hope to carry out satisfactorily with the support of his expedition; the Roman Catholic party then became less aggressive, and peace seemed to be patched up between the Christian parties for a time.

In May Jackson left for the coast, and Gedge remained in Uganda to represent the Company's interests. With him were some seventy Swahilis and a fair number of rifles, but his force was quite inadequate to give his advice or opinions any weight at the Court. No one can form any idea of the terribly trying time the Company's representative had during the next six months. Whenever the Mohammedans raided within sight of the capital, as they did more than once, the King became Gedge's humble servant, and begged for rifles and asked his advice; but as soon as the immediate danger was past, Mwanga once again proceeded to disregard him, and to laugh at the Company's authority. Gedge, however, boldly stuck to his post, and did his best in these trying circumstances. Later on, in connection with some political business, he went to the south of the lake to see Emin Pasha, who was then the German representative there. Emin and he worked cordially together, but before he could return to Uganda he fell seriously ill. Ophthalmia also attacked him, and for some time he was blind. The German officials could not, or would not, help him to secure canoes, but with much difficulty, and greatly shattered in health, he ultimately returned to Mengo.

In December, 1890, Lugard, with a strong expedition, entered the country, and at once proceeded to take command. Gedge, weakened by illness and by the trials he had been through, though his senior in the Company's service, handed over charge to Lugard, and zealously assisted him in establishing himself at Mengo. In January, 1891, Gedge left for the coast, but within three days he was again prostrated by illness, and was supposed to be dying. He recovered, but was so weak that Lugard detailed Auburn, a European, to accompany him to the coast.

On December 26th, Lugard, by a display of great firmness, induced Mwanga to sign a treaty, placing his territories under the protection of the Imperial British East African Company. For some weeks the position was one of constant anxiety, and Lugard had to take precautions against his camp being attacked while his fort was still unbuilt. He relied on obtaining food from Usoga, and made arrangements to that end, but the Wasoga did not fulfil their promises. Meanwhile he pushed on building operations, and had the fort at Kampala, a small hill about 1,200 yards from the King's palace, traced out before the end of January, 1891, when Captain Williams, R.A., arrived with reinforcements. He, though Lugard's senior in military service, became second in command in Uganda, and loyally served his chief.

Lugard's position was now secure, and he began to try to settle some of the more burning questions between the two Christian parties, while Williams raised and drilled a picked company of Zanzibar askaris. In February civil war nearly broke out; both factions got under arms, and a conflict was only averted by the determined attitude adopted by Lugard and Williams. But Lugard was steadily gaining ground. By prudence, firmness and determination, he was making his influence apparent. The two gravest questions of all he postponed, but many minor ones that threatened the peace of the country were happily settled by the end of March. Lugard then suggested that an expedition should be sent out against the Mohammedans, who were again making themselves felt, and were reported to have re-established themselves in great force in Singo. Preparations were accordingly at once begun. By tact and good management, Lugard got the Katikiro appointed as the general of the Waganda force, and on April 8, 1891, the arrangements were so far advanced that he moved out of Kampala to join the Waganda contingent, and embark on the second Mohammedan war. He has himself narrated the history of this war at length, but a short description of these operations and their results, which ultimately led up to the last Mohammedan outbreak, may not be out of place.

We may preface the account by saying that this was the

rainy season, and that, as cloth was not available for tents, or even extra clothing for his men, his force suffered considerable hardship. Lugard had, however, laid in a supply of 129 loads of flour, and a herd of goats and sheep, a wise provision, to which it was due that his little column did not experience famine in the devastated country where his military operations were to lie.

The expedition, exclusive of Waganda, consisted of four Europeans—Captain Lugard, Captain Williams, Mr. Grant, and Dr. Macpherson; 139 Soudanese from Egypt, an excellent and trustworthy set of men enlisted by Williams; 153 of the Zanzibar levy, raised by Williams in February by picking out the best of the Swahili askaris; 308 headmen, askaris and porters, who were also armed, but formed more indifferent fighting material. The Company's contingent thus mustered about 300 soldiers and 300 armed porters.

The Waganda, under the command of Apollo, were not yet completely mobilized; they continued to pour in for the next fortnight, when their total strength amounted to 4,700 guns, and over 12,000 spearmen. Lugard's whole force thus reached the respectable total of over 16,000 men.

We may now follow the march. This is somewhat difficult from his map and despatches, as names are rarely given, and the natural features noted are few and far between. But by subsequent maps made by myself and Owen, on which a few of Lugard's camps have been identified, his route can now be fairly well traced.

He left Kampala, as we saw, on April 8, 1894, crossed the Lubegi, a broad swampy branch of the Maanja, to the north-west of the capital, and thence marched through the Mugema's country by Sentema, along the right bank of the Maanja River. This river appears to have been crossed at the Neko ford, on the road to Matiana, the Makwenda's capital. This distance was traversed in six marches, or at an average rate of about five miles per day. From this point Lugard left the Makwenda's road, and struck more north, across the comparatively open country on the left side of the Maanja River, toward the small but lofty plateau of Matamba. The country was now quite deserted, and food was scarce among the Waganda. On April 18th he descended into the valley of the Mata, a tributary of the Maanja; this stream is several hundred yards wide, covered with papyrus, and requires bridging in the rainy season. Here Lugard halted a day, no doubt to allow a bridge, or, more properly speaking, a causeway, to be made, and on April 20th we find him camped somewhere among the rock-crowned spurs of Kaitabia.

Next day he had climbed the long gradual ascent which leads to the summit of the great mass of mountains that separates the drainage areas of the Maanja and Kitumbui Rivers, and from which a magnificent view can be obtained of the great plains of the Maanja and Kafu Rivers. From this point two roads run to the north-west: one keeps along the tops and upper slopes of the mountains, and is thus free from serious cross-drainage, while the other descends into the plain north of the mountains, and, keeping along near their base, has to pass many streams, which in the rains are troublesome. Lugard chose the lower route, probably from considerations of food-supply for his Waganda allies, for we must remember that all this country was desolate, and food could only be got in small quantities from the plantations, which had been allowed to run wild, and which had been greatly damaged by elephants and game.

On April 23rd we find his camp pitched below the main hills, somewhere near Kawawa, in the little valley flanked to the north by the low rocky ridge of Kawanda. From Kawawa he marched close under the outer spurs of the mountain range, and on April 25th reached the slopes of Kiboga Hill, the site of the Christian camp before the great battle of Vumba in the last war. Still pressing slowly on, he passed the fertile and sheltered valley of Mwebia, now also deserted, crossed the low wooded range that juts out to the north-west from the Peak of Kikabala, and on April 29th reached Ntuti; a short march next day brought him to the Kitumbui River, near the small hill on which was afterwards built one of my two frontier forts, which was named, after the leader of the expedition we are at present considering, Fort Lugard.

The Christian army was now in touch with the Mohammedans, and Lugard was anxious to get the latter to make peace without fighting. The negotiations were carried out at first through prisoners, and later through envoys sent by the enemy to ascertain Lugard's terms. These terms were liberal enough, as the enemy were to be allowed to return to Uganda if they became peaceful subjects of Mwanga, and handed over to the Company's representatives their leader Mbogo and the young son of Karema. At first it appeared that these terms would be accepted, as there were many amongst the rebels who were weary of a life of exile; but the younger and more impetuous party, thinking, no doubt, that an offer of peace when the hostile armies were almost face to face was a sign of weakness, carried the day, and the Mohammedans, in a courteous letter, declined the proffered terms and elected for war. This was a great disappointment to Lugard, but not to the Christian chiefs, who had all along been opposed to treating with the enemy, of whose treacherous nature they were the best judges. Nothing now remained but battle.

The Mohammedans, who had been reinforced by 1,300 Unyoro musketeers, established themselves behind the Kyangora River, which was difficult at any time, and was now, thanks to the incessant rain, almost impassable. Williams reconnoitred the enemy's position, only to find that a direct attack would be very hazardous. The Christian army halted,

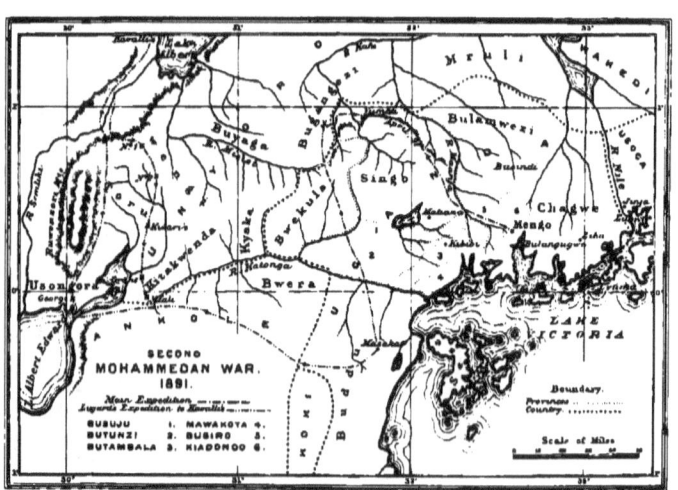

and a council of war followed, in which various schemes were discussed. Finally, by a clever flank march, Lugard crossed the river and circumvented the enemy, who fell back on a second position of great natural strength on a rocky range, which somewhat resembled that occupied by Karema's forces at Vumba in 1889. The Christian army decided to attack the position, which could not well be turned. The Waganda formed the front line, while Lugard and the Company's men constituted a support in rear of the centre. The Waganda Christians advanced with their usual impetuosity, and the engagement was soon general along a front of nearly a mile. The enemy fought well, with the exception of their Wanyoro allies, who broke and fled. One wing of the Christians was checked, and Lugard wheeled round to support it, but, before he could bring his men into action, the success of the other wing and centre decided the day. The Mohammedans retired, and, pressed vigorously by the victorious Christians, their retreat soon resolved itself into a disorderly flight. This, the decisive and only battle of the second Mohammedan war, was fought and won on May 7, 1891, in the neighbourhood of Kowar, and, strange to say, two of the actions of the Unyoro war of 1893-94 took place within ten miles of the scene of Lugard's victory.

Kowar is a district of the great Unyoro province of Bugangezi, ruled by the powerful chief Chikakure. The province was a fertile one, and contained numerous inhabitants who had assisted and encouraged the Mohammedans. From Chikakure's headquarters two main roads ran into the interior of Unyoro. One of these led north-west to Kijambi, where it bifurcated, the left branch leading to Lake Albert, and the right-hand one to Kabarega's capital. The other highway ran direct to the Baranwa crossing of the Kafu River, and hence to the capital of Unyoro, but was very difficult in the rainy season, as it crossed the Kyangora and Kitumbui

Rivers, as well as the Kafu itself and some minor swampy streams.

Lugard fully intended, after the defeat of the Mohammedans, to carry the war into Unyoro, and march straight on Kabarega's capital. His Waganda allies, however, opposed this scheme, as they considered the state of the rivers, after the heavy rains, rendered its execution impossible. They informed him that three large rivers must be crossed, and that the passage of one of them, the Kafu, was out of the question if the Mohammedans, aided by Kabarega, occupied its further bank; they also drew attention to the lack of supplies. Lugard therefore reluctantly abandoned the idea and marched southward. There can be little doubt that the Waganda were tired of military operations during the rains, and made out as bad a case as possible. Had the expedition retraced its steps to Ntuti, and then advanced by the old trade route into Unyoro, through Kaduma's to the Baranwa crossing of Kafu, they would have not only found a fertile and productive country, but have encountered only one bad river on the way to Kabarega's headquarters. This one river, the Kafu, was undoubtedly very difficult, but ample materials existed on its banks for the construction of a bridge or causeway, and as at the Baranwa crossing the river narrowed to about a quarter of a mile, and the comparatively open left bank could have been completely commanded by the Maxims from high ground on the right bank, the passage could not have been seriously opposed. This information was not, however, acquired until long afterwards, and Lugard, dependent on the Waganda for information as to the country ahead, no doubt acted wisely in not committing his expedition to a further campaign at that season of the year, especially as he had accomplished his immediate object, and shattered for the time being the power of the Mohammedan rebels.

The season was most unsuitable for military operations, as

not only was there almost incessant rain, but the new crops were not ripe, and thus the commissariat arrangements for so large a force were very difficult. The cattle of Unyoro had died in the great plague which had devastated the herds from Lake Nyassa to Somaliland, and from Mombasa to the Soudan. The enemy had driven off their sheep and goats, and hidden away their reserves of grain in caves or pits cunningly constructed in the ground. Small-pox had as usual broken out amongst the Waganda, who were, moreover, burdened with wounded. His own men, too, were much exhausted by the hardships of the campaign. So on May 11th Lugard broke up the force, at the same time sending a message to the beaten Mohammedans that he was still ready to offer them the same terms as before, and allow them to settle in Uganda under the Company's protection.

Before closing this brief narrative of Lugard's successful campaign, it may be interesting and instructive to explain the comparative slowness of the movements of the expeditionary force. It left Kampala on April 8th and fought and won the decisive battle on May 7th, at a distance of about 140 miles from the capital of Uganda. Its average rate of progress, including halts, was thus only 4·7 miles a day. Several stoppages at the beginning were, indeed, necessary to allow time for the Waganda contingents to arrive, and others were unavoidable, as bridges had to be built over rivers swollen by the rains. Time was also lost towards the end of the march in unsuccessful negotiations with the enemy; but even when allowance is made for these, the marches only averaged 5·9 miles a day.

This compares badly with the results obtained in Colonel Colvile's advance against Unyoro in 1893. As his chief staff officer, the arrangements for this advance fell mainly on my shoulders, and resulted in our marching a body of about 12,000 men a distance of over 130 miles, through very much the same country, at an average rate, if we include halts, of 8·8 miles a day, or excluding halts, of 10 miles a day.

But, though at first sight the cases appear similar, in reality they were not so, for in the Unyoro campaign we started with many advantages which Lugard did not enjoy. Before Colvile's arrival in Uganda I had already caused to be reconnoitred, and more or less mapped, 110 miles of the route, and had constructed on the Unyoro frontier two forts, which covered the first portion of the advance. Thus, when Colonel Colvile's expedition moved forwards, we were able to arrange for the Waganda contingents to use several roads, for the greater portion of the distance, under cover of these forts, and this materially quickened our movements. A favourable season, at the close of the rains, was also chosen for the military operations, and this not only lessened the hardships incurred by all ranks, but gave us the inestimable advantage of plenty of food, as the crops were just ripening, and had not yet been reaped.

If we compare the conditions of Lugard's expedition in 1891, we see at once he had many drawbacks to contend with. The season was unfavourable, and food was scarce. The country, though known to the Waganda, was unknown to him, and thus he had to be largely guided by their reports. The district traversed produced but scanty supplies, and this meant that the Waganda foragers had immense distances to travel, and hence that the marches for the main body must be short. Moreover, for the latter portion of his march, at all events, he did not know when he might encounter the enemy, and thus had to spare his men as much as possible, and keep them more concentrated. If all this be taken into consideration, one can hardly marvel at the comparative slowness of his movements.

Lugard, after dismissing the Waganda on May 11th, marched to Buddu, with the bulk of the Company's force, while

Williams, with a small party, returned to Kampala, and took over charge from De Winton, who had remained at the capital on the departure of the expeditionary force. Lugard, having reorganized his caravan, proceeded to Kavalli's on Lake Albert, won over Selim Bey and his Soudanese colony, and established them in a line of forts in Southern Unyoro. He then returned to Mengo, and about three weeks after his arrival the civil war amongst the Christians broke out. The incidents of this war I have already described, and have mentioned that at the close of it the Mohammedans were brought back into Uganda; but it is now advisable to give a more detailed account of the circumstances under which they were repatriated. Lugard allotted them three out of the ten provinces of Uganda, and believed that this settlement would be productive of permanent peace. Had the Mohammedans been loyal to their promises, this belief was not unjustifiable, but, unfortunately, from their misconduct and treachery their return to Uganda brought on the third and last Mohammedan war, with which I will deal in later chapters.

When in the spring of 1892 the unfortunate civil strife between the Protestants and Catholics was raging in Uganda, the Mohammedans, who, though much reduced in strength owing to desertions after Lugard's victory at the Kyangora, were still a powerful and compact faction, considered a favourable time had come to attempt to regain their hold on Uganda. Lugard's despatches show how apprehensive he was of a Mohammedan attack immediately after the capture of Bulangugwe, on January 30, 1892, and subsequent information shows his apprehensions were well grounded. The Mohammedans prepared for war, but, fortunately, they were divided in their counsels. One party wished an immediate advance on Uganda, a movement which, had it been adopted, would have placed the Company's representative in a very precarious position. The other advocated an alliance with Selim Bey's

Soudanese in the chain of forts on the Toru frontier, as preliminary to an attempt to reconquer Uganda. The latter counsels prevailed, and the Mohammedans wasted time by endeavouring to persuade the Soudanese to join them. The Soudanese, however, regarded them with suspicion, as they were the allies of Kabarega, who was at war with the forts in a vain attempt to rid himself of this incubus which Lugard had located in his south-western provinces. Many of their comrades also were in Uganda, serving with Lugard. The Soudanese, therefore, refused to join hands with the Waganda Mohammedans. Mbogo's followers had thus wasted a considerable period of precious time to no purpose, and had also alienated Kabarega's friendship by their overtures to his enemies, so they were now quite willing to enter on the negotiations which Lugard had opened after his defeat of the Roman Catholics and the escape of Mwanga.

Lugard considered that the Mohammedans could take Bulamwezi and Chagwe unopposed, while they were already masters of their old battle-grounds in the north-west of Singo. He also, no doubt, thought that a Mohammedan party in Uganda would strengthen his hand against the doubtful allegiance of the beaten Catholics, and would, at all events, cause the cessation of the destructive raids which had rendered the frontier districts of Uganda untenable. But meanwhile the Mohammedans had heard, from a captured spy, that Mwanga had fled, and, as there was no King in Uganda, that Mbogo, their Sultan, would be welcomed as Kabaka. Accordingly, the whole Mohammedan force marched for that country with great rejoicing. But by this time Mwanga had returned to the capital and been recognised as King. Envoys from the Mohammedan party arrived the day after this event, but they were too late, and Lugard had to tell them that under no considerations whatever could Mbogo be King of Uganda. The envoys feared to return with this intelligence, and, moreover, with the message that Mbogo must be given up preliminary to entering on definite negotiations. They wished to be in a position to say what territory in Uganda the Mohammedan party would receive should they make their peace with Lugard, and urged the claims of their party to more liberal terms than were proposed to the Catholics, giving as a reason for this, that they had not invaded Uganda when their opportunity offered. After some manœuvring, Lugard satisfied them by promising to give their party the three provinces of Busuju, Butambala, and Butunzi. The western portions of Busuju and Butunzi had been harried by themselves, and were in an almost deserted condition, but their eastern portions and the whole of Butambala contained fertile districts, which had not suffered to any great extent from the wars. These three provinces amounted to a considerable area, and, what was more important, they carried a much larger proportion of political power. In all Uganda there were ten great provincial chiefs, each of whom had under him numerous minor district chiefs. Three of these provinces, with all that they embraced, were to be handed over to the Mohammedans, should they agree to Lugard's terms. The envoys were completely satisfied, as their faction would thus, though they mustered only about 5 per cent. of the total population at this time, acquire both territory and political power out of all proportion to their numbers.

On April 11th Selim Bey was deputed to return with the Mohammedan envoys to their camp, and endeavour to gain over their party to Lugard's views. Shortly after came the disquieting news that Mr. de Winton, the Company's officer, was in the hands of the Mohammedans, and this was closely followed by the sad intelligence that this young officer had fallen a victim to fever. Alone in the wilds of Unyoro he was struck down, and died without the consolation of having a man of his own race to attend him in his last moments.

14

The sad news of the loss of this zealous and energetic officer was a great blow to the little knot of Europeans who were battling against such odds, and straining every nerve, each in his own way and in his own department, to evolve peace out of disorder, and prosperity out of desolation. But the times were too stirring to allow of idle regret; work, constant work, was a daily necessity, and no doubt this, under the circumstances, was a good thing for all, preventing them from brooding over the blow; for it must be remembered in the interior of Africa it is doubly dispiriting to lose a trusty comrade.

On May 8th the Mohammedan envoys returned with the news that they could not restrain the masses of their people, who, after a definite rupture with Kabarega, had entered Uganda, but they asserted that nothing need be feared from this advance. A few days later, however, the chief of Singo sent in to the capital to say that the Mohammedan party were advancing in great force, and had broken off negotiations. Lugard had previously sent Achmed Effendi to warn Selim Bey that disquieting rumours regarding the intentions of the Mohammedans had reached him, and directing him to order the Soudanese in the Unyoro forts to attack the Mohammedans in rear should their intention be hostile. He was also to retard a Mohammedan advance by every means in his power. From the latest intelligence, there was no doubt that an advance in force was being made, though whether with a hostile intention, as reported by the Makwenda, or from stress of circumstances, as stated by the envoys, was still uncertain. Lugard was in a most trying position, as Williams was absent, quelling disturbances in Usoga, and numerous rumours were current of fresh movements among the Catholics; the heathen, too, might at any moment renew their insurrection if an opportunity occurred, so Lugard sent orders for Williams to return at once from Usoga, while he himself started with a small force to meet the Mohammedans.

On May 16th he reached Merowa in Busuju, where he was met by the disquieting report that the Mohammedan Katikiro, the leader of the moderate faction, had, with a following of only thirty men, abandoned Mbogo's party, who would no longer listen to him, and had openly insulted him. This looked like war. Lugard now sent his confidential interpreter, Dualla, ahead by forced marches, to warn Selim Bey that his life might be in danger, and to report the true state of affairs; at the same time the Protestants were ordered to concentrate their army at the capital, so as to be ready for emergencies. Dualla reported that the Mohammedans asserted they would neither work for nor obey Mwanga, but would acknowledge the authority of Lugard alone. Lugard also heard that there was a talk of treachery, and that he might even be assassinated.

On May 23rd Mbogo, the Mohammedan Sultan, with a large following, reached Lugard's camp. On the following day Lugard concluded these exceedingly difficult negotiations, and had the satisfaction of knowing that by his firmness and persistence he had gained his point.

'The chiefs rose and placed one of their King's hands in Selim's, and the other in Dualla's, who undertook to be sureties for him. They in turn, with nice feeling, said all their confidence was in me, and placed his hands in mine, and the Baraza broke up amid acclamations and general joy.' Thus writes Lugard in his despatch. The Mohammedan party entered into possession of their three provinces, and Lugard, accompanied by Mbogo, returned in triumph to the capital. The Catholic party accepted his terms; and Williams, after some fighting and much hard marching, had established peace in Usoga. Then, with sanguine anticipations of 'permanent peace' in Uganda, Lugard left for the coast.

CHAPTER XIV.

EVENTS THAT LED TO THE THIRD MOHAMMEDAN WAR.

THE reader will have observed, in the negotiations mentioned at the close of the last chapter, that the Mohammedans objected to work for the King or to obey him, and that they had made Selim Bey and Dualla sureties for their late Sultan Mbogo. If we wish to condense into a few lines the causes that led to the third Mohammedan war, we have them in this last sentence.

On Lugard's departure for England Williams entered on his charge, and on no one could the responsibility have more fittingly devolved. To this gallant officer Uganda owes much more than has ever been recognised. Though Lugard's senior in the service, he had loyally worked under him rather than dislocate his early administration by a change of authority; moreover, the troops who gained Lugard's victories had been raised and trained by him. During the long, weary months when Lugard was absent at Kavalli's, Williams had maintained peace in Uganda with an inadequate force. No one can realize the anxiety and strain that this involved. Day and night he had to be on the *qui vive*. Not only had he to conduct difficult negotiations between the embittered Christian parties, but he had again and again to personally patrol the streets to prevent hostile assemblages which might have precipitated a conflict. From his weak garrison he had to detach men to maintain order in Usoga, and to provide Lugard with stores and ammunition, although his own supply of the latter was absurdly small. In addition to this his Maxim was utterly unreliable. Still, during his period of command peace had been maintained at Kampala.

When in January, 1892, after Lugard's return, it was found that the Company had ordered the abandonment of Uganda, Williams nobly offered to sacrifice his private means to maintain a garrison and administration in the country, rather than that such a blot should fall on the name of England. In the Christian civil war, which broke out shortly after, it was Williams who led the decisive attack on the King's Hill in the battle of Mengo; it was he who conducted the successful assault on Bulingugwe and subdued the Sese Islands. When insurrection broke out in Usoga, Williams was again the means of restoring peace and order.

A gallant soldier, a clear-headed and firm administrator, it was under him that, during the close of the Company's rule in Uganda, that divided country had, after many years, its first glimpse of prosperity. When I returned to Uganda in December, 1892, the progress in the country was most marked. Roads and cultivation had advanced, and from the borders of Kavirondo to the confines of Buddu Williams' rule was respected and obeyed. The only cause for misgiving was the attitude of the Mohammedan party.

This faction, compact and united in the three provinces which had been allotted to them, did not rest in peace and cultivate their shambas. Their constitution was peculiar. They had lost by desertion many of their peasantry, the cultivating class, partly from the cruelty with which they enforced Mohammedan rites and partly because the Bakopi were tired of an unsettled life, and preferred to take service under Christian chiefs. These desertions reacted on the party in two ways. The chiefs were owners of fertile lands which they had not sufficient hands to till, and the proportion of armed men, who had found pleasure and profit in a life of war, was high as compared with the more peaceful portion of the community. This led to a good deal of dacoity on their borders, which were on that account gradually being deserted by their Christian neighbours, and the Mohammedan territory was rapidly being surrounded by a belt of desert, in which the shambas were allowed to run wild, and where no one dared to settle. In the autumn of 1892 Williams caused one notorious robber to be executed at the capital, but this acted only as a slight deterrent. Raids and dacoity were rife, the former outside, the latter within, the borders of Uganda.

There was a large settlement of Mohammedans at Natete, Mackay's old mission-station at the capital, and thefts, with or without violence, became of frequent occurrence. Abdool Rasud, whom Lugard had left as chief of Butunzi and recognised head of the Waganda Mohammedans, a man with the reputation of a lover of peace, had lost his influence, and Juma, a young and daring chief, was now styled by his party their Katikiro. He lived at Natete, where he had assembled round him a number of the young and impetuous bloods of his faction. This colony at the capital made little or no attempt to cultivate, yet constantly complained that they had not sufficient food. They studied to maintain the closest intimacy with Selim Bey and the Soudanese, and the fort mosque became their habitual meeting-place.

The Mohammedan party had intrigued with the Catholics, with a view to a combined attack on the Protestants, but the Catholics refused their overtures. They were also intimately connected with the Soudanese in the Unyoro forts, instigating them to raids which resulted in the capture and sale of slaves. The hope that the repatriated Mohammedans would settle down into peaceable citizens was thus daily proving more and more illusory; instead, the tension was growing greater and greater. Williams, though slow to move, was not unmindful of the increasing gravity of the situation.

In the winter of 1892-93 there came a crisis. A serious disturbance had been caused by the Mohammedans near their border, and Williams demanded that the offenders should be handed over to him for trial. No notice was taken of his order. This led to an ultimatum, and the Mohammedans were given a limited period in which to submit to the terms imposed. As the time gradually passed, and no sign of submission was made, the excitement in the capital increased.

At length the period of grace allowed was over, and the Mohammedans remained defiant. War seemed the only solution. Selim Bey now stepped in and did his utmost to induce Williams to extend the period, backing up his other arguments by hints that his men would not fight against their co-religionists. At the same time he and Mbogo persuaded their party to nominally fulfil the stipulated conditions, and, though the ringleaders in the late disturbance were never surrendered, Williams professed himself satisfied, and allowed the matter to drop. This produced but a temporary lull, for Juma's party was gaining confidence, and on January 8, 1893, there was very nearly war in the capital. Early that Sunday morning the fort bugles rang out the alarm, and the whole garrison rapidly fell in under arms, while the Maxims were prepared for action. The Protestants could be seen streaming out of church and rushing for their weapons, while bodies of men, already armed, were running towards the hills overlooking the Mohammedan quarter.

The Soudanese guard, which had been stationed on the outskirts of Natete as a precautionary measure, reported that there had been a disturbance, in which some Protestant houses had been looted and burnt, and that both sides were preparing for war. Williams, leaving the fort in a state of defence under Major Smith, hastily set out with a small guard to visit the Mohammedans, having already sent urgent messages to the Protestant chiefs to restrain their followers. As we reached the commanding little hill by the Pokino's quarter, a fine view was obtained of Natete and a great panorama of hill and dale, but a most disquieting sight was the rapidly-accumulating bands of armed men which crowned every hill surrounding the Mohammedan quarter. Messages were at once sent to them to dismiss, and Williams, descending amongst the Mohammedans, patiently investigated the details of the original disturbance.

The Soudanese report proved true, and we saw the smoking embers of what had been a Protestant's house, surrounded by unmistakable signs of violence. In the end two Mohammedans were made prisoners, and the matter appeared settled. While Williams had been away, several minor disturbances had occurred in the Mohammedan settlement which had sprung up round Mbogo's residence, and the guard-room at Kampala was full of prisoners arrested by Smith. Later in the day a few shots were fired, and that night Williams considered it desirable to put a strong picquet over the Roman Catholic mission-station, while the Protestants placed a guard on Namirembe.

Next day there were more disturbances, and Monseigneur Hirth reported that an alarming rumour was abroad to the effect that the Soudanese meant to make common cause with the Mohammedans. On January 10th renewed disturbances occurred during the night, and war-drums were beaten. So great was the anxiety in the capital that the Roman Catholic missionaries packed up their effects preparatory to leaving for Buddu. Peace was, however, again restored, but so strained were the relations that a few days later there was another rush to arms because a few shots had been fired at a leopard in an outlying garden.

Williams, feeling that the Roman Catholics had not at the

close of the late civil war got enough territory, had opened negotiations between the two Christian sects, with a view to increasing the Catholic territory. These negotiations, much to his disappointment, broke down. The Mohammedans, hearing of them, decided they, too, must have additional land. About this time news was received of the approach of an Imperial Commissioner, and all such questions were left over till after his arrival.

In due course the Imperial Commissioner, Sir Gerald Portal, arrived, accompanied by a large staff, with an escort of 200 Zanzibar troops. On April 1, 1893, the Company's flag at Kampala was replaced by the Union Jack, and a few days later Williams left for the coast with the proud satisfaction that, during both his periods of administration, civil war in Uganda had been averted. He took with him all the old Soudanese, except eighteen who remained as drill-instructors and officers for the new troops that were to be raised.

This appears a fitting time to glance at the general state of affairs, not only as regards Uganda, but in the adjacent countries, in order that we may the better follow and understand the development of the Mohammedan outbreak that ensued.

In Uganda, as we have seen, there was a general increase of prosperity: roads had been cleared, cultivation had increased, and the markets were flourishing. In the north-west of Singo, and in the north of Bulamwezi and Chagwe, promising settlements were springing up where formerly had been nothing but jungle and deserted shambas. The Mohammedan provinces were in a more unsatisfactory state, and many properties had been neglected, while others had passed out of cultivation altogether. Round the Mohammedan borders people were afraid to settle, owing to the lawless propensities of their neighbours, and South-west Singo had for the same reason been but sparsely inhabited. The dread of a fresh Mohammedan outbreak was gaining ground in the land, but so far nothing had occurred beyond dacoity and isolated disturbances. The Catholics in Buddu, though complaining bitterly of their cramped condition, had adhered to the treaty they had made with Lugard.

Beyond the western border things were more unpromising. After nine months' absence, Mr. Reddie had just returned from Unyoro and Usongora, where he had been sent in June, 1892. He had travelled over a great deal of country, and had made valuable maps of his routes, but reported that the temper of the people in many districts was distinctly hostile to Europeans. In Unyoro he had been attacked more than once, and in Kitakwenda had lost several men in beating off the assaults of the natives. This hostile feeling was due to the misconduct of the Soudanese who had been left to hold the chain of forts, and whose high-handed proceedings I have referred to in a previous chapter.

In Usongora itself, the once peaceful district north of Lake Albert Edward, there had been trouble, although Fort George was held by Swahilis, who got on better with the natives than the Soudanese did. Lugard had appointed Karakwanzi paramount chief of Usongora, but, as Owen afterwards found out, Karakwanzi had no claim to the position, and had to live close to the fort and under its protection. The Wasongora would not obey his orders, and the Swahili garrison, and afterwards Owen himself, found it much easier to deal with their district chiefs direct. The Manyema slave-hunters had returned to the Semiliki River in great force, after having devastated the country near Mazamboni and Kavalli's on the withdrawal of Selim Bey's Soudanese, and had established themselves in a strong stockaded position. From this fortress they raided Usongora and carried off many slaves. The small Swahili garrison of Fort George, which was guarding the Salt Lake, moved out to assist the Wasongora, but was roughly handled by the slave-raiders, and lost several killed and wounded. News of this reverse had reached the Soudanese forts, and a reinforcement of these wild soldiers had marched to Fort George, where their advent had complicated matters by alienating the Wasongora.

I have already mentioned that Sir Gerald Portal sent Major Owen and Captain Portal to Unyoro to enlist three companies of Soudanese. One of these companies was to be despatched at once to Uganda for duty in that country, while the others were to be concentrated as far as possible on the two eastern forts near the borders of Uganda, with a detached post to keep open communication with, and protect, Kasagama of Toru. There were also a number of old officers and others whom it was not considered desirable to enlist, and these, with their wives, families and slaves, amounting to about 2,000 souls, were to be brought into Uganda and granted land on which to settle. But such difficulties attended the satisfactory settlement of the 1,200 or 1,300 people who came to Mengo with the newly-enlisted company, that Sir Gerald Portal sent counter-orders to Major Owen directing him to retain the unenlisted for the present in Unyoro until arrangements could be made for them in Uganda.

As these orders took some fifteen days in reaching Owen, they were too late, for that energetic officer had already sent off the unenlisted towards Uganda, and all he could now do was to halt them at Fort de Winton to await further orders. There was very little food at this fort, and at its neighbour, Fort Briggs, and the scarcity was still further aggravated by this large caravan which had now to encamp there. Moreover, these counter-orders created great dissatisfaction amongst the old officers and their followers, who had been taken from the comparative plenty of the western forts under the impression that they were being led to a still richer land in Uganda, and now found themselves stopped in a desolate and devastated region, where famine loomed in the imminent future. I shall have more to say of this in its proper place. In the meantime, leaving Major Owen, Captain Portal, and Mr. Grant busily engaged in training and disciplining their new troops, and contending against the enormous difficulty of feeding 4,700 people in a wasted country now parched by long-continued drought, let us see what was happening in Uganda.

Sir Gerald Portal had built a small fort at Kibibi, in the Mohammedan province of Butambala, and garrisoned it with twenty Swahilis. It lay on the road to the Unyoro forts, for Lugard's circuitous route through Ankole had been already abandoned by Williams in favour of the shorter though more difficult one, which ran through the western provinces of Uganda. The questions at issue between the Protestants and Roman Catholics had been satisfactorily arranged, and the latter party had been granted a large accession of territory.

The Mohammedan problem alone remained unsolved. They demanded an additional province, Busiro, which was at this time one of the most flourishing and best cultivated in Uganda. Lawful claims to this they had none. Though, at the outside, mustering only five per cent. of the population, they had already got territory far in excess of what their numbers warranted, and an even larger proportion of chieftainships. In the provinces allotted to them they had allowed a number of shambas to go out of cultivation, while others were sadly neglected; yet they complained that food was scarce in their districts. Their conduct also told against them. They had not settled down peaceably in the country assigned to them, like the Roman Catholics, but had been a constant source of trouble and annoyance, which had culminated in an extreme state of tension. Robberies, not to say murders, at their hands were of common occurrence.

By virtue of the provinces and chieftainships allotted to them, they were bound to pay certain taxes to the King, and to furnish a certain amount of labour; they had not fulfilled these conditions, but acted as if they constituted an independent State. To give them an opportunity of settling down and developing their country, these taxes had at first been remitted, but now that they were legally due they refused to pay, unless granted the new province they wanted. Their motive was obvious. Through their own idleness and restlessness they had allowed the country they held to deteriorate, and now they wished to move into and enjoy the luxuriant plantations of Busiro, which had been developed by the toil of others. Busiro exhausted, they would no doubt in another year clamour for a fresh district, on the plea of renewed scarcity of food.

They were told that their claims to a new province were not recognised, that they had already more land than their numbers entitled them to, and that their condition, prosperous or the reverse, depended on their own industry. I was, however, detailed privately to ascertain if it would be feasible, or desirable, to allot them a few small shambas midway between the capital and the nearest Mohammedan province of Butambala. I reported in favour of giving them a few in Busiro, close to the Namaya River, which were enclosed, by natural features of the ground, in a small well-marked group. Before Sir Gerald Portal could take any action on this report, the attitude of the party had become so defiant that it was out of the question to make them any concessions whatever.

The immediate effect of the Imperial Commissioner's refusal to extend their territory was an increase of crime at the capital, where matters were becoming more unsatisfactory than ever. The Mohammedan party at Natete were further reinforced, and became correspondingly independent. During the month of May they killed or wounded four Protestants in the capital or its immediate vicinity—an unprecedented record. A case was referred to Sir Gerald Portal, on which he gave his decision, but the Mohammedans paid no attention to his ruling. Meanwhile, rumours revived that the Soudanese would make common cause with the Mohammedans, no doubt from the fact that their intimacy was steadily increasing.

The attitude of Selim Bey was also far from satisfactory. He was annoyed that the unenlisted at the Unyoro forts had not been brought into Uganda *in toto*, as he had said would be done in his letter which was read on parade at the enrolment of the Soudanese troops. When the third company sent off by Owen arrived at Kampala, they were ordered by Sir Gerald Portal to the new headquarters he had founded at Port Alice; with this company came a certain number of unenlisted men who were also to be located there.

Sir Gerald was himself at Port Alice, and it fell to Lieutenant Villiers, who was commanding at Kampala, to see these orders carried out. He instructed Selim Bey accordingly, and was greatly surprised when the latter distinctly refused to allow the unenlisted to proceed to Port Alice. I was just marching through Kampala, on return to headquarters from deputation duty, and Villiers reported to me the deadlock which had occurred. We went to see Selim Bey, who stoutly adhered to his position. He said we could do as we pleased with the enlisted soldiers and their families who were under our orders, but that he was still the chief of all who had not been enlisted, and could not recognise that the British officers had any authority over them, and, finally, that he wished these men located at Kampala, and would not allow them to go to Port Alice.

This, of course, could not be tolerated, and Selim Bey was made to clearly understand the fact. Though discontented and dissatisfied, he was not yet ripe for active mutiny, and ultimately promised to issue the necessary orders. This he did not do, and so effectually did he thwart the efforts Villiers made to carry out Sir Gerald Portal's wishes, that only a small portion of the unenlisted reached Port Alice. Sir Gerald, to whom this serious affair was duly reported, took no action in the matter, in spite of the representations of the military officers of his staff, who viewed with misgiving any loosening of the bonds of discipline. It happened in the early part of May, and produced, as might be expected, a renewal of activity on the part of the Mohammedans, who looked on Selim Bey as their head and representative in the councils of the Europeans.

On May 15th a somewhat serious disturbance occurred in the Mohammedan quarter, and about twenty shots were fired. A few nights later the Protestant chief Mukasa was killed by a Mohammedan on one of the roads near Natete. Towards the end of the month both the Mohammedans and Selim Bey became more active. The former repeatedly pressed their claims to be granted the province of Busiro, and Selim Bey sent a party of soldiers with some Mohammedan chiefs to intimidate the King into granting their demand. This was reported to the Imperial Commissioner, who was, however, satisfied by Selim's denial of any knowledge of the transaction. That the story was true is undoubted; the plan was made in Selim's own house, as afterwards admitted by chiefs concerned, and the party of soldiers was then and there told off by Selim himself, as the non-commissioned officer who commanded it confessed.

A few days later Selim Bey followed this up by a letter to Sir Gerald Portal, in which he urged him to grant the Mohammedan request, and allot them additional territory. This was the first open move that Selim Bey had made in support of the Mohammedan party, and it was ominous of future trouble. After the fast-approaching departure of Sir Gerald Portal for the coast, and with him his Zanzibar troops, Selim Bey's Soudanese would form the only military body with which British authority was to be upheld in the country. Selim was supposed to exercise unlimited influence over his men, and it was for this very reason that he had been engaged at the high rate of pay of 400 rupees a month, and constituted native Commandant of the battalion. If the native Commandant of the troops was to be permitted to take up the Mohammedan cause and constitute himself their partisan, the future work of British officials in Uganda would be rendered impossible.

Sir Gerald Portal demanded an explanation from Selim Bey, who contented himself with asserting that his letter had no political significance whatever. With this excuse Sir Gerald appeared satisfied, but at that time he was not in a condition of either mind or body to deal with the matter in his usual firm and decided manner. Not only had long and arduous work, anxious negotiations and an immense amount of sedentary office work lowered his general tone, but he had only a few days before been prostrated with fever, and was worn out with anxiety for his brother, who lay dying in Kampala.

On May 27th Captain Raymond Portal died. He had become seriously ill when alone at the eastern Unyoro forts, and had made a gallant effort to reach Kampala. The greater part of the way to the intermediate post of Kibibi he had been carried by his men, and he arrived in a terrible state of exhaustion, having had very little food he could touch. At Kibibi he was met by Villiers, who, as soon as it was known that Captain Portal was ill, left the capital and pushed on by forced marches to meet him. He and Dr. Baxter, of the Church Missionary Society, who followed a day later, brought the sick man to Kampala, where he could be properly housed and given a chance for his life. Here he was attended with unremitting care by Drs. Baxter and Moffat, the latter of whom was at once summoned from Port Alice. But medical skill and careful nursing proved of no avail, and a most promising career was brought to an untimely end. Next day he was buried with military honours in the churchyard at Namirembe, where he sleeps next to De Winton, who also lost his life in the swamps of Southern Unyoro.

The blow to Sir Gerald was crushing, for he had all along believed that his brother would recover. He looked a different man, and the officers of his staff were agreed that the sooner he marched for the coast the better, as change of scene and the varied incidents of marching life would enable him to recover, while if he remained in Uganda a total collapse was feared.

Sir Gerald Portal had promised the King and chiefs to hold a farewell durbar at which he would settle the Mohammedan question once for all. On May 29, 1893, this memorable durbar was held, and to prevent all possibility of mistake, Mr. Pilkington, of the Church Missionary Society, was asked to act as interpreter. The result of this durbar I have already mentioned—the Mohammedan chiefs openly threatened rebellion if their demands were not acceded to. These demands were refused, and Sir Gerald Portal warned them that he had given me instructions to deport their leaders if they gave trouble, and that he himself would await in Kavirondo a further report of their conduct before marching onward to the coast. The following day he left for Kavirondo.

Sir Gerald Portal had done an immense amount of work in a very short space of time, and had nearly worn himself out by his ceaseless energy. He solved two of the great problems of Uganda, but the cloud of Mohammedan rebellion, which before his arrival already loomed above the horizon, had rapidly increased and spread, until, on his departure, it completely overshadowed the land.

CHAPTER XV.

THE LAST FORTNIGHT BEFORE THE OUTBREAK—SELIM BEY'S INTRIGUES.

No sooner had the Mohammedan chiefs left Sir Gerald Portal's final durbar, than they went in a body to interview Selim Bey, with whom they were closeted for some time. When this meeting broke up, they did not wear the mien of disappointed men whose last hope of securing advantage for their party had been rudely shattered, but, on the contrary, they seemed elated and in good spirits. What occurred at this consultation was not known until some weeks later, when some of the Mohammedan chiefs were put on their trial for their share in the rebellion, and the truth became known.

From the information of chiefs concerned, the gist of what took place at this memorable interview was somewhat as follows. The Mohammedan chiefs asked Selim Bey to make a last effort to induce the Imperial Commissioner to grant their demands before he left for the coast. But Selim pointed out that the departure of Sir Gerald Portal was not a disadvantage, but in itself an advantage to the cause, for with him also departed his escort of Zanzibar troops. After these had left, none but Selim's men would remain to guard the forts, with their stores and supplies of arms and ammunition. So all that had to be done was to wait patiently until Sir Gerald was well clear of Uganda, when he, Selim Bey, could speak to the new Commissioner with much greater weight. If the latter should prove as obdurate as the Imperial Commissioner had done, nothing was easier than to arrest him and his European staff in their beds, any night he chose. Then the reserve arms and ammunition in the forts could be served out to faithful followers of the Prophet, and the combined force of the Soudanese and Mohammedan Waganda, with over 1,000 breechloading rifles in their hands, could sweep the Christians out of the country, and set up a Mohammedan State, with Mbogo as Sultan. Meanwhile the Mohammedans must secretly prepare for war, and assemble as many of their followers as possible at Natete until the signal should be given. Such was the story of the Mohammedan chiefs, and, if absolutely correct, the blame would be thrown entirely on Selim Bey. But it is more probable that this well-laid plot had been discussed before, and that on Sir Gerald Portal's final refusal to grant the Mohammedan party the additional land they desired, their chiefs resorted to Selim Bey to report their non-success, and to see if he was prepared to back them up in carrying the plan into execution.

Whoever may have been most to blame, there appears no doubt that as early as May 29th the plot of future mutiny and rebellion was thought out, and that the chiefs of the Mohammedan faction were only waiting till their organization was complete, and the caravan of the Imperial Commissioner at a safe distance.

But when I took over charge from Sir Gerald Portal I did not know this, and, though I could see that a crisis was inevitable in the near future, I trusted, as did Sir Gerald himself, that only the Mohammedans were concerned, and that Selim Bey would keep out of it.

On May 31, 1893, Mr. Berkeley, who had been left behind by the Imperial Commissioner to settle the outstanding question of a road for the Catholics from Mawakota to the

15—2

capital, announced Sir Gerald Portal's decision, and then left to catch up his caravan. I had hardly returned to the fort, after accompanying Berkeley a mile or two on his road, when I almost simultaneously received two letters, from the heads of the two missions in the capital, protesting warmly against the decision, each considering that the other party had got an unfair advantage. However, both these worthy gentlemen, after a personal interview with me, expressed themselves satisfied, and regretted that the native information on which they based their letters had been somewhat exaggerated.

On June 1st Selim Bey began to test the strength of the new administration. He sent up a message by his confidential sergeant to say that he wished a meeting of all the Europeans in the capital convened with as little delay as possible, as he desired to expound his views. Mr. Gedge, the *Times* correspondent, was with me when the message was delivered, and remarked that the Bey had lost no time in asserting himself. But though we joked about it, the affair was in reality serious. I at once visited Selim, and, on his assuring me that the message had been correctly delivered, I informed him that such conduct could not be tolerated, and that if he had anything to say he must say it to me. The Bey began by adopting an independent attitude. He explained that he was not originally a Company's servant, but the independent commander of a large body of Soudanese; that he had been invited into Uganda by Lugard; and that all orders to the Soudanese had passed through him, while he had been consulted in all matters relating to the Mohammedans. He also added, that the Christian Waganda had Europeans to bring forward their claims, but the Mohammedan Waganda had no one but him. I informed him that, whatever might have been the case in the past, he was now an officer in the service of the British, Commandant of the Soudanese battalion, and as such would be treated with all the customary respect due to his position and rank; but I warned him that it was impossible to allow him to interfere in the politics of the country. He then admitted that, as Commandant of the Soudanese troops, he, as well as those troops, was under the orders of the British Commissioner, but maintained that he was also the independent head of the unenlisted Soudanese, and must be recognised as such. These unenlisted, we may note, were, in point of numbers and fighting spirit, not far inferior to the enlisted soldiery. To this argument I naturally replied that I recognised no such distinction; that the unenlisted, as long as they remained in the country for which I was responsible to Her Majesty's Government, were under my orders, and would be treated as an integral portion of the population; that any who objected to be so dealt with were at perfect liberty to return to Kavilli's or the Soudan if they pleased, but that as long as they remained in Uganda they must obey my orders, and not those of the native Commandant of the Soudanese battalion.

On Selim Bey still objecting, I quietly but firmly informed him that, as Acting Commissioner, I had been given extensive powers, and was prepared to use them should my orders be trifled with or disobeyed. The Bey then judged it wise to moderate his language, but, however, again brought forward the Mohammedan claims to fresh territory, and said, if they were not satisfied, they talked of again migrating to Unyoro. I listened to what he had to say, and then stated that the Mohammedan claims had already been investigated by Sir Gerald Portal and his decision announced, and that, though Selim had for this occasion been allowed to have his say, he must in future avoid mixing himself up in the Mohammedan question, which was a purely political, and not a religious, one.

Later on I had an interview with Juma, the so-called Mohammedan Katikiro, and impressed on him the necessity of the Mohammedans submitting to the King, and doing their duty as subjects of the Kabaka of Uganda. Juma, though polite, did not, to judge from his somewhat diplomatic language, hold out much hope of a satisfactory settlement. Meanwhile it appeared to me that the first thing to do was to move Selim Bey to Port Alice, where it would be more difficult for the Mohammedan chiefs to intrigue with him, as they were habitually doing. When he should be removed from their councils, I hoped that by patience a peaceful settlement of the Mohammedan question might yet be obtained. Selim Bey's health had been poor at Kampala, and he had often talked of paying a visit to Munyunyu, so I told him to go from that place to Port Alice by the steel boat which I ordered to Munyunyu for the purpose. At the same time the Soudanese in Kampala were paid up in full, and Mr. Wilson was sent to Port Alice to pay the two companies there. This left me alone in Kampala, for Dr. Moffat and Mr. Gedge were already at Port Alice, but I thought it desirable, in the approaching crisis, that the soldiery should have no grievance as regards arrears of pay.

On June 4th bad news was received from Owen in Unyoro, who wrote very full despatches and requested most strongly that these might be sent after Sir Gerald Portal, should he have already left Uganda, as Owen wished him to fully understand, before he went home, the extreme difficulties of the position in Unyoro.

The situation there during the last few weeks was somewhat as follows: Major Owen, after enlisting the required Soudanese troops, had left Captain Portal in charge, and marched to the Salt Lake, accompanied by Mr. Grant. He had also taken with him Kasagama of Toru, to show him the district of Kitakwenda, where Sir Gerald Portal had suggested he might settle, if he did not care to remain in Toru, after the northern forts were abandoned. At Fort George Owen found that the mixed garrison of Soudanese and Swahilis had not proved acceptable to the Wasongora, who were passively hostile and could hardly be prevailed on to furnish sufficient food for the garrison. He also heard of the Manyema raid, and that they were in large force in a strong stockade west of the Semiliki River, in the territories of the Congo Free State. Owen sent messages to them, informing them that the British Government had now replaced the Company in Uganda, and warning them against future raiding. The Manyema made prisoners of his envoys and laughed at his threats. Owen also got hold of two letters from the Manyema; one was a defiance to the Commandant of Fort George, while the other appeared to be addressed to the Waganda Mohammedans, telling them of the reverses the troops of the Congo Free State had suffered, saying that all the white men had been expelled from Tanganyika westwards, and advising the Mohammedan party in Uganda to fortify themselves and not submit to the white men, as the Manyema were coming to their assistance.

Owen had not a sufficient force to take immediate action, and was, moreover, himself in ill-health. In a few days, however, being recovered sufficiently to march again, he crossed Beatrice Gulf and entered Northern Ankole. He found the inhabitants of this district far from as friendly as he had expected, owing to the fact that he had not trade goods, to give them the handsome presents to which they appeared accustomed. After some difficulty he got guides, who led him astray. When a day or two later he discovered their treachery, he dismissed them, and proceeded to strike out his own line through Kitakwenda to Fort Briggs. In Kitakwenda the people were distinctly hostile, and Owen was further hampered by having to march without roads through a difficult and overgrown country, where he suffered from want of water. Mr. Grant was with him, but his escort consisted of only about twenty Soudanese, and his whole caravan did not exceed fifty men. He pushed stubbornly on, in spite of the daily increasing boldness of the natives, who now crowded round his caravan on the march, threatening it with their spears. At last they swooped down on the rear guard, and attempted to carry off the few goats his column possessed, and he was obliged to fight in self-defence. Small as his party was, he gave the enemy a sharp lesson, and was after this fight permitted to proceed in peace.

Food difficulties were very great, and Owen and Grant had to subsist for days on a few sweet-potatoes and such pigeons as they could shoot. The former had the further anxiety that he might miss the fort, and march past it into hostile Unyoro with his small party. However, his compass-line was nearly correct, and he reached Fort Briggs without further accident.

The prospect had not materially brightened. During his absence, the Wanyoro, seeing the northern forts weakened, had attacked in great force; the garrison had beaten them off successfully, but the Wanyoro army had then marched south and occupied the road between Forts Lorne and Briggs, and thus completely severed the line of communications. Bimbashi Shukri, who was at Fort Briggs at the time, had sallied out with a party of thirty Soudanese to reconnoitre, and had fallen into an ambuscade. At the first volley Shukri had been killed, and the Soudanese soldiers, making but a poor stand, finally fled in disorder to Fort Briggs, having lost, in addition to their Bimbashi, a Mulazin and several men. Grant was at once despatched to relieve the garrison, but found that the Wanyoro, satisfied with the success they had achieved, had retired northwards. Shukri's death was a great loss, as he was not only a capable and energetic officer, but one of proved loyalty to the British.

At Forts Briggs (No. 3) and De Winton (No. 4) Owen found the garrisons were almost in a state of mutiny. The long-continued drought had ruined the partial attempts at cultivation round the forts, while the active operations of Kabarega's army, and the defeat and death of Shukri, deterred them from sending parties far afield, and prevented supplies from being forwarded from Toru. Scarcity, amounting to famine, had already made itself felt. When Owen arrived, the soldiers fell in armed, and respectfully asked for food; the weeping and wailing women and children crowded round with the same request, while amongst the great mass of unenlisted it took the form of a demand. But for Owen's cool and collected demeanour, there might even now have been a catastrophe. He, however, succeeded in quieting them, in imparting to them some of his own confidence, and immediately despatched an immense caravan to Toru for provisions.

In his letters he pointed out that it was necessary he should have reinforcements, a Maxim, reserve ammunition, and stores, to enable him to defeat the Wanyoro, who were still in the field, and to attack the Manyema, who had seized his envoys.

In forwarding these despatches, I gave a brief account of the state of affairs in Uganda, stating that the Mohammedans were in a condition of veiled rebellion, and intriguing with Selim Bey, who was in a very uncertain frame of mind, and considered the defeat and death of Shukri was directly due to our retention of the Unyoro forts with reduced garrisons, a measure which he had informed Sir Gerald Portal would prove a mistake. He also made capital out of the famine that prevailed at the forts, and was generally sullen and dissatisfied. I pointed out that a renewal of the alliance between the Mohammedans in Uganda and the Arab or Manyema party outside must be prevented at all costs, and proposed to strengthen Owen and to make a counter-raid on Kabarega's capital, and so relieve the pressure on the former's communications. These despatches reached Sir Gerald Portal, whose health was already much improved by change of life at Wakoli's in Usoga, and he at once replied. His letter was headed 'One march beyond Wakoli's,' and dated 'June 8,

1893.' In this he positively forbade any military operations against the Manyema in the territory of the Congo Free State, and any attempt to recover the prisoners by force. He also ordered the immediate evacuation of Fort George at the Salt Lake, and, as soon as the immediate difficulties were settled, to let Toru go, and withdraw into Uganda. With reference to my suggested counter-attack on Unyoro, he agreed in the following terms : ' If Owen has got his people together and can hold his own, but is still threatened by a force of Wanyoro, then it may be wise to make a counter-raid into Unyoro.' Sir Gerald expected to reach Mumia's in Kavirondo in a few days, and announced his intention of halting there until June 21st, when, if the gravity of the situation had not lessened, he would return to Uganda.

The position all round was thus very serious. The main idea of concentrating the bulk of the Unyoro garrisons at the western forts, near the Uganda border, had been that, in case of internal trouble in Uganda itself, they would be available to support the central authority. Now, however, not only was Owen unable to do this, but he was also in pressing need of reinforcements. I was the only military officer in Uganda, where I had two civilian assistants and the doctor ; in Usoga was Captain Arthur with one civil assistant, and in Unyoro was Major Owen with another civil assistant, Mr. Grant. The post in the Mohammedan country was now a source of weakness, as its small garrison of twenty Swahilis could not successfully oppose the large force of Mohammedans in the vicinity, should there be a rising, so on June 5th I sent a small party with letters to Owen detailing the general situation in Uganda, and the probability of a Mohammedan rising, and despatched orders to Kibibi that the garrison of that post were to accompany the mail-carriers to Major Owen, and place themselves under his orders. This was successfully done, and Owen thus warned of what was happening in Uganda. By this time a fresh despatch from Owen was received, to the effect that the Unyoro army had retired, that his communications were now open, and that he was anxiously awaiting reinforcements before attacking the Manyema.

On June 6th Mbogo paid me a visit, and assured me that he had no part in the Mohammedan trouble, and that personally he was in favour of his party settling down into peaceable citizens, but that Juma, the Mahommedan Mujasi, and other chiefs had a strong faction who were opposed to this course. The same day it was announced by the King, on my suggestion, that a full baraza would meet on June 12th to deal with the Mohammedan question, and the chiefs of the malcontents were directed to attend.

On June 9th Selim Bey left for Port Alice. He had, before his departure, undoubtedly caused some discontent amongst the soldiery by insinuating that the defeat and death of Shukri and the famine at the forts were due to a careless disregard of the well-being of the Soudanese. Two kidnapping cases in which Soudanese women were reported to have been carried off by the Protestants also caused ill feeling. Both of the missing women turned up in a few days, and I held a most searching inquiry into the circumstances, with the result that, though I could not legally prove that Selim Bey or any of his officers had purposely secluded the women, there was little doubt that both cases were got-up jobs, with a view to embittering the soldiery against the Protestant Waganda.

Selim Bey took five days over the twenty odd miles that lay between Port Alice and Munyunyu, the port of Mengo, and his men amused themselves *en route* by looting a station which belonged to the Church Missionary Society. But events were now rapidly drawing to a climax, and before there was time to deal with this misconduct, fresh offences followed in rapid succession. Selim Bey landed at Port Alice, marched in state to his new quarters, flying the Mohammedan flag, and at once took up an attitude of opposition towards Mr. Reddie, who was then commanding at Port Alice, and countermanded some of his orders, especially those regarding the reserve. Sir Gerald Portal, before his departure, had sanctioned my raising from amongst the unenlisted Soudanese a reserve force of 250 men on a reduced scale of pay. This was not only with a view to increasing discipline, but also because, after having gone into the matter carefully, I pointed out that the pay and rations of 600 soldiers on the active list was not sufficient to feed themselves and their 6,000 to 7,000 followers, while the increased emoluments due to a reserve of 250 men would enable this to be done, and put us in a position to stop the looting and stealing which was so prevalent amongst the Soudanese followers. Certain non-fighting men were also to be formed into a regularly-paid coolie corps.

Selim Bey had been consulted, and had announced that he would do his best to further the scheme. His utmost efforts, however, only produced seven candidates for the reserve, so it was evident he was secretly working against the scheme, which would have deprived him of much of the power he had claimed over the unenlisted. Mr. Reddie, at Port Alice, had got together some twelve to fifteen reservists, and was daily drilling them, when Selim Bey arrived, and issued a proclamation that they were to be disbanded and in future the unenlisted must not obey Reddie's orders.

On June 11th, the day before the big baraza, a Mohammedan reinforcement arrived at Natete, and a regular fusillade was opened to celebrate the event. I succeeded in quieting the disturbance, but had to place picquets on the Protestant and Roman Catholic mission-stations. This demonstration on the part of the Mohammedans was supposed to be with a view to intimidating the King, and thus influencing his decision at the baraza next day.

On June 12th the baraza assembled at the King's Court, and

several minor Mohammedan chiefs attended it. The King asked for a definite answer as to whether their party were prepared to be loyal subjects, or wished to be considered rebels against his authority. They replied they were not of sufficient rank to take upon themselves to speak for all, but would refer his question to their principal chiefs, and an answer would be given next day. Twenty-four hours later the Mohammedan Mujasi came to see me, told me the King had threatened war unless the Mohammedans paid their taxes and did their share of work, and asked me to interfere. I replied that the King was within his rights, and that the Mohammedans must either do their duty as subjects of Mwanga or take the consequences. I explained that their religion was in no danger, and that the question was purely a political one.

On the Mujasi saying there would be war the following day, I replied that war or peace depended on the action of his own party; that if they decided to fight, I should certainly not protect them; but if they elected for peace, they might depend on me to see that they were justly, and even generously, treated. Then in his presence I gave orders, to the native officers commanding the Soudanese company in Kampala, that no armed Mohammedans were to be allowed within our boundaries, as they talked of rebelling within a few hours against their rightful King. The Mujasi left me, and for several hours I was in uncertainty as to what his party proposed to do; but finally he returned to say that he and the other chiefs had considered the matter, and had decided to submit. The following day a few petty Mohammedan chiefs began their share of work on the royal buildings, and everyone hoped that at the eleventh hour peace had been secured.

Sir Gerald Portal wrote to me a most eulogistic letter on my conduct of these negotiations, which he considered finally settled the Mohammedan question; but we had all reckoned without Selim Bey.

The Mohammedan submission was only a blind to gain time while the matter was reported to Selim Bey at Port Alice and their preparations hastened. Had he even then refused to interfere, the matter would no doubt have dropped, and the Mohammedans have settled down in peace—for the time, at all events. But Selim did not dream of relinquishing his championship of the cause of Islam. He encouraged the party to persevere, with the result that the war-drums were beaten in the Mohammedan provinces, and their army assembled in the east of Busuju, some thirty-five miles from Mengo, close to the spot where Lugard had concluded his negotiations at the close of the second Mohammedan war. So numerous and aggressive did they appear that Sekiwala, the Protestant chief who ruled the district of Singo, nearest to the border of Busuju, abandoned his property and fell back on Matiana with all his people. The Mohammedans at Natete, in the capital, were also further reinforced till they mustered 1,200 guns. Selim Bey evidently thought the time was now nearly ripe for him to take action. So on June 16th he sent me, by his confidential sergeant, an intimidating and mutinous message, to the following effect:

That he heard there was a probability of a fight between the King Mwanga and the Waganda Mohammedans; that he had told Mbogo not to fight, but warned me that if I allowed the King Mwanga to fight the Mohammedans, he would consider such an action on the part of Mwanga as hostile action against himself; and that his reason for adopting this position was that in conjunction with Captain Lugard he had brought back the Waganda Mohammedans to Uganda.

This was nothing more nor less than rank mutiny, and I was now alive to the truly serious crisis that was impending. I

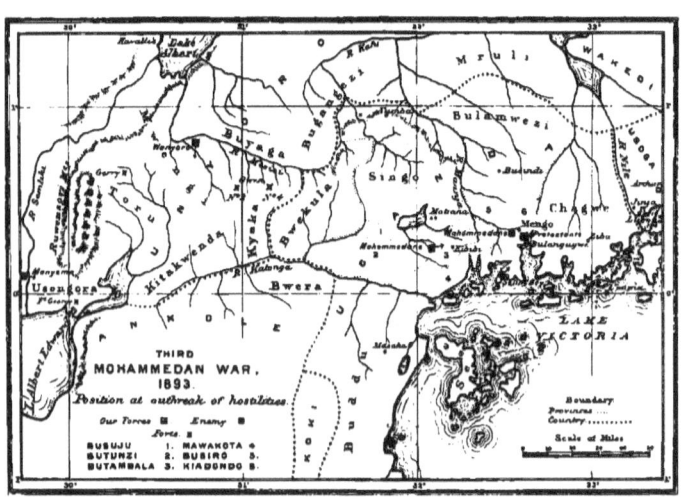

had to bear in mind that Selim Bey and his men had been concerned in one successful mutiny already in Equatoria; that a fate similar to Emin Pasha's might be mine, should I, like that unfortunate officer, attempt to temporize or let the matter slide. If Selim Bey had that influence over his men that he was supposed to exert, the Soudanese troops could not be depended on. Whatever was done must be very risky, but the best chance of success seemed to rest in a rapid initiative, and this I decided to take.

I had already been informed by the Protestant chiefs that, if Selim Bey and his men made common cause with the Mohammedans, they dare not face such odds, and that the people would break and flee. The Roman Catholic party were for the most part distant, and could not help in the crisis that was now upon us. I do not think I am wrong in saying that the native chiefs and gentlemen of both missions considered my position well-nigh desperate, and even amongst the Government officials defeat was looked on as almost inevitable. Mr. Gedge had only a few days before said that such a combination would sweep us out of the country, and asked me what I could do to avert it. I had then made up my mind what course to pursue, if it came to the worst, but had hardly expected that the time for action would come so speedily.

I knew enough of the Waganda to see that our best, and indeed only, chance of a successful issue out of this gloomy situation lay in a rapid movement, which might disorganize the plans of the rebels, and enable us to beat them in detail, or even to cow them into submission.

Having made up my mind to act, and act quickly, there was still much left to be done before the morrow. I had not only the Government officers and Government property to consider, but the safety of the many missionaries scattered about the country, and till a late hour that night I was busy issuing my orders. Owen was in a very critical position if the mutiny and rebellion broke out, so my first duty was to write to him. I told him that the long-expected outbreak was upon us, related the attitude which Selim Bey had now adopted, warned him that the road between his forts and Uganda would be no longer safe for small parties, and that in case of trouble with the Unyoro garrisons he should endeavour to take up a position in Toru, till I could send him reinforcements. Arthur was ordered to return to the capital from Usoga by forced marches, while his assistant, with all the men at his disposal, was to occupy the Nile ferry, and keep open our communications with the coast. Reddie and Gedge at Port Alice were to leave the Soudanese in charge of the stores, with strict orders not to leave the station, and themselves with their Swahilis join me at Kampala next day.

The missionaries at the capital I meant to get into the fort the following day, and those in Singo were warned to take refuge in Bagwe Island in Lake Isolt. The mission-stations in Chagwe and Buddu I considered fairly safe for the present. I was in hopes that the company of Soudanese at Kampala would stand by me, as I had daily been drilling them, and was well known to the officers, but I meant to test their loyalty very soon. If they proved doubtful, my only force consisted of some eight Egyptian Soudanese and my Swahilis.

I intended to get the missionaries into Kampala the succeeding morning, and bring Mbogo and the son of Karema into the same place for security, and then demand four of the principal Mohammedan chiefs as hostages for the peaceful behaviour of their party until I could deal with Selim Bey. If they refused to do this, they would be attacked at Natete on June 18th, before they could get reinforcements from Port Alice. The Protestants were already in considerable force at the capital, and I had directed the Katikiro to quietly increase their strength by drawing in additional men from the provinces.

The only remaining matter of any great importance was the recall of Sir Gerald Portal and his caravan. I was thoroughly aware that Sir Gerald's caravan could not reach me under three weeks at the earliest, and so could in no way assist me in the actual struggle that must come off in the next few days.

But I might fairly urge that in the terribly despondent state of the Protestant Waganda, on whom I must chiefly rely, and, indeed, of the Europeans, the knowledge that Sir Gerald Portal with his strong, well-armed caravan was hastening to our assistance would prove a moral factor of immense value. I might argue that if beaten in the field, as most people seemed to expect, I could still hope to hold out in Kampala with the Europeans and Swahilis, and, while thus guarding the reserve rifles and ammunition, hold a large body of the enemy at bay, and allow of Sir Gerald rallying round him the Protestant Waganda in the east of Uganda, and perhaps turning the tables.

Other reasons might be urged, but it will be sufficient to mention the chief one of all. Sir Gerald Portal was recalled in accordance with his own wishes expressed in the letter of June 8th, from which I have already given certain quotations.

NOTE.—The following quotation from another letter dated July 8th may be interesting. Sir Gerald says:

'Both of us [Colonel Rhodes and himself] are perfectly ready and willing to put in another five months in Uganda. For myself, I should not mind it at all.'

CHAPTER XVI.

THE CRISIS—VICTORY AT RUBAGA.

ON the morning of June 17, 1893, one of the two eventful days which were destined to decide whether British authority and missionary enterprise were to retain their position in Uganda, or to be swept away by a violent revival of Mohammedanism, there was little to show that such momentous issues hung in the balance. The fort bugles sounded the *reveillé* at the customary hour, and the Soudanese paraded for drill as usual; the ordinary routine work of the fort was dealt with, and the Swahilis were told off to their daily tasks, the only difference being that the headmen in charge were warned to return with their parties to the fort by noon.

In the town there was little to mark this day as different from many that had preceded it. To the critical observer there might have appeared rather more armed Waganda than usual moving about, but this was not very apparent. Yet, though outwardly all seemed calm and peaceful, there was a suppressed something in the atmosphere, an undefined tension, like that heavy feeling in the unnatural calm which precedes the tropical thunderstorm.

That morning at an early hour the Katikiro paid me a visit. In this itself there was nothing unusual, as interviews on matters of political or judicial moment were of almost daily occurrence. He reported that, in accordance with my instructions, he had secretly and unostentatiously assembled over 2,000 guns in the capital in case of a Mohammedan rising, and that more were coming in. This had been admirably managed without the fuss and show that usually formed a marked feature in the concentration of an army at the capital.

The Katikiro said the minds of men had been much agitated by a report which had been circulated by a few of the Mohammedans, that the Soudanese were in very truth to join hands with their party, and at one fell swoop do away with British supremacy and Christian teaching. It must be remembered that families in Uganda were much divided—one brother might be a Protestant, another a follower of Rome, a third a devout adherent of Islam. During the previous wars there had been numerous cases of relatives warning each other to escape from some impending stroke planned by the opposite faction, and this had happened in the present case. Some Mohammedans had advised their Christian kinsfolk to seek safety in the provinces, and remain in concealment, as there was a great combined revolution impending at Mengo, where Selim Bey had promised to assist the Mohammedan party in recovering the kingdom and upsetting the British rule.

Up to this time I had invariably laughed at any idea of there being truth in such rumours, but now I knew from the Bey himself that they were correct, and informed the Katikiro of the fact. He, though he had dreaded this for some time owing to the otherwise unaccountable boldness of the Waislam, was perceptibly staggered by the realization of his fears. He said the confirmation of this report would have a disastrous result on the morale of the Protestants; they were prepared to fight the Mohammedans if necessary, but to expect men to fight a daring foe in front with the fear of a Soudanese attack on the rear was out of the question. He pointed out, if the

16—2

Soudanese and Mohammedans got possession of the Maxims and the 400 reserve breech-loading rifles in Kampala, with the large amount of ammunition and powder stored there, that it was utterly out of the question to expect the Protestants to face them, as for that matter the combined Christians would be unequal to the task.

Many weaker spirits amongst the Protestants had already counselled flight, and he greatly feared the result of this last piece of news would be a general retreat into Chagwe and Usoga. However, he and several other chiefs had decided, whatever the odds, to stand by Her Majesty's representative, and carry out any scheme I might propose.

I explained my plans: The Europeans and Swahilis were to garrison Kampala; the Soudanese, whose loyalty could not be depended on, were to be disarmed, and hostages were to be obtained from the Islam party, or they would be attacked before assistance could reach them from Selim Bey. I informed him that all the necessary orders had been issued overnight, and only the arrival of Reddie and Gedge was necessary for the execution of my plans. Meanwhile the Katikiro was to increase his strength in the capital, but not to unfold the full gravity of the situation, except to such chiefs as could be depended on to stand steadfast and free from panic.

I visited the Church Missionary Society in Namirembe, where I saw Mr. Pilkington, who at once summoned the head of the mission, the Rev. J. Roscoe, at that time engaged at the church in superintending classes. To these two gentlemen the situation was explained. I told them my hopes that a rapid initiative would defeat the proposed combination in detail, and that the best chance of success appeared to be in all the Europeans showing a united front, irrespective of creed or profession. At the same time, should they prefer to do so, they were free to withdraw to the eastern provinces while there was yet time; but I explained that such a proceeding would necessarily have a very dispiriting effect on the Protestant Waganda, and might lead to their flight from the capital. Other members of the mission were called in, and it need hardly be said that, in an assemblage of Englishmen confronted with a crisis like this, there was no dissentient voice, but one and all decided to stand or fall by me, as the representative of British authority.

I then went to the Roman Catholic mission-station at Rubaga, and explained the situation and proposals in almost the same words I had used at Namirembe. Here, too, the missionaries resolved to stand by the Government. Both missions having thus decided to support me, it was arranged that the missionaries should come to Kampala in the afternoon—not in a body, so as to create alarm, but dropping in by twos and threes.

Meanwhile, the Europeans in the fort had seen to all internal arrangements. Rifles and ammunition were ready stored to hand in case of emergencies, and such other details attended to as forethought could suggest.

As the afternoon wore on, many impatient glances were cast to the southward for signs of the approaching column under Messrs. Reddie and Gedge. My order had been sent off at one a.m., and, as Port Alice was only twenty-one miles distant, the special messengers, even allowing for the darkness, should have placed the letters in the hands of the officers concerned by six a.m., as the road was good and well known. Allowing two hours for the necessary arrangements, the column should easily reach Kampala by four p.m. Without this reinforcement I should be much hampered, as I had only some fifty Swahilis at Kampala, and nearly half of them were partially or wholly incapacitated by that insect disease 'jiggers.'

From the fort a stretch of the Port Alice road, about three

miles distant, was easily seen, but no signs of any reinforcements could be made out. The missionaries had now arrived, and as it was four p.m., and but two hours' daylight remained, reinforcement or no reinforcement, action could not be much longer delayed. It was useless to indulge in speculations as to what had occurred at Port Alice to delay Reddie and Gedge. Our messengers had possibly been delayed, or Selim Bey might have made the two Europeans prisoners, and retained them as hostages. One thing only was clear, that their non-arrival had rendered the situation at Kampala much more serious, and might even lose us the initiative.

Mbogo and the infant son of Karema, who was in his charge, were brought into the fort, and Juma and another Mohammedan chief, who were found consulting with Selim Bey's Vakil, were arrested. The Soudanese officers were called up, and I investigated their loyalty, and that of the men under their command. The result was not wholly satisfactory, as, though they professed unbounded attachment to the British authority, they refused to take an oath of allegiance to Her Majesty, 'in case they might subsequently break it.' Owing to my reinforcements from Port Alice not having arrived, I had not sufficient force at my disposal to make sure of overawing and disarming the Soudanese without bloodshed, and so had to express myself satisfied. The question of the oath was waived for the time being, and the captain of the company was directed to put on extra sentries at night, and generally be prepared for emergencies.

At the same time I picked out eight of the most reliable men, as I was determined to visit the Mohammedan quarter, and endeavour to secure the remaining hostages I wanted. The Europeans considered this a somewhat reckless performance, but I was convinced that a fearless bearing was the only course open to me in the weak state of Kampala.

The Soudanese guard had fallen in, and I prepared to leave for Natete, having placed Dr. Moffat in charge of the fort during my absence, with instructions how to act in case of disturbance. Juma I decided to take with me, to his own great satisfaction, as he no doubt hoped to escape or be rescued. When, however, two Soudanese were directed to load with buckshot, and told in his presence that he was to be immediately shot if any attempt were made at rescue or should he attempt to escape, he prayed and entreated to be left behind in the guard-room. However, his presence was necessary to my plans, and my little party set out amidst the misgivings of many present, who fully expected that the next news would be that I was a prisoner in the hands of the rebels.

Marching rapidly, we reached Natete about five p.m., and halted on a small cleared space on the outskirts of the Mohammedan quarter. Here the chiefs were summoned to meet me, and came in considerable numbers; but only leading men were allowed on the clearing, the lesser fry being kept back by the Soudanese. In the centre I sat on a small ant-hill, with my Winchester by my side, and near me, guarded by the two stolid Soudanese with loaded rifles, stood Juma. The further proceedings were rapid. I demanded two additional hostages, one of them being the Mohammedan Mujasi, who had not put in an appearance, being reported very ill.

In addition to these two hostages, my demands were that the Mohammedans resident at the capital should deposit their arms in Kampala, or retire and remain quietly in their provinces until such time as the present disturbance should be satisfactorily settled. They were given clearly to understand that a refusal of these terms meant war.

They were undecided how to act, as their arrangements with Selim Bey had not contemplated such rapid action on the part of the Europeans, and the loss of Juma was also a great blow to them. They were given but brief time for consideration, and, after a hurried consultation, they agreed to the terms imposed, promised that all who had not gone to their provinces would surrender their arms the following morning, and handed over a chief as a hostage for the fulfilment of their conditions, promising, as it was then near sunset, to deliver up the Mujasi next day.

With this measure of success I returned to Kampala, where I was gladly welcomed. As nothing further could be done till the morrow, the missionaries went back to their quarters, and the apprehensions of all were somewhat quieted by the fact that three hostages were secure in the fort. This eventful day thus closed with a faint chance of a bloodless solution of the difficulty, but it was only the last flicker of the taper of peace before it expired.

While these things were taking place at the capital, Messrs. Gedge and Reddie were having a most trying time at Port Alice. The messengers, bearing the news of the critical state of affairs at the capital and the orders for concentration, had been greatly delayed, and not till late in the morning did they reach their destination. This delay was very unfortunate. My orders were that the sick, of whom there were a good number at Port Alice, should be at once embarked on the boats, which were at that station, and sent to Munyunya by water, and that Messrs. Gedge and Reddie should then rapidly march to Kampala with the sound men. But one boat had already sailed before the messengers arrived, and that belonging to the mission had broken from its moorings and been driven high and dry during a recent gale. It was thus necessary to organize land transport for the sick. Moreover, the porters had been sent out to their work, and further delay resulted while they were being recalled. Mr. Gedge, who had a private caravan, soon got his men together, but he could not desert Mr. Reddie and leave him hampered with sick.

The delay was a cause of great anxiety. The Soudanese, collecting in sullen groups, watched the preparations for departure with suspicion, and it was felt the non-arrival of the reinforcements in Kampala that afternoon might disarrange my plans. When all the arrangements were complete, Mr. Reddie went to see Selim Bey, and gave him my order. He at once threw off the mask, and told Mr. Reddie he might inform the Acting-Commissioner that, should the Protestants fight with the Mohammedans, he, with all his soldiers, would join the latter party. In these most unpleasant circumstances Mr. Reddie behaved with great coolness, and, as soon as he had rejoined Mr. Gedge, the column got under way and were clear of Port Alice before Selim Bey or his Soudanese had made up their minds what to do.

It was now late in the afternoon, and a toilsome night march to Kampala was unavoidable. Danger might lie in front from the Mohammedans, and in rear from the Soudanese, and no further news had been received of events at the capital. Mr. Gedge commanded the advance guard, Mr. Reddie brought up the rear; and so the caravan, burdened with sick, marched slowly on. Early on the morning of the 18th Mr. Gedge arrived in Kampala, and at once roused me from sleep with the disastrous news that the Bey had announced his intention of joining the Mohammedans with all his men. Later, when Mr. Reddie arrived, I heard the whole story.

During the night the insurgents had heard from Selim Bey, and had received reinforcements of fighting men from the provinces. Juma, too, by the connivance of some member of the Soudanese guard, sent a letter to Natete informing the Mujasi where to find a concealed store of ammunition, and advising him to hold out, as the Soudanese would support him. Juma's demeanour was far from that of a man in peril of his life; indeed, he was evidently quite sure that, in the confusion of an outbreak, his Soudanese custodians would allow him to escape. The Mohammedans were now prepared for war. The fighting element in their councils had again gained the ascendant, and those few who wished for peace had left their camp during the night. Information of their decision was sent to Selim Bey, who was urged to advance to their assistance with all speed, while they gained time by pretending to negotiate.

As soon as I received the reports of Messrs. Gedge and Reddie, I realized that I could no longer delay the disarmament of the Soudanese troops at Kampala, and had now at my disposal sufficient force for the purpose. Mr. Reddie had brought in a good many men, but they were mostly sick; Mr. Gedge, however, had a well-disciplined caravan of seventy men, and he at once, in the most public-spirited way, placed himself and his men under my orders. There were thus about one hundred and twenty fairly-sound Swahilis in Fort Kampala, and, though as fighting material they were most indifferent, I decided to act at once.

A message was sent to the gentlemen of the Church Missionary Society at Namirembe to immediately repair to the fort, as the crisis was at hand. The Katikiro was ordered to get his men under arms, tell off the main portion to guard the Namirembe-Rubaga ridge, thus cutting off Natete from Kampala, and to retain a smaller body in the plantations adjacent to the fort, with a view to an immediate attack on the Soudanese should they not lay down their arms when ordered to do so.

It was not necessary to summon the Roman Catholic missionaries, as during the night they had judged it wise to abandon their mission-station, and make their way as rapidly as possible to their *confrères* in Buddu. This information was conveyed to me in a letter delivered on the Sunday morning, and it also contained the announcement that I need not attempt to recall them, as, by the time the letter was put into my hands, they would already be far on their way. It must not be hastily assumed that these gentlemen were deficient in the bravery characteristic of the French nation, as later it appeared that they had only acted in accordance with a rigid order issued by their Bishop in view of such a contingency. At the same time, this sudden departure had undoubtedly a very bad effect on the Roman Catholic Waganda. Only some fifty remained at the capital, and the inhabitants of Kaima's province, whose border was not twelve miles from Mengo, instead of coming to the assistance of the King, fled towards Buddu.

As soon as the English missionaries arrived at Kampala, the disarmament of the Soudanese was taken in hand as a first step, and an order was issued for the troops to parade on the glacis of the fort at once.

While this was being done, the arms and ammunition kept in readiness for the purpose were issued to the Europeans and Swahilis, who proceeded to the posts that had been previously assigned to them. Mr. Gedge took charge of one Maxim, Mr. Wilson of the other. The Soudanese sentries were relieved by Swahilis, and fell in before the guard-room. All arrangements being now complete, I took command of the old guard and marched it outside on to the right of the troops, who had by this time formed in line with their backs to the fort. Simultaneously the Swahilis and Europeans, detailed to man the parapet overlooking the parade-ground, moved into position, and both Maxims were run out.

I gave no time for panic to supervene, but immediately through my interpreter addressed the assembled troops. They were informed that Selim Bey had mutinied, and that, though I believed the Soudanese company at Kampala was loyal, I wished to be distinctly informed, in view of their refusal the day before to take the oath of allegiance, whether they meant to obey my orders or to follow the Bey. Had they had any doubt as to which way their interests lay, they had only to look over their shoulders at the stern, determined line of white and black faces that lined the parapet, and the muzzles of the two Maxims already covering their flanks. They did not hesitate, and officers and men loudly protested their loyalty.

After having established silence, I said I was truly glad of their decision, which had saved their lives, and believed in their declaration of loyalty; but it was yet necessary to disarm them for a time till these troubles fomented by the Bey should be settled. Without allowing them time to think, I gave the order, 'Ground arms.' At once, with only one exception, the rifles were grounded, and that one only paused long enough to glance along the line and see that his comrades had obeyed, when his rifle was down like lightning. The Soudanese were then turned about and marched well clear of their arms, on which a party of porters, previously detailed for the purpose, at once swooped down, and the rifles were tied in bundles and removed to the fort. The Soudanese were afterwards without trouble deprived of their side-arms and ammunition. Four rifles were returned to them to enable them to put a guard on their quarters, and they were informed they had nothing to fear, but must remain quietly in their lines; and the officers, who were allowed to retain their arms, were directed to see to the good behaviour of the men.

This most anxious performance was now over, and the Europeans had won the first move in the game. It still remained to disarm or defeat the Mohammedan rebels before they could receive assistance from Port Alice; they had fulfilled none of their promises, and had taken up a defiant attitude under arms at Natete. The next move was to clear out the small Mohammedan settlement near the fort, containing the immediate followers of Mbogo and others who had joined them. They were given one hour to lay down their arms or leave the capital. This particular section, though no doubt more or less involved in the general intrigue, were not clearly implicated in the rebellion, and an opportunity was accordingly given them to secure their own safety before the fighting began. Mbogo was particularly anxious that this should be done. A few gave up their arms and were admitted to the protection of the fort, while the rest were passed outside the Protestant lines under escort. Some apparently went off into concealment, and others joined the hostile force at Natete.

A picquet had already been placed on the commanding range north of Kesubi on the Port Alice road, to watch and report any hostile advance of the Bey's troops, and an envoy was now sent to the Mohammedan quarter to say that, if they did not before one p.m. completely fulfil the terms offered and agreed to on the previous day, they would be forthwith attacked.

The Mohammedans saw that only by a bold stroke could they hope for success against the rapid initiative of Kampala. The combined rising had apparently been planned for June 19th, and they had not yet completed their arrangements or received their last reinforcements from the provinces. They had, however, sent messages to Selim Bey to hasten his advance, and thought if they could only maintain themselves at the capital till nightfall his force would be able to reach them, and they could still hope for a successful result. They were inferior to the Protestant army in strength, it was true, but, still, they had 1,300 guns in a compact force, while the Protestants had to defend a long line from Namirembe to Rubaga. Accordingly they decided to make a feint against Namirembe, the Protestant church and mission-station, where they not unnaturally concluded the main bulk of the opposing force would be collected, and at the same time deliver their main attack on the Catholic mission-station of Rubaga. If they succeeded in occupying this, they would have gained a strong position on the highest hill but one in Mengo, from which they would command the road to Port Alice, along which Selim Bey's reinforcement was expected.

In the confusion which would result from the left flank of the Protestants being attacked, they were not without hopes that they might succeed in setting fire to the royal inclosure and buildings, and so disorganize their opponents and prolong the conflict on favourable terms till the arrival of Selim Bey; then a combined attack in the darkness could be made on Kampala Fort itself. This was a bold plan made by men who saw their chance of victory slipping away if they did not risk much to gain time.

Before recounting the farther events that lead up to the battle, it will be well to glance briefly at the topographical details of the respective positions. The capital of Uganda, Mengo, is generally described as being situated on a number of hills; this is true, but these hills are all members of the main ridge whose culminating points are Rubaga and Namirembe. This main ridge, commencing from the dominant hill of Rubaga, on which the Roman Catholic Fathers had established their mission-station, church and schools, runs in a northerly direction to Namirembe, a slightly higher peak, on which stands the imposing Protestant church, and on whose slopes are clustered the quarters of the Church Missionary Society. The ridge then bends more to the north-west, and, swelling into some minor grassy summits, finally ends abruptly on the bank of the papyrus-covered river Lubegi.

The main ridge thus forms a crescent about three and a half miles long, with its concavity towards the north-west. Between the horns of the crescent the ground lies much lower, and is bounded by the swampy Lubegi on the north, and the almost equally difficult Nalukorongo River on the west. In the western portion of this low-lying district rises the minor hill of Natete, on which the scattered shambas of the Mohammedan quarter were situated. From the main ridge two principal spurs run out to the eastward, both radiating from the shoulders of Namirembe : the more southern spur culminates in the King's Hill, the more northern in the somewhat lower hill of Kampala. In the west, a flat, high-lying spur runs in a north-west direction from the northern shoulder of Rubaga, and terminates abruptly in a steep descent towards Natete, with which it is connected by a low ridge.

The main Protestant force extended from Namirembe to Rubaga in a line about 1,500 yards long, but smaller parties were also posted on the north-western prolongation of the ridge. Namirembe was about 900 yards from Fort Kampala, while Rubaga was about 2,200 yards; the King's Hill was distant about 1,200 yards from Kampala, and a trifle more from Rubaga. The Mohammedans, concentrated at Natete, were about 1,700 yards from Rubaga, and not much more from Namirembe, and were thus in a position to attack either of the dominant points in the Protestant line, while if they stood their ground at Natete they were exposed to a converging attack.

They mustered about 1,300 guns and an equal body of spearmen, while the force at my disposal consisted of about 2,200 guns and perhaps 4,000 spearmen; but our superiority in numbers was partly counterbalanced by the somewhat extended line we had to occupy. As I have previously stated, a fight amongst the Waganda is decided by the musketeers, the spearmen taking little, if any, part in the action, but joining in the pursuit.

As I could not be sure that the Mohammedans, instead of acting on the defensive, might not attack us, the order of battle was somewhat as follows. About 1,500 guns occupied the front line from Namirembe to Rubaga, with 500 in support behind the centre. The Europeans and Swahilis formed a reserve in Kampala, from which, in case of reverse, we could have efficiently supported the front line by our Maxim fire, the ranges having been accurately established. About 100 guns remained with the King, and the others formed detached posts on our right flank. When the rebels were defeated, the support of 500 guns was to return to Kampala to accompany me at once against Selim Bey.

As one o'clock, the hour by which the Mohammedans must submit or take the consequences, approached, the excitement became intense; but the Protestant army, now relieved of all apprehension with regard to a possible attack in rear by the Soudanese at Kampala, patiently stood their ground, confident of success. Every order given by me was at once communicated to the units concerned, either by running foot-messengers or by mounted chiefs. Kakanguru, a brave Protestant leader, was in immediate command of the fighting line, and was ably assisted by the principal chiefs of the party. About one p.m. the Katikiro galloped up to Kampala with the news that the rebels refused all terms, and were gradually advancing their people, apparently with the intention of attacking. I at once gave the order that they were to be attacked and driven out of Natete. The Katikiro galloped off with the order, while the garrison of the fort fell into their fighting positions, and the Maxims were run out to be ready to support the Protestants, should any part of their line be forced.

Suddenly the first few shots were heard, and the firing became hot and incessant. The Mohammedans did not wait to be attacked, but, feinting to their left to hold the Protestant right wing, made a rapid attack with the main portion of their force on the flat spur which runs north-west from Rubaga. The Protestants on this spur offered a stubborn resistance, but the Waislam attack, led by their Mujasi, who had conveniently recovered from his bed of sickness, was not to be gainsaid, and at the first rush the head of the spur was captured. The enemy pressed on, and were steadily gaining ground towards their objective, Rubaga, from which they were now only a few hundred yards distant. But the Protestant support and reinforcements from the right wing were rapidly hurried up to the assistance of the hard-pushed left, and the Mohammedan advance was checked. The Mujasi fell fighting, and the column he had so gallantly led wavered, and finally fled down the spur towards Natete, hotly pursued by the victorious Protestants.

The Mohammedan defeat was now complete, and they fled in absolute disorder towards the fords of the Nalukorongo River. They were, however, given no rest, the Protestants following up their advantage and charging into the fugitives, who were jammed up in the papyrus-grown bed of the river. The young Christian chief of Brussi greatly distinguished himself, dashing into the midst of the enemy, where he fell fighting; but his valour was not in vain, for his charge had frustrated an attempted rally to cover the ford. The Mohammedans, finding they could make no stand at this river, fled westward to their own provinces, unceasingly pursued by Kakanguru with the whole victorious army, who allowed them no chance of reforming till they were driven across the Namaya River, the western border of Busiro. Here he detached the gallant Makwenda, paramount chief of Singo, with some four hundred guns, to follow up the flying and now greatly scattered rebels, and with orders to take up a position to the north of them at Matiana, after driving the enemy into Butambala.

Our victory was thus complete, but one small *contretemps* had occurred. The Waganda were not accustomed to the use of supports, and my reserve of five hundred men, instead of rejoining me after the defeat of the rebels at Rubaga, had taken part in the pursuit, and thus left me with hardly two hundred Waganda guns at the capital.

The second move in the game had also been won by the Europeans, and none too soon; for hardly had the Mohammedans been defeated, when a report came in from the picquets near Kesubi to the effect that a Soudanese force had left Port Alice, and had reached the hill of Kitasa, about four hours' march from Mengo.

The Battle of Rubaga had lasted barely thirty minutes from the time the first shot had been fired till the rebels were in full flight over the Nalukorongo, but in that time the casualties had been many. Some five Protestants were killed, and twenty or so of the severely wounded were brought to the fort for treatment. (Those who were only slightly hurt did not report themselves, so our actual loss in killed and wounded was perhaps twice as heavy as would appear from these figures.) The Mohammedans—some of whom were also brought to the fort to be attended to—suffered more heavily, but the exact number killed and wounded was uncertain, though estimated at about one hundred and fifty.

Dr. Moffat, assisted by Mr. Lecky, of the Church Missionary Society, was indefatigable, and was occupied till after dark dressing wounds and performing operations in the more serious cases. The young chief of Brussi, whose gallant attack has been mentioned, had been shot through the thigh, but the bullet had passed through without injuring the bone or any of the principal bloodvessels; he was, to the great satisfaction of all, pronounced out of danger.

I had given orders that, after the defeat of the Mohammedans, a force of five hundred guns was to remain in Mengo, as I intended next day to personally lead this detachment against Selim Bey. In the excitement of the victory, however, the reserve had joined in the pursuit, and the Sekebobo, who was the chief detailed to accompany me, had barely two hundred men, and some of them without guns. With such a force it was impossible to attack Selim Bey, who, it was estimated, had over two hundred and fifty breechloaders in the hands of more or less disciplined men. I had accordingly to forego an immediate advance on Port Alice; all that could be done was to send messengers after Kakanguru, directing him to send back five hundred men, and meanwhile to strengthen the picquets on the hill north of Kesubi.

The close of that stirring day showed every prospect of a successful issue out of the crisis, though in the morning many had thought that, in the face of such a powerful combination, we could hardly achieve success. Our victory produced such a moral effect that the native chiefs enthusiastically volunteered to follow me anywhere against any odds. A few days before they would have hesitated to fight Selim Bey's force on almost any terms; now they were ready, nay eager, to be led against those very troops posted in the strong position of Port Alice. The Roman Catholic Kimbugwe, who, with about fifty men, had remained in the capital, now left to raise a Catholic force in Buddu and attack the Mohammedans in flank; and the native captain of the Soudanese company at Kampala came forward to say that he and the bulk of his men were prepared to fight against Selim Bey and the Port Alice force, should they refuse to surrender.

We had put the fort in a thorough state of defence, and the gates, somewhat flimsy affairs, made of elephant-grass canes, were replaced by removable barriers of palm-logs. Three Swahilis were put on duty at each sentry post, but even then they had to be visited every half-hour to insure that they remained awake. This duty would have been very severe on the four Government officers in the fort, but the missionaries and Mr. Gedge came forward and volunteered to relieve us of this night-work, as we had so many other duties

17—2

to attend to. Dr. Moffat had his wounded to look after, and Mr. Wilson had his hands full with routine duties.

The supply of food was somewhat difficult, as the markets were of course closed; but there was a reserve in the fort, and the Katikiro did his best to get in supplies from the districts immediately adjoining Kampala.

In such a crisis no one could have more loyal and willing assistants than I had at this time. No one seemed to care how much work was placed on his shoulders provided it helped on the common cause.

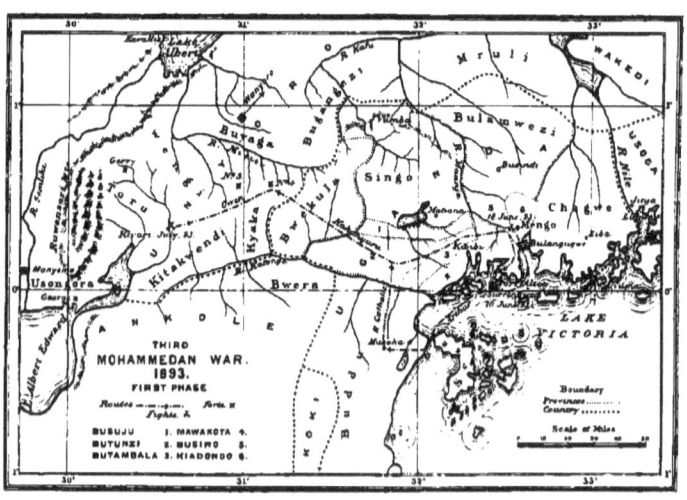

CHAPTER XVII.

FALL OF SELIM BEY—UGANDA SAVED.

THE night passed quietly, and everyone hoped that next morning Kakanguru would have sent back the five hundred men I wanted for the contemplated move against Port Alice. But when morning dawned there was no report of him except that he had pursued the beaten rebels to the borders of Busiro. Selim Bey's force which had advanced on Kesubi had fallen back on Port Alice on hearing of the Mohammedan defeat. But otherwise the news was meagre.

A letter, however, arrived from Arthur to say that he would reach Kampala that evening, as he was making forced marches to join me. He had received most conflicting accounts of the events of the 18th. One account declared that the Europeans had been victorious, another that the Soudanese had joined the rebels, and that the Europeans were invested in Kampala. Rightly reflecting that, had the result gone against us, he would have heard from me, he pushed on by forced marches and regardless of alarming rumours.

The morning passed slowly and anxiously, as I was impatient of delay in settling the Port Alice question. There was, however, nothing to be done. To have attacked the position with too weak a force would have been to court disaster, and thus infuse fresh courage into the beaten Mohammedans, whereas to move on Port Alice with an overwhelming force would probably result in Selim Bey's surrender without bloodshed. And bloodshed was to be avoided if possible in dealing with the Soudanese, as, though the European party in Uganda appeared to be winning the day, Owen and Grant, in Unyoro, were practically in the hands of Selim's followers.

After noon Kakanguru and the victorious army returned to Mengo, and immediate steps were taken to tell off the men who were to accompany me to Port Alice. Before all the details were arranged, however, a breathless messenger arrived, followed almost immediately by a second, to say that Selim Bey was ferrying his men across the western creek at Port Alice with a view to joining the Mohammedans in their provinces. This was most disquieting news, and not a moment was to be lost in attempting to prevent a junction between these two parties. If the report was true, Selim had only some sixteen miles to march to reach the Mohammedan province of Butambala, while a force from the capital had a distance to traverse of quite thirty miles. The Protestant chiefs, relying on the speed the Waganda can attain in emergency, said they thought they could get in front of Selim Bey, as the Soudanese, hampered by his presence, could only march slowly.

The necessary orders were accordingly issued, some rifles and ammunition served out, and the Protestant army was on the point of setting forth, when further messages arrived to announce that Selim was advancing on the capital. This latter report was confirmed by the foremost party of the Protestants, who had already reached the Matundwi Ridge. The army was accordingly moved into position along the Nalukorongo River, the fort was got under arms, and everyone, more or less calmly, awaited the result.

Shortly white-coated Soudanese could be seen from the fort filing along the path descending the Matundwi range towards the river, but their numbers were small. The Protestants, seeing how few they were, and that they did not intend hostile action, allowed them to pass, and the little party under a native officer marched on to the parade-ground at Kampala. I went out to meet them, and received the news that Selim Bey reported that all was quiet at Port Alice, and no disturbance had occurred in that part of the country, but that the trouble between Mohammedans and Protestants should at once be stopped.

This detachment, whose advent had led to such exaggerated reports, and so much excitement, laid down their arms, and were accommodated in the Soudanese lines at Kampala. It was by no means evident that Selim Bey regretted the part he had taken in fomenting the tragic occurrence of the last few days, or that he had yet given up all hopes of still playing a political part. His last message might be merely a ruse to gain time, in accordance with his previous habit. In any case, I could not overlook his former conduct, so orders were issued that a force of seven hundred guns should be ready to accompany me to Port Alice next day to enforce the surrender of Selim Bey and his men. A little later Captain Arthur arrived in Kampala, where his presence was a great assistance to me, as up to this time I had been the only military officer in the fort. Arthur had done marvellous marching, and, despite all sorts of alarming rumours he had received on the road, pressed on to the seat of danger. Now that I could leave him in command at Kampala, I was free to embark on the expedition to Port Alice.

About this time a letter was sent to the chiefs of the Mohammedan party in the provinces, informing them that, although a section of their party had fought against me, I would still grant peace to all who remained quietly in certain specified districts. This was also backed up by a letter from Mbogo himself, in which he urged the Mohammedans to accept my terms, especially considering that Juma was a prisoner in Kampala, and the Mujasi had been killed in action.

On June 20th, at 8.30 a.m. the expedition against Port Alice left Kampala. It consisted of five Europeans, Moffat, Reddie, Gedge, Forster, and myself, eight Soudanese, and about forty Swahilis with a Maxim; the Waganda contingent amounted to about 700 guns and 1,400 spearmen under the Sekebobo. On our way out of the capital we met the Roman Catholic missionaries returning to Rubaga, looking very dishevelled and worn-out after their experiences in the swamps of Southern Mawakota. I asked them to go to the fort, if Arthur considered it desirable, and warned them that any further movement to the west might be dangerous, as the Mohammedan rebels were now between them and Buddu. We pushed on rapidly, till the small mountain stream near Kesubi was reached. A short halt was made here to let the column close up, and then it again advanced towards Port Alice.

The country was now open and covered with short grass, with isolated clumps of fine trees, while on the right lay a great swampy arm of the lake. We had thus gained the neck of the great peninsula of which Port Alice is a lesser offshoot, and if Selim Bey had no canoes, he must either fight or surrender. But there was little time to view the scenery. Everyone wished to get that day's work well over. About 3.30 p.m. the head of the column entered the dense forest belt that shuts in the open peninsula of Port Alice on the landward side, and an hour later the advanced guard was in front of the Soudanese position. Groups of Selim's men were seen crowning the heights on which the new headquarter station founded by Sir Gerald Portal was situated. This position, viewed from the landward, was a high ridge completely barring all advance along the peninsula to Ntebi; on this ridge were two summits—on the higher and more western one, the European station and stores had been located; on the reverse slope of the lower and more eastern the Soudanese lines had been built. The slopes of the ridge were clear of cultivation, and presented a beautifully grassy, yet somewhat steep, incline. Held by determined men, the position, though somewhat too extensive, was naturally one of great strength.

I advanced without a pause to within 1,400 yards of the position, and then halted to give final orders. The Maxim was placed on a small knoll with a clear field of fire, and was put in charge of Mr. Reddie; as the Waganda came up, they were formed into two wings and a centre, commanded by Moffat, Gedge, and Forster respectively, and were to halt in that position while I went on, with a few Soudanese, to interview the garrison of Port Alice and endeavour to secure a bloodless surrender. Should I be made prisoner, or should there be any treachery, an immediate attack was to be delivered on the Soudanese position. In making such an attack, the Europeans and native leaders were informed that there must be no pausing to open a fire action. The Soudanese were better armed and better trained, and would have the advantage at that game. Under cover of the Maxim, the columns were to charge straight at the Soudanese, reserving their fire until they got to close quarters, and then overwhelm the soldiery with the spear.

This settled, and Mr. Reddie placed in command, I advanced with six Soudanese and the flag, sending two men ahead to order a parade on the smaller of the two hills above the market-place. Some excitement could be seen amidst Selim's men as we formed up, but when they saw my small party, a native officer—Bilal—with one or two non-commissioned officers, came to meet me. Bilal announced that the Soudanese troops had resolved to surrender, and then accompanied me to the parade-ground. Here the Soudanese were drawn up in column with their flank to the Maxim, as ordered.

The officers came forward and informed me that they would lay down their arms as a sign of submission, but expected to have them returned to them after doing so. To this I said nothing, but gave the order to ground arms, which was immediately done. The column was then turned about and retired, and before they had halted and fronted, my small guard were in possession of the grounded arms. The rifles were tied into bundles and stacked by my men, and a signal to Reddie brought up the porters, who removed them and the ammunition to the guard-room. I also wrote to Reddie, telling him to dismiss the Waganda spearmen and all the guns except two hundred, which the Sekebobo was to bring on as a guard.

All this was rapidly carried out, and in an hour from the time the expeditionary force had halted before Port Alice, the Soudanese were disarmed and dismissed to their quarters, while the Europeans were in possession of the Headquarter Hill, with the rifles and ammunition under a Swahili guard, and with the Sekebobo's force supplying picquets round the station. I then proceeded to Selim Bey's quarters, for he had not attended the parade, and made him a prisoner; this was accomplished without difficulty, and the Bey's private followers were disarmed.

The Sekebobo managed his men excellently. When I went to arrest the Bey, several small columns were drawn up, concealed by a fold in the ground, but ready to rush into the Soudanese quarter had the Bey's private following offered any resistance; and when, before nightfall, a European inspected the Sekebobo's arrangement of picquets and sentries, there was really nothing to alter. With this stern old Waganda chief, it was like a return to the ancient Covenanting days in Scotland, for every evening the day's work closed with a prayer-meeting, conducted by the Sekebobo in person, and always largely attended by his followers. The discipline he maintained in his contingent was particularly good, and he carried out my orders in the spirit, not merely to the letter.

The surrender of Port Alice was immediately reported to the capital, where the result of our operations was awaited with intense anxiety. This, my third success in rapid succession, produced a still greater feeling of confidence throughout the country, and, indeed, constituted us masters of the situation in Uganda itself, though we knew not what might happen on the frontier.

The day after the capture of Port Alice, Selim Bey was brought up for trial, charged with mutinous conduct and treason. The scene was an impressive one, and we could not help thinking how the tables were turned since the occasion, not many years before, when the Bey and his mutinous comrades sat in judgment on the unfortunate Emin Pasha. It is needless to go into the details of the trial. Mutinous conduct was clearly proved, but there was a slight doubt in the matter of treason. The defence was that there had been an error in the interpretation of Selim's statement to Reddie, and that he had merely announced his intention of accompanying the Mohammedans who proposed to withdraw out of Uganda, and of quitting the British service should war break out between the Protestants and Waislam.

As a matter of fact, the result would have been the same, and the offence of deserting, and inducing his men to desert, in order to join the enemies of the British authority, was hardly less a crime than had he directly fought against the British officers. But the court, being formed of the victors, was lenient, and Selim Bey was sentenced to degradation and deportation to an island in the Victoria Lake, till he could be sent to the coast. Meanwhile he was allowed a small monthly sum for the support of his numerous family, out of consideration for the help he had rendered Lugard in the past. When the Bey heard his sentence, he appeared unaffected, till the portion about deportation was read out to him; then he became most violent and abusive, but was promptly marched off under a guard. Arrangements were at once made to collect the necessary canoes to transport him to the small island of Nzaze, which had been selected for his prison, and was situated some ten miles out in the lake.

In a few hours Selim Bey sent a deputation of officers to me, who, in his name, admitted the justice of his punishment, but prayed for pardon—at all events, in so far that the sentence of deportation might be remitted; he made the most profuse promises for good conduct in the future, and said he would consider himself the slave of the British for life, if only permitted to remain with his own people. I was, however, obdurate, and Selim was informed that warning and leniency had been of no use in the past, that he had brought this evil on himself by his disloyalty, and ought to be grateful that he had not been shot. The officers did not seem particularly disappointed that Selim Bey must go, and agreed in throwing the whole blame for recent events on his intrigues with Juma and the other warlike spirits amongst the Mohammedan party —a clear case of worshipping the rising sun.

Early in the morning of June 22nd news was received that the canoes were ready for Selim Bey's removal, so Mr. Gedge took charge of him, his wives, and a few unarmed servants, and embarked them under protection of a strong guard commanded by Mr. Reddie. The embarkation took place without any difficulty or any demonstration of either joy or sorrow on the part of the Soudanese, and Gedge was soon paddling to the eastward.

The rifles and ammunition taken from the Soudanese were then packed in the mission sailing boat, and Mr. Forster, with a crew of Swahilis, set sail for Munyunyu. About twenty rifles were retained to arm a guard to be left at Port Alice, under command of Mr. Reddie, in order to protect the

Government stores. The whole of the Soudanese then fell in, and without hesitation took the oath of allegiance to Her Majesty on the Koran.

This done, Moffat and I, leaving Reddie in command of Port Alice, marched for Kampala. Moffat pushed on and reached it that night, but I was tired out by the anxiety, not to say physical exertion, of the last few days, and camped for the night at Kesubi.

On June 23rd I returned to Kampala. Mr. Gedge also arrived, having safely located Selim Bey on the island of Nzaze under the surveillance of the local chief. This chief was warned by my order that no communication should be allowed between the Bey and the Soudanese or Mohammedans, and that if he attempted to escape he was to be immediately put to death. Mr. Forster, with the mission boat and the arms, also turned up safely at Munyunyu.

News had come in the day before regarding the attitude of the rebel Mohammedans. On receipt of the letter from Mbogo and myself, eight Mohammedan chiefs declared for peace, but the larger number determined to continue the struggle. The war-party had captured a small detachment of Swahilis, sent to Uganda by Owen with mails and stores, including the Berthon boat; his men had been robbed of all their stores and arms, stripped of their clothes, and then allowed to escape.

I at once wrote to the Mohammedan chiefs that all who wanted peace must remain in the province of Busuju, where they would not be attacked, but that armed Mohammedans found outside that province would be treated as enemies. This letter emphasized the split in the Mohammedan party. Those who wished for war, having now heard of Selim Bey's fall, determined to march to Unyoro, and persuade the Soudanese there to join them, or, failing that, to unite themselves with the Manyema beyond the Semiliki. The peace party decided to take the terms offered, separated themselves from the rebels, and on marching towards Busuju were fired on by their exasperated co-religionists.

On June 25th, the necessary preliminaries having been settled, I sent a letter to the Roman Catholics in Buddu ordering them to assemble an army and join the Protestants in a rapid advance against the rebels. At the same time the Protestants collected, and on the 26th Kakanguru, who had been appointed General, advanced westwards with a force of about 7,000 men. His directions were to drive the rebels out of Uganda, and move at once to the assistance of Owen, for whom he had letters. The same day Captain Arthur and Mr. Gedge, with ten Soudanese, fifteen Swahilis, and a Maxim, set out for Buddu by canoe, in order to restore confidence there, and to expedite the despatch of the Roman Catholic contingent for the war. They had a very stormy and trying passage, but reached Villamaria in three days. Arthur's presence at Villamaria undoubtedly had the effect intended, and immediately after his arrival the Roman Catholic contingent, under the command of the Kakanguru, marched to join hands with the Protestants, who were by this time at Kibibi.

The movements of this special expeditionary force will be dealt with in a separate chapter.

A most alarming report had a few days before been sent in by the Mohammedans, to the effect that they had captured Major Owen and Mr. Grant, who with seventy Soudanese and a Maxim had advanced into Uganda from the west. They offered to give up the prisoners if we would hand over to them the chiefs we had in our hands, as well as Mbogo and the young Prince his nephew. I did not believe this report, and replied that, even if it were true, it was a complete mistake to suppose that we would alter the course of the war, even if they succeeded in capturing half the Europeans in Uganda. At the

A STORM ON THE VICTORIA NYANZA.

same time, if harm came to any Europeans they might make prisoners, the rebels were told that the punishment meted out to them would be many times more severe than otherwise. This report, floated by the Mohammedans, apparently reached the English newspapers, and unfortunately caused much needless anxiety amongst Major Owen's relations and friends. His reported capture was false from beginning to end.

On June 25th and 26th Messrs. Gunther and Fisher, of the Church Missionary Society in Singo, arrived at the capital. They had taken refuge on Bagwe, the largest of the six islands in Lake Isolt, but had experienced a very anxious time indeed. They confirmed the report that for several days before the actual outbreak of the war at the capital the Mohammedans had been beating war-drums and collecting their armed men, and that the Sekiwala had in consequence abandoned his shambas on the Busuju border.

On June 26th I sent despatches to Sir Gerald Portal, reporting the complete success, as far as Uganda was concerned, of my operations against the Mohammedan rebels and Selim Bey, and informed him that an expedition of about 10,000 men had been sent to Owen's assistance in Unyoro. I also reported the good services of the Europeans who had so gallantly assisted me.

To this Sir Gerald Portal replied officially on July 7th. He said he would come on to Uganda as soon as Colonel Rhodes could be moved, unless he heard that his presence was no longer necessary, and informed me that he had sent to England for four additional officers with a knowledge of Arabic to assist in training the Soudanese troops. He also entirely approved of the 'active, energetic, and apparently successful measures' I had taken, and informed me that he was sending Lieutenant Villiers back to Uganda as an additional assistant. He also requested that the Government officers, Captain Arthur, Dr. Moffat, Mr. Reddie and Mr.

Wilson, might be informed that a report of their good services would be laid before Her Majesty's Secretary of State, and that an expression of his thanks might be conveyed to the gentlemen of the mission, Messrs. Roscoe, Pilkington, Miller, Lecky, and Forster of the Church Missionary Society, and Messrs. Guillermain and Gaudibert of the Algerian Mission. He also wrote unofficially, congratulating me on my 'eminently successful management of the whole episode,' and regretting that he and Colonel Rhodes had missed this excitement, as they felt they had 'been out of a good thing.'

Before closing this chapter, we may glance at Sir Gerald Portal's movements. He had written to me on June 8th that he would halt at Mumia's, in Kavirondo, till June 21st, for further news of the crisis. When he reached Mumia's, he, however, altered his plans, and marched for the hills of Elbourgoloti, some thirty-five miles towards the coast, where he was prostrated with fever, due to the arduous and swampy marches between Usoga and Kavirondo. He halted here till June 14th, and then marched to the Guaso Masa, one day's journey further towards the coast, when he received the news of Selim Bey's mutinous message and the crisis thereby developed. Sir Gerald then divided his caravan, sending Messrs. Berkeley and Foaker, with two-thirds of his Zanzibar troops and the bulk of the porters, to the coast, and returned towards Mumia's with Colonel Rhodes and Mr. Villiers, fifty Zanzibar troops, and a few porters. On the way Colonel Rhodes was taken seriously ill, and Sir Gerald halted with him at Mumia's, and sent Villiers with some twenty Swahilis to reinforce Uganda. Lieutenant Villiers did the march of about one hundred and eighty miles, from Mumia's to Kampala, at an average pace of twenty miles a day—wonderfully good marching. Fortuuately for him, the trouble in Uganda was over, as with twenty men he would have stood no chance had things gone against us. When Villiers arrived with the news of Colonel Rhodes' serious condition, Dr. Moffat was sent to Mumia's, but fortunately before his arrival the Colonel had recovered.

On July 5th Arthur and Gedge returned from Buddu, as Monseigneur Hirth considered confidence completely restored in that province, and their further stay therefore unnecessary. They had throughout their visit been treated by the French priests with their customary hospitality. On July 7th the Soudanese were re-armed, and next day, assisted by Arthur, I tried various Mohammedan chiefs implicated in the rebellion. Three days later Mr. Gedge, the *Times* correspondent, who had throughout most loyally assisted me, left for the coast, taking with him Juma, the Mohammedan Katikiro, as a prisoner, and Mbogo with a small following. Mbogo was not a prisoner, but I judged it wise that both he and the young Mohammedan Prince, Karema's son, should be removed to Zanzibar, in order that the Mohammedan party might be deprived of a head, and thus more readily led to recognise Mwanga as sole King in Uganda. Dr. Moffat, who went to Kavirondo by boat, called in at Nzaze, and took on Selim Bey, who was also to be deported to the coast. Through the connivance of some of Selim Bey's men, Juma was supplied with a file, cut through his chains, and escaped on the confines of Kavirondo. With this exception, Mbogo and his following, and the prisoners, were handed over to Sir Gerald Portal at Mumia's, for conveyance to the coast. Selim Bey died on the way; his Soudanese were located at Kikuyu, and Mbogo and his people were shipped to Zanzibar, where he received an annual grant charged against the revenues of Uganda.

The final removal of Selim Bey, Mbogo, and the young Prince, completely cut away the ground from under the feet of the Mohammedan faction, and the good results of this action were at once noticeable in the increased confidence

18

and resultant prosperity that followed, even before the end of the war. The Soudanese reserve, which under Selim Bey had with difficulty reached a total of some ten men, rose in a few days to over one hundred and twenty; the Lendus also enlisted as porters to a very fair extent, both at Kampala and Port Alice, and worked well and contentedly, as every man enrolled became *ipso facto* a free man; the Soudanese, with the increased pay and emoluments which thus came to them as a whole, were much more contented, and the robbing of plantations, which in the past had been of daily occurrence, now practically ceased.

In those few weeks I had gained such a position and influence in the country that I had no misgivings for Uganda, even although the war was not actually over; but the position of Owen and Grant was still necessarily an anxious one.

Sir Gerald Portal, who had remained at Mumia's, now left for the coast, after writing to me that he would do his best at home to convert my appointment as Acting Commissioner into a permanent one. With this parting promise I had every incentive to do my best, not only in completing the repression of the rebellion, but in establishing peace on somewhat more permanent lines than heretofore in this unfortunate country.

CHAPTER XVIII.

OWEN VICTORIOUS IN UNYORO—CLOSE OF THE CAMPAIGN.

IN the last chapter we left the Mohammedan party split into two portions. The smaller, with nominally about three hundred guns, had accepted my terms and were holding themselves aloof in Busuju, where their neutrality was respected; the larger portion had moved westward towards the frontier of Unyoro. Kakanguru, a Protestant chief who had been appointed General of the Waganda for the war, was following up the rebels with about 7,000 Protestants, and was to be joined by a Roman Catholic contingent of 3,000 men under the Kimbugwe. News from the front was somewhat meagre, but it was known that Kakanguru, on whom the necessity for speed had been enjoined, had in three marches reached Kibibi, a rich district in Butambala, some thirty miles from the capital. After this the Protestant part of the force moved more slowly, in order that time might be afforded for the Roman Catholic contingent to join them. The combined force then pushed on more rapidly, the Mohammedan rebels retiring in front of them without fighting.

In about twelve days the combined Christian army had reached Fort de Winton (No. 4), about one hundred and twenty miles from Kampala, and put themselves under Major Owen's orders. Their rate of marching, for so large a force, had not been bad, averaging as it did about ten miles a day.

Before dealing with subsequent movements, it is necessary to refer to what had occurred in the Unyoro garrisons during the recent crisis in Uganda. Major Owen had succeeded in reopening the road between Fort Briggs and Fort Lorne, and the hostile Wanyoro army had apparently definitely retired to the north-east. He was now devoting his whole energy to the question of a regular and sufficient food-supply for the half-starving garrisons of the two eastern forts. He was himself at these forts when he received my letter of June 5th, warning him that the Mohammedans were in a state of incipient rebellion, and that Selim Bey was intriguing in their favour. None of my subsequent letters reached him, as the mail-runners were either intercepted on the road or had been afraid to proceed. From this he concluded that the expected rebellion had broken out, but of its details he knew nothing till the Mohammedans approached and camped near the fort.

He had, on receipt of the news of June 5th, taken the wise precaution to issue an order prohibiting under any circumstances the admittance of Waganda Mohammedans into the forts. Now, however, he found that his orders had been disregarded, and that, not only had Mohammedan envoys been allowed into Fort de Winton, but that, with the connivance of the Soudanese officers, most dangerous and alarming reports were being circulated amongst his men.

It must be remembered that not only had Owen the Soudanese garrison of the eastern forts to consider, but also the great body of unenlisted. The latter consisted of old officers and non-commissioned officers who, for reasons of age or doubtful character, had not been engaged as soldiers, but who, with their wives, families, ferruks, and slaves, mustered some 1,200 in all. In fact, at Fort de Winton the old unenlisted officers, who had been detained there by Sir Gerald Portal's orders, had as many armed men in their following as

Owen had enlisted soldiers in the garrison. These old officers had been in constant communication with Selim Bey, and no doubt were in his confidence; probably this was the reason that he was so excessively put out when Sir Gerald Portal issued orders that they should stay at Fort de Winton instead of coming into Uganda.

It is evident that amongst such material the circulation of alarmist reports by the Mohammedan envoys was most dangerous, especially when we consider what those reports were. Their gist was as follows—that, on the departure of Sir Gerald Portal, the Acting Commissioner, being actuated by a hatred of the Mohammedan religion in general, had pushed matters to extremes because the Waganda Mohammedans stood by their faith; that the Soudanese of Kampala had been ordered to fire on the innocent Mohammedans, and, because they refused, had been disarmed; that Selim Bey had been sent to an island with the large bulk of the Soudanese (the Port Alice peninsula was probably meant), that after the Mohammedans had been brutally expelled from the capital, all the Soudanese at Port Alice, without regard for sex or age, had been massacred in cold blood; and lastly, that Mbogo, Juma, and the Mohammedan Mujasi had been put to death, and the bloodthirsty and triumphant Commissioner was now coming at the head of a large Christian army, bent on the wholesale slaughter of the Soudanese in Unyoro. The Mohammedans urged that these latter should unite with them and make a stand for their faith, which was in danger of being destroyed, assuring them that the united forces of the Soudanese and Mohammedans could defy the Europeans, and found a separate State in Toru, where the religion of Islam could flourish in peace and quietness, without the absurd restrictions against slave-dealing and raiding which the Europeans tried to enforce.

No doubt a truer account of recent events had been privately conveyed to the old Soudanese officers, who had been aware of the Bey's intrigues, and who now saw the complete failure of his plans as regards Uganda; but these false and exaggerated reports were those that were circulated amongst the soldiery and people of inferior grade.

Naturally, the garrison was in a ferment, and the officers who had not been privileged to learn the true story came to Owen to ask if what they heard was true or false. He was as ignorant of what had actually happened as they were, but he knew that the Mohammedans had for some time been fomenting rebellion, and informed the Soudanese officers of this fact. He said they might rest assured that the Mohammedans had not been attacked without cause, and that if anything had happened to Selim Bey, of which he was ignorant, Selim Bey had no doubt brought it on himself by misconduct, and as for the idea of a general Soudanese massacre, he laughed at the story. He informed the Soudanese that, in his command, whatever might have happened in Uganda, all who obeyed orders and followed his lead implicitly need fear no harm. In conclusion, he again issued orders against any intimacy with the Mohammedans.

The old officers were not, however, idle. They had a personal following equal in strength to Owen's enlisted garrison, and were not without hopes of winning many, if not most, of the latter to their views. They accordingly formed a plan that the Soudanese should murder Owen and Grant, seize all the arms, ammunition, and stores in the forts, and make common cause with the Mohammedans, settling with them in Toru, forming there an independent Mohammedan State. As some of the more timorous were, however, afraid that they might be attacked in Toru, a supplementary modification in the scheme was made, to the effect that the Soudanese should again retire to Kavalli's and quit all connection with the English and Uganda.

These bold schemes were gaining ground, for, although the bulk of the enlisted soldiery, with a certainty of regular pay, etc., were not desirous of leaving the British service and returning to the wilds, the unenlisted and followers had no such reasons to restrain them, and had already found the discipline and restrictions against raiding, plundering, and outraging to be irksome. They looked back with regret on the unfettered freedom they had enjoyed west of Lake Albert, where, thanks to their arms and training, they had been lords of the country round.

One of the leading spirits in these plots was an old Soudanese officer called Bilal Bey, though what legal right he had to the title Bey is uncertain. He was at the head of a large number of armed followers, who had not been enlisted, and who were equal in numbers to three-quarters of the garrison at Fort de Winton. He apparently argued, not without sense, that if he accomplished a *coup d'état* at Fort de Winton, the garrisons of the other forts would follow his lead. He had been in close correspondence with Selim Bey, and was now in equally close intimacy with the Mohammedan chiefs camped near the fort. There can be little doubt that Owen and Grant at this time were in most imminent danger of assassination, for the Christian relieving force had not yet come up, and their very approach was converted by the Mohammedan chiefs and disaffected officers into a threat to the Soudanese.

Owen, though it was not till later that he fully realized the danger he ran at this time, was aware of the serious plots that were being fostered by the disaffected officers, and, to counteract them, devised a plan which, though fraught with terrible risk, can only be considered in the light of its success as a stroke of genius. He placed under arrest the officer commanding Fort de Winton for disobeying his orders and admitting Waganda Mohammedans into the fort, tried and cashiered him. He then appointed in his place as Commandant the head of the disaffected party, Bilal Bey, in whom he publicly gave out he had every confidence. Fortunately for the success of this stroke, Bilal was a selfish man, seeking only his own safety. The plots he had fomented had not been from a love of Islam, but because he feared that his secret correspondence with Selim Bey might be known, and might involve him in disaster similar to that which had attended his late chief. Now he unexpectedly saw a chance of reinstating himself in good odour, and, by pointing to a loyal command of Fort de Winton, of escaping the consequences of complicity with Selim Bey.

He was accordingly installed in his new office, whereupon he promptly deserted the failing Mohammedan cause. This defection completely took the heart out of the mutinous party, for, their leading and most powerful adherent having joined the side of the British, they saw little chance of success in a mutiny against Owen, to whom they naturally supposed Bilal had exposed their plots.

Had they possessed anyone of sufficient hardihood to have even now assassinated Owen, they would no doubt have again drawn Bilal Bey to their side, and succeeded in their designs. But they had no such man. On the contrary, they now vied with each other in expressions of loyalty, and negotiations with the Waganda Mohammedans were broken off. Owen's desperate expedient and unfaltering bearing had won the day as far as the Soudanese mutiny was concerned.

The Mohammedan Waganda, seeing that all chance of an alliance with the Soudanese in Unyoro was hopeless, began to negotiate with Owen for peace, and professed to be willing to accept any terms he offered. He informed them that the ultimate decision must rest with me as Acting Commissioner, but that, if they really wished for peace, he would do his best to effect a satisfactory settlement. The chiefs accordingly made a show of discussing terms, while actually, in pursuance of their alternative plan of joining hands with the Manyema beyond the Semiliki, they were quietly forwarding their women, children, and goods towards the Salt Lake.

About July 8th the Christian army under Kakanguru camped near Fort de Winton, and placed itself under the orders of Major Owen. My letters had, however, been unfortunately lost, and thus, although he was now made aware of the true course of events in Uganda, he was uninformed of my views regarding the disposal of the Mohammedans. On Kakanguru's approaching Fort de Winton, he had sent my letters ahead with a small party, which had encountered a superior force of Mohammedan foragers, and had been compelled to retire northwards, in this way losing touch with the main body of their army and with the forts. It was not till later that these important letters were placed in Owen's hands.

On the approach of the Christian army the Mohammedans had shifted camp and moved a little to the west; they were, however, to all appearances, still desirous of negotiating for peace. Owen continued his endeavours to effect a settlement, but at the same time took the precaution of sending orders to Grant to watch the roads to the Salt Lake with about one hundred Soudanese, in case the Mohammedans should march in that direction.

The food difficulties in the neighbourhood of Fort de Winton were now tremendous. I have already described what trouble Owen had in feeding the Soudanese at the eastern forts, and now there were some 17,000 additional mouths drawing what food they could from this already exhausted district. It was quite evident that the peace negotiations must come to a rapid conclusion one way or the other, or famine would compel the dispersion of both forces.

With unwearying patience Owen interviewed the chiefs of the opposing armies, and even succeeded in arranging a meeting between them. Satisfactory terms seemed on the verge of attainment, when one morning it was found that the Mohammedans had bodily marched westwards, and thus broken off all hopes of a peaceful conclusion.

Owen was now as prompt in action as he had been patient in negotiation. He at once placed himself, with a small force of Soudanese, at the head of the combined Christian army, and started in pursuit, at the same time sending orders to Grant to co-operate by cutting off the Mohammedan rebels from the Salt Lake.

Through the difficult and almost foodless tracts to the west the two armies pressed on, both having the greatest trouble in obtaining supplies. About July 18th, in the neighbourhood of Lugard's old fort at Kivari's, the pursuers overtook the pursued. The Christian army, expecting to fight next day, formed line of battle with the Protestants on the right wing, Owen and his small handful of Soudanese in the centre, and the Catholics on the left. In this order they advanced westwards in a line of parallel columns, the usual fighting formation of the Waganda.

Suddenly it was discovered that the Mohammedans had turned to the north, and were about to place a very difficult papyrus swamp between them and their enemy. Owen at once issued orders to wheel to the right and attack the rebels before they had succeeded in effecting the crossing. The order was promptly obeyed, but, as a change of front of the whole line would have caused such delay that the Mohammedans would have got clear, the wheel was by wings, so that the actual attack was made by the Protestants of the right wing, with Owen in support and the Catholics or left wing in reserve. The former advanced with their usual impetuous rush, and the Mohammedans saw that their assailants must of necessity close with them while they were actually engaged in effecting the difficult crossing of a dangerous swamp.

The Mohammedan chiefs behaved well, and, though taken at a great disadvantage, rallied round them some of their best fighting men, and prepared to offer an obstinate resistance at the edge of the swamp amidst the bush and papyrus which fringed its bank, hoping to thus gain time for the remainder of their army to occupy a very strong position on the further side. They had not time, however, to properly form their line before the Protestant force was upon them. The fight was brief, and the Mohammedan rear guard was driven into the swamp, with the loss of its principal chiefs.

The victorious Protestants gave the enemy no time to take up a position on the far bank of the swamp, but crossed it with the fugitives. The Catholics, determined to have their share of the victory, pressed on and joined their fellow-Christians, and the allies scattered the disordered Mohammedans like chaff. Many of the rebel chiefs were slain in attempting to rally groups of men or make head against the victors, and before night the rebel army was completely dispersed, with the loss of about 600 men. The Christians, who suffered but slightly, captured a great many of the Mohammedan women and children, and most of their goods.

After this victory, Owen again sent offers of peace to the Mohammedans, and promised to give them back their women and children if they submitted and returned to Uganda, to be dealt with as the Commissioner might decide. These offers were now eagerly accepted by the surviving Mohammedan chiefs, and the next few days were spent in collecting their people from the forests and swamps in which they had taken refuge. Seventy of the leading men placed themselves in Owen's hands, and the whole of the remaining rebel force accompanied him back to Fort de Winton, escorted by the Christian army.

At Fort de Winton the Christian army was broken up, and with great rapidity each chief led off his column to his own district, to recover from the effects of the famine they had suffered from for days. The lesser people amidst the Mohammedans also made all haste into Uganda, in scattered bodies, and the chiefs accompanied Owen, who, with Grant and about sixty Soudanese, escorted them into Uganda, there to submit themselves to the decision of the Commissioner.

We must now return to events in Uganda, which was rapidly settling down into unexampled peace and prosperity. The deportation of Selim Bey and Mbogo had given a feeling of confidence to the country; news had been received of the safety of Owen and Grant, and that, thanks to the successful management of the former, the Soudanese had remained loyal. The Mohammedans who had taken no part in the rebellion were established in the fertile province of Butambala under a new and trustworthy chief, and their two former provinces of Busuju and Butunzi were given to the Roman Catholics and Protestants respectively.

This was not done without a little interference on the part of Monseigneur Hirth, who claimed that the Catholics should have both these provinces, in recognition of their past misfortunes. I pointed out that all former claims had been settled by Sir Gerald Portal, when he increased the Catholic territory, and could not now be reopened. Monseigneur Hirth then suggested that the Catholics should have Butunzi, the larger of the two captured provinces, because they had 'not only not assisted the Mohammedans, but had even fought against them,' and because they had sent a far larger contingent to the war than the Protestants had.

To this I replied that the fact of the Roman Catholics having refrained from rebellion hardly constituted a claim to additional territory; I also explained that the Protestants had borne the brunt of the fighting, had, practically, without Catholic aid, beaten the Mohammedans at Natete, and had alone faced Selim Bey at Port Alice and enforced his surrender; they had also sent their fair contingent to Unyoro, and in my opinion should have the larger province as their share of the spoils of war. Monseigneur Hirth then protested that the Catholics would not avail themselves of the new province assigned to them, as they could not live in it for fear of Protestant aggression. His views were, however, as it turned out, not those of the Catholic Waganda, who occupied Busuju without demur, and settled down contentedly enough.

No anxiety was felt with reference to the Mohammedans who had been expelled from Uganda. Judging from past history, they might be expected to raid; but the troops at the disposal of the Commissioner were amply sufficient to guard the frontier, if Sir Gerald Portal's views as regards concentration were carried out. It was known that Kabarega was no longer disposed to allow these turbulent and treacherous Waganda to settle in his territories; it was also certain that, as had happened in the past, the lesser people amongst the expelled Mohammedans would filter back, and that the Mohammedan party would shortly cease to exist as a dangerous factor in frontier politics.

On August 2nd I was at the new headquarters at Port Alice, when I received an urgent summons from Arthur, who was commanding at Kampala. News had just been received that the whole Mohammedan party was returning to Uganda. I at once marched to Kampala, and next day there was a council, at which the facts were declared. The Mohammedans had returned to their old provinces, and were proceeding to drive out the new Christian settlers and the loyal Waislam indiscriminately. Owen was supposed to be marching on Matiana, but his exact position was not certain. The greatest consternation prevailed in the capital, as the army which had been sent to Unyoro against the rebels had been disbanded, and those who had taken part in that expedition were hardly in a condition to face fresh fighting. A new army could not be collected in a day, and meanwhile the Mohammedans were reoccupying their old positions by force.

I decided to march to Matiana to meet Owen and ascertain exactly what had happened, and take steps to move against the rebels from the northward, while Arthur organized a force at Kampala to proceed against them from the east. Owen had, however, marched fast, and I met him about twenty-two miles from Mengo. Here the actual state of matters was disclosed. Of the seventy rebel chiefs who had started with Owen from Fort de Winton, only four were left; the rest had deserted and rejoined their people, who had moved straight into their old provinces.

Without delay we had a meeting with the four Mohammedan chiefs who remained, and informed them that the rebel party had lost all claim to their old provinces and properties, and that they had now the option of three courses left to them. Either they must give up their arms, when they would be allowed to settle among their Christian kinsfolk, or they must leave the country and seek their fortunes elsewhere, or they might face a renewal of hostilities. The action of the beaten Mohammedan party in coming back in the guise of suppliants for peace, and immediately endeavouring to forcibly repossess themselves of their old estates, was strongly condemned, and the four chiefs were at once sent off to their people with the terms mentioned above. They were given five days in which to make up their minds, but were informed that if no decision had been come to by August 10th, they would be forthwith attacked.

This having been settled, it was arranged that Owen, strengthened by my escort of about forty Soudanese, should return to Matiana with the Makwenda, raise as many of the Waganda as he could, and move into Busuju from the north. I myself decided to return to Kampala, raise a similar force there, and advance into Butambala from the west. Both columns were to endeavour to form a junction at Kibibi on the 9th—that is to say, in four days' time. It was not anticipated that either would be able to secure many Waganda at such short notice, so that in case of hostilities each would have to depend mainly on its hundred odd Soudanese. Though the numbers available were thus small, I thought that the rapidity of our movement into two of the three disputed provinces, and the low morale of the rebel party after their late defeats, would minimize the danger due to the weakness of our forces.

On August 6th we separated, and respectively reached Matiana and Kampala. Matiana was about seventeen miles, while Kampala was thirty-two miles, distant from Kibibi. On August 7th I marched westwards with Arthur and Villiers, one Maxim, and one hundred and twelve Soudanese, accompanied by one hundred Waganda guns under the Sekebobo. This latter contingent, however, rose in the next couple of days to two hundred guns.

On August 8th Owen marched south with Grant, a hundred Soudanese, and two hundred Waganda guns under the Makwenda, and was joined by the Catholic Katikiro with a small following.

On the 9th my column camped at the capital of Butambala, while Owen's was at the capital of Busuju. The former was some five miles east, and the latter about the same distance north, of Kibibi. From his position Owen overlooked a considerable party of the rebels who had agreed to surrender. He informed me of this fact, and suggested that the attack should be postponed a day to give time for a settlement to be arrived at with this section of Mohammedans. To this I agreed, and next day moved to Kibibi. The Mohammedans who wanted peace began to surrender guns the same day, both to Owen at Busuju and to me at Kibibi. News was also brought in that the Katikiro Apollo, in person, was leading up a fresh contingent of five hundred guns to support us, as the Waganda thought our columns dangerously weak.

By August 12th Owen's force had joined me at Kibibi, and Dr. Moffat had also arrived from Kavirondo with a few additional men. The Mohammedan party in the neighbourhood had complied with my terms, and peace was secured in the districts near. There was, however, a large body of the rebels at Butabuzi who had declined to accept the terms as regards surrendering their arms, and did not make any overtures for peace; they had made themselves masters of that district of Butunzi, and had settled down under a number of the worst characters amongst their chiefs.

It was necessary to move against this section and compel their surrender, or drive them out of the country. Arthur and Moffat were detailed to remain at Kibibi to receive arms, which were still being surrendered, while Owen, Villiers and myself with about one hundred and twenty Soudanese, a Maxim, and a force of five hundred Waganda guns, advanced on Butabuzi. The direct road was impracticable, as there was no food left near it; so the column would have to march south-west to near the Katonga River, and then west along its northern bank, as along this route, it was hoped, supplies could be obtained in sufficient quantities for our column of about two thousand men.

Before following the course of this column, and its subsequent development into the Koki expedition under Lieutenant Villiers, we may review the results of the last ten days. On August 5th Owen and I had formed our plans, and in four days we had organized our columns and moved into positions commanding the capitals of two of the disputed provinces, and within supporting distance of each other, having covered in the time fifty-four and forty-seven miles respectively. This rapid action had broken up the cohesion of the rebel party; the smaller people in large numbers had deserted their

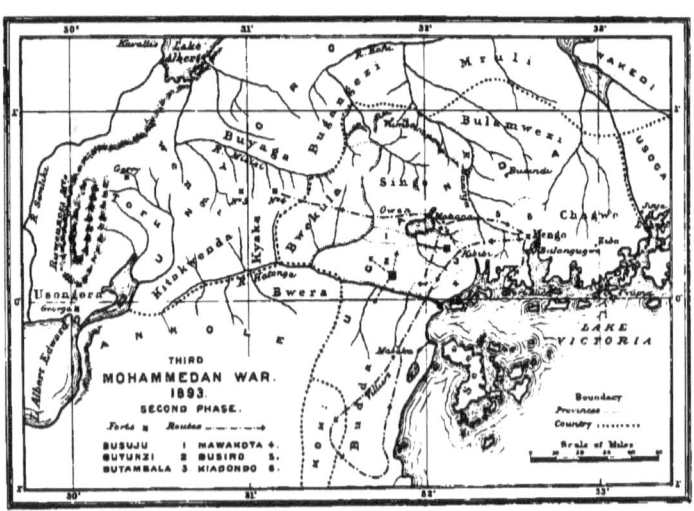

chiefs and taken refuge with their Christian kinsfolk; a great number of the principal men had surrendered, and had been told off to different provinces, where the Christian chiefs gave them small properties; and the outstanding rebels had been reduced to a small force of about twelve hundred in Butabuzi.

On August 13th we moved south-west, and next day reached Batauka, on the southern border of Butambala, about ten miles from the Katonga. Here it was definitely ascertained that the last intact body of rebels had fled from Butabuzi, feeling that further resistance on their part was vain. Lutaia, a pestilent chief, for whose arrest a warrant was already out, had fled to German territory with a few men, the bulk of the rebels had dispersed, but about six hundred had located themselves in Koki. Koki was a small, dependent kingdom on the west of Buddu, and had possessed in the past a particularly bad reputation for aiding slave-dealers and conducting a smuggling traffic in guns and gunpowder. It was most undesirable to allow a Mohammedan settlement there; and, moreover, there were several outstanding questions to be settled with Kamswaga, the ruler of that kingdom. I accordingly sent on Lieutenant Villiers with a small force to clear Koki of rebel Mohammedans, and to settle the questions in dispute. Reddie, then at Port Alice, was ordered at the same time to proceed by boat to Buddu, and place himself under Villiers' orders.

Next day the latter started with seventy Soudanese and the Maxim, and the remainder of the expedition broke up, the Waganda contingent returning, with Arthur's detachment at Kibibi, direct to the capital, while Owen and myself, with a small escort, took a circuitous route to Kampala, through Butunzi and Singo.

Thus ended the last phase of the third Mohammedan war. The Kampala and Matiana columns had, it is true, encountered no resistance, probably because of the rapidity of their movements, but had for the same reason experienced considerable hardships. The conclusion of the war was eminently satisfactory, and the Mohammedan problem ceased to weigh in Uganda politics.

Before concluding the chapter, however, I must note the complete success of the Koki expedition, under the command of Villiers. Not only were the rebel Mohammedans compelled to abandon their last refuge in British territory, but, thanks to his tact and judgment, all the questions at issue as regards Koki itself were satisfactorily settled. A considerable amount of accurate geographical information was also the result of this expedition.

Leaving Batauka on August 15th, Villiers marched to the Katonga River, and next day crossed the broad, level valley through which it flows. The river has here three well-defined channels of moderate width, which are in the dry season waist-deep, and overgrown, as usual, with papyrus. These channels meander about over a breadth of five miles, and the intermediate islands, as well as the flat ground on the south bank, are but slightly swampy, and covered with luxuriant grass, which supports an immense amount of game. Another march brought Villiers to Villamaria, the headquarters of the Roman Catholic Mission in Uganda. Though this station has not been long in existence, its condition and the beautiful gardens which surround it are a testimony to the industry of the Roman Catholic Fathers, who have also persuaded their followers to construct excellent roads all round the station. Here Villiers halted for a day or two to await the arrival of Reddie, and to arrange certain details with the Catholic chiefs. During this time he was most hospitably entertained by the Roman Catholic missionaries.

Leaving Villamaria, the expedition reached the borders of Koki in three marches, and next day arrived at Kamswaga's capital. Here a beautiful view was obtained of the little lake of Koki, the size of which had been previously exaggerated. This lake has been named after the leader of the expedition, he being the first white man who saw it. Villiers found his work in Koki much simplified as far as the Mohammedan rebels were concerned, as they had judged it wise to retire before his arrival. He had still questions regarding Koki itself to settle—notably the suppression of illicit trade in slaves, arms, and ammunition, and the enforcement of the annual tribute due to Uganda. At first it seemed not unlikely that Kamswaga, who was terribly afraid, might from sheer panic resort to arms. He collected a considerable force of fighting-men in his capital, but Villiers' wise, yet firm, management removed his apprehensions, and induced him to make a satisfactory settlement of all the points at issue.

The Royal Family of Koki is Wahuma, and its members are very fair, almost white in colour. The population, however, though classed as Wahuma, is so intermixed with other races that all shades of colour are to be met with. The country is full of hills, which are composed of much-altered sandstone, the strata of which have a great angle of dip, and are in places almost on edge. There is good grazing on the hills, while in the valleys, and round the lake, is a large extent of excellent cultivation.

In accordance with instructions, Villiers then marched to the south of Buddu to look for a site for a port near the coast of the lake, which would be a suitable place to allow of a check being placed on illicit trade in arms and ammunition. He found a very good situation on the lofty, though somewhat blunted, peninsula of Sango.

Much useful work was also done by Mr. Reddie, under Villiers' orders, in investigating and mapping the roads and natural features of the south of Buddu. The results showed that the Kagera River was navigable for steam-launches, and could not be crossed by canoes except at certain points, owing to the extensive papyrus and other growth, which, except at these points, completely blocked all approach to the banks. The approximate limits of the large Loonga Forest, which covers a considerable tract in South Buddu, were mapped, and it was ascertained that a good deal of this stretch was in the rains nothing but a swamp.

On September 13th Villiers returned to Port Alice, after having accomplished a great deal of capital work during his eminently successful expedition, and with the satisfactory close of the Koki expedition ended the Mohammedan wars. Since this the Mohammedans have given no trouble; and perhaps the most instructive illustration of the great change in feeling that was produced is the significant fact that those of the sect who had received properties out of Butambela assembled for the Unyoro war of 1893-94 under the banners of their Christian chiefs.

CHAPTER XIX.

CONCENTRATION AND PREPARATION AGAINST KABAREGA.

AFTER my settlement of the Mohammedan question (I may fairly call it a settlement, as it has stood the test of three and a half years), there was still a good deal left to be done in connection with the Soudanese; not in the way of more mutiny, for they had seen where that led under British rule, but in bringing them under still better discipline and organization. But I had better begin from the beginning.

In a previous chapter I mentioned that Sir Gerald Portal was originally averse to the retention of Toru, and, in fact, of the whole of South Unyoro, but had yielded to the representations of Owen and myself, and allowed us to retain two forts in Unyoro and an outpost towards Toru, as well as Fort George on the Salt Lake. This he did with some reluctance, as, rightly or wrongly, he did not apparently consider the Company's treaties outside Uganda as binding on the Imperial Government. When Owen's despatches reached him at Wakoli's on his way to the coast—despatches relating the Manyema attack on Usongora, and the Wanyoro attack on the forts, which resulted in the death of Shukri—Sir Gerald evidently reverted to his original idea, that our possession of these outlying districts weakened Uganda, without conferring on us any equivalent compensation. In his letter dated 'One march beyond Wakoli's, June 8, 1893,' Sir Gerald expressed very decided views on the subject. I need only give the following extracts :

'To evacuate the Salt Lake fort. As soon as immediate difficulties are settled, I would let the whole of Toru go.'

So much for the definitely-expressed views of my official superior, whose instructions I was supposed to be following in Uganda.

Let us see what was the state of matters in the country he proposed to evacuate, not considered from the purely sentimental view of a temporary retrocession of the British flag from districts where the company had made treaties, but from the practical report of Major Owen, whom none can accuse of wishing anything but good for the country. Thanks to the Soudanese oppression, before Government had taken over Uganda, he found that about fifteen hundred square miles in Southern Unyoro were desolate, that Kitakwanda had been rendered actively hostile, and that in Usongora the people would gladly be without us. In fact, he estimated that all the friends we could reckon in those regions, and these only friendly because they feared Kabarega, amounted to two thousand Wanyoro settled at the forts, and Kasagama of Toru with, he estimated, five thousand people. The remaining population of the great extent of country we were occupying, at considerable cost in money and blood, would, he considered, be far from averse to our departure, for the Soudanese had proved more dreaded than Kabarega, and had alienated or expelled almost the whole of the inhabitants.

So much for the views of the natives concerned, as interpreted by a capable officer, who had travelled throughout these districts, and whose opinions coincided with those of others of experience in Unyoro.

Let us now look at the question from an administrative point of view. By the Imperial Commissioner's arrangements we had at our disposal six hundred troops. Of these, ' three hundred and fifty were stationed in Uganda, and had to look after a population of perhaps four hundred thousand people, with whom we had treaty obligations. Three hundred and fifty soldiers were none too many for this work, and an increase of this number was very desirable. In Unyoro we had garrisons aggregating two hundred and fifty men to guard a number of districts, the friendly inhabitants of which only amounted to a few thousands, while the bulk of the population would have gladly welcomed our departure. The proportion seems somewhat unfair, and it must be remembered that Owen considered more troops necessary in Unyoro if we were to maintain our position as we should. The Unyoro garrisons occupied posts the most distant of which was twenty days' march from Kampala, thus necessitating a considerable transport caravan to keep up the supply of trade goods for the pay and maintenance of the men. This had not been so apparent during the Company's *régime*, as the Soudanese in Unyoro were unpaid, and maintained themselves.

These scattered forts, with their weak garrisons, also tempted Wanyoro attacks, and it was evident from recent events that we could not be sure of maintaining our communications at all times, even between the forts themselves. The difficulty of feeding the garrisons has already been referred to, and had become still greater.

These forts had a further disadvantage in times of trouble, for, being in hostile country, a considerable portion of their garrisons had to stand fast to guard them, and the mass of women, children, and followers that remained in them. Thus, less than half the garrison could be relied on for offensive or defensive combinations, and such combinations were rendered still more difficult by the distance between individual forts and the nature of the country. In fact, we were wasting and frittering away our strength by holding these positions. Should offensive measures against Kabarega, or any of the surrounding monarchs, be necessary, I could not make use of more than a fraction of my troops unless I abandoned some of these detached posts; and it would be far more damaging to our prestige to do so on the outbreak of war than in peace time. I think this was made sufficiently clear in the latter part of the Mohammedan war, when Owen and I, after dangerously depleting our garrisons, could only put about two hundred soldiers in the field. Thus, practical considerations of organization and efficiency dictated a concentration of our force in Uganda.

I had yet another point to think of. Since Lugard in the early days had refused Kabarega's proffered friendship, that dusky potentate had been our inveterate enemy, and had practically cast off the allegiance he owed to his suzerain, Mwanga. He had been still further embittered against us by the location of irresponsible Soudanese in his southern provinces, and by the desolation they had caused. Having regard to the development and prosperity of Uganda, I could see that at no distant date Kabarega's power must be broken and his prestige destroyed. But to do this with our troops distributed as they were would be an almost hopeless task, unless we denuded Uganda of its garrison, and this, of course, was impossible.

I had thus to take upon myself the responsibility of deciding what was best. On the one side I had the clearly-expressed views of my superior officer, the Consul-General of Zanzibar, backed up by every argument of common-sense; on the other, the sentimental objection to withdrawal, which I might be sure some people would make capital of at home. Being averse to breaking faith with our friends, I decided on the only course open to me. The Soudanese were to be withdrawn into Uganda, where they could be efficiently organized; the whole of our useless territory in South Unyoro was to be temporarily given up, but our friends were not ' on that account to be abandoned, as I proposed to bring them into Uganda with us, and settle them in that country, which was much under-populated. As Owen, after careful investigation, had come to the conclusion that those well disposed towards us amounted to only seven thousand people, this could be easily done. The King and the Waganda chiefs were agreeable, and certain districts of Singo were placed at my disposal for the new settlers, whose advent would increase our strength while lessening our difficulties.

The undertaking was, however, a formidable one, as the Soudanese alone mustered four thousand five hundred souls, and to this had to be added about seven thousand friendly natives. It was essential that the movement should be thoroughly organized, or the immigration of such a large body would do immense damage to the districts of Uganda through which they marched. My predecessors had moved through Uganda bodies of Soudanese mustering one thousand to thirteen hundred men, women, and children, but had found it difficult to provide food for even this number without entailing hardship on the natives of the country traversed; and the task before us was to conduct a far larger migration without eating our friends out of house and home.

I had already in August thought out my plans, and took the opportunity afforded by the meeting with Owen and Grant to make the proposed arrangements clear to them. About the middle of that month the latter officer was sent back to Unyoro to commence the arrangements for evacuation. The Salt Lake was first to be abandoned, and the garrison moved to Toru. From this district considerable food-supplies could be got, and Grant was to arrange that ten days' provision for the whole assemblage should be collected before the end of September, by which time we hoped to withdraw the garrisons bodily into Uganda.

'We had already garrisons at Kampala and Port Alice, and I

intended to form an additional station at Matiana, the capital of Singo. These three stations were near enough to support each other in case of internal trouble in Uganda, and would enable us to concentrate a field force of about three hundred men on any portion of the probable area in which complications might arise between the Roman Catholics and Protestants. At the same time, by thus dividing the force into three garrisons the food difficulty was much simplified.

On the extreme north-west frontier of Singo, in that salient angle of Uganda which juts out into Unyoro, and approaches within four or five days' march of Kabarega's capital, I decided to build two forts, with a garrison of about seventy men each. The great mass of old officers and their followers who had not been enlisted were to be located at Lubwa's, in Usoga, where I had arranged to provide them with land on which to settle, thus carrying out the original proposal of my late chief, which, however, he had found impracticable up to the date of his departure. On the conclusion of the Mohammedan war, Owen was to visit Singo and personally select the sites for these three new stations; he was then to join Grant in Unyoro, take command of the whole column there assembled, and march to Matiana, where orders had already been issued for the collection of great supplies of food to await the immigrants.

Two additional assistants were sent to Matiana, to aid him in distributing the mass of Soudanese amongst the various stations that formed their ultimate destination. About one thousand would remain at Matiana under one assistant, while Owen took fourteen hundred and distributed them between the two frontier forts; Villiers would conduct about five hundred to Port Alice, to bring that station to its proposed strength; and Grant would march a column of about fifteen hundred to Lubwa's by a road which avoided Mengo; with the few additional men I wanted at Kampala, this disposed of the whole of the Unyoro garrisons.

The friendly people of Unyoro and Toru, who would accompany Owen into Uganda, were to be taken care of by Waganda chiefs, and conducted independently to their allotted districts. Such was the general scheme, and preparations were at once pushed forward towards its execution. Not only was food collected at Matiana, but orders were also issued through the King that food should be stored at various points on the line of march of the smaller columns.

While we hoped that Kasagama of Toru would accept our offer of territory in Singo, Owen was given latitude to make another arrangement if this petty King preferred it. I intended in December, at the close of the approaching rains, to direct an expedition against Kabarega, if Unyoro remained hostile, as there was every prospect of its doing. If Kasagama preferred to retain Toru, and thought he could hold his own for a few months, with the assistance of some extra guns, Owen was authorized to hand over to him some of our muskets to the number of two hundred. As the Unyoro Chief of Bugangezi, Chikakure by name, had played a prominent part in the recent attacks on the Unyoro forts, I also authorized Owen to punish him, which he could have done on his way into Uganda with the Soudanese garrisons.

At the end of September the great exodus commenced. So thoroughly had Grant arranged all the details, that Owen on his arrival found everything ready. The friendly Wanyoro, to the number of two thousand, willingly agreed to settle in Singo, but Kasagama had accepted the alternative proposal, and considered that he could hold his own with the additional muskets which he had received. He was also assured that we would send an expedition, before many months were over, to furnish him with fresh supplies. Then the great mass of

Soudanese and Wanyoro moved into Uganda in two columns, a day's march apart from each other.

Owen decided not to attack Chikakure, as that chief had made proffers of friendship and peace; needless to say, he broke these promises later on. Owen led his crowd to Matiana, where he found three assistants waiting for him. The rest of the programme was carried out like clockwork, and in a little over a week the Soudanese and Wanyoro were settled as had been arranged. So admirably did my staff fulfil my plans that this great immigration was accomplished without a single complaint from the Waganda through whose districts they had marched, and greater praise than this it is impossible to give. This portion of our arrangements having been successfully carried out, it remained to organize the Soudanese into a fighting machine, which would be equal to maintaining order in Uganda, and at the same time conducting a probable expedition against Unyoro in December.

Sir Gerald Portal had authorized our enlisting six hundred soldiers, but had subsequently modified his original proposals, and fixed five hundred as the maximum. As we had already enlisted about five hundred and sixty before his second order was promulgated, I did not consider it necessary to dismiss the extra men. Sir Gerald had estimated that the retention of Uganda would cost an annual sum of £27,000, and I was enjoined to work to this estimate, which provided for five hundred soldiers and, on my representation, an additional body of two hundred reservists. On going through the estimates carefully, I found that I could effect economies under several heads, and resolved to devote the resulting surplus to still further increasing the military force to a total of nearly nine hundred men, of whom six hundred would be on the active list.

The regular troops already enlisted were not to be increased, except as regards Usoga, where I sanctioned the formation of a half-company of Soudanese to take the place of the half-company of Zanzibar troops, who were shortly to proceed to the coast. Since Selim Bey's fall we had found it easy to raise a reserve force of very fair material. We accordingly devoted ourselves to its formation.

These reserves were mainly intended for garrison work in time of trouble, in order that as large a number of regular troops as possible might be available for operations in the field. Each reservist was given a month's steady drill before he was entitled to pay, but after having thus passed through the recruit stage he was entitled to half the pay of a man on the active list and a scale of ration money, which enabled him to keep himself and family. He was also given a uniform—we could not run to much in those days—and had to put in a specified number of drills a month. This scheme worked well, and, in addition to being very popular, had the incidental advantage that it put a stop to the daily robberies which had marked the former *régime*. The distribution of troops was now as follows:

Kampala	120	on active list, and	60	reserve.
Port Alice	200	,,	,,	,,	60	,,
Fort Raymond (Matiana)	100	,,	,,	,,	50	,,
Fort Grant (Singo frontier)	70	,,	,,	,,	35	,,
Fort Lugard (Singo frontier)	70	,,	,,	,,	35	,,
Fort Lubwa (Usoga)	40	,,	,,	,,	60	,,
Totals	600	,,	,,	,,	300	,,

While the reorganized troops were daily gaining in cohesion and usefulness, we had many other matters to attend to, one of the most important being to persuade the Soudanese to cultivate private land round their various stations, and to get the settlement at Lubwa's put on a proper basis. This was done with very satisfactory results, and round all but the frontier forts there soon sprang up many acres of excellent cultivation, the produce of which made our troops and followers more independent of the local markets, and at the same time increased their prosperity.

The internal state of Uganda now gave little trouble, and we were able to take up other questions. At Port Alice a number of commodious stores were built, and I set to work to get some brick houses constructed for the Europeans at that station. This was a matter of some difficulty, as we had neither brickmakers nor bricklayers. But a Commissioner of Uganda in the early days had to turn his hand to many things, and I became head brickmaker and chief bricklayer. Not only had I to design these houses, but at first to lay a large proportion of the actual bricks. Later, however, after I had drawn large scale drawings of the arrangements necessary for proper bonding, we found that some of our Swahilis picked up the work very quickly. The result of our labours was that by November two small brick houses had been finished, and another was in course of construction.

In addition to bricklayer, I had also to turn rigger and sail-maker in chief, and, though familiar with sailing before my visit to Uganda, I had no idea that the new duties required so much technical knowledge. We had hired the Church Missionary Society boat, which had proved rather a white elephant to the mission, more especially so after the native skipper managed to fall overboard and get drowned. One stipulation, however, was made, that we must be at liberty to re-rig the boat. It had been sent out very completely fitted up in every detail, even to possessing a beaker for fresh water; but it was evidently intended to withstand very rough weather indeed, as it could hardly be persuaded to move at all except in a regular gale, so small was its sail area. It had been built as a schooner, but by unstepping the foremast, using it as a bowsprit, and putting in a much larger spar in its stead, we converted it into a serviceable yawl.

The sail-making was a great difficulty. The sails were made

of American drill, and, though carefully cut, we found that when sewn they altered their shape considerably; indeed, I have rarely seen such a grotesque object as our first attempt at a jib. Ultimately, at the third attempt we succeeded, and the mission boat, though not exactly a thing of beauty, was equal to sailing the waters in any wind. It was made still more serviceable later on by the valuable assistance of James Martin, an ex-sailor, who accompanied Smith's caravan to Uganda in October.

We were not, even in these piping times of peace, without some little occasional excitement. The Germans had discovered a great colony of slave-dealing Arabs at Kitangole in the north of their territory, and, with praiseworthy zeal for their own interests, decided to pass them on to Uganda. The first consignment had scarcely reached Mengo, when my assistant there sent a message to Port Alice that a consignment of slaves were about to start for German territory. He endeavoured to intercept them, but, though he rescued some, several canoe-loads had pushed off before his arrival, and were making their way down Murchison Bay.

On getting this message I sailed in the Government steel boat, hoping to intercept the canoes, and, sure enough, when we got near the mouth of the bay, a large and suspicious-looking craft hove in sight. We got within hailing distance and inquired its intentions, when the slave-dealers took the alarm, and were soon paddling west with all speed. The wind had dropped, and we had to row in pursuit in a glassy calm. This told against us, and, although I encouraged my men to exert themselves to the utmost, the canoe was steadily getting away from us. For about eight miles this unequal race continued, when a brisk breeze sprang up from the south, and we hoisted sail and began to turn the tables on our friends.

The breeze held and, indeed, freshened, and, while this increased our speed, the sea that rose delayed the slave-dealers. We passed Port Alice, with which we endeavoured to communicate by signal, and were rapidly overhauling the canoe, when it altered its course and began to paddle straight in the teeth of the wind. The steel boat, though fitted with leeboards, was not good to windward, and we feared the rascals might escape; but the sea was too much for them, and they beached their canoe on the island of Mfu and took refuge in the bushes. As this was a small island and contained no canoes, except a small fishing one, all we had to do was to remove the Arab vessel. As we sailed off with it in tow, we saw several of the Arabs regarding our movements with blank faces of dismay. We were only a few miles from Ntebe, and I sent word to Villiers to have a party of Soudanese ready at nightfall to land on the island.

It was a fine moonlight night when we put off, and in our own boat and the captured canoe made slowly and without noise for the dark outline of the island. As we approached its swampy margin, a number of hippopotami, whose midnight prowls we had disturbed, dashed past us into the water with much grumbling and bellowing. But after we had made our way through the swamps, we were delighted to find that the Arabs were encamped about their fires, and quite unsuspicious of danger. We approached softly, but in crossing a patch of moonlight they saw us, and vanished into the bushes. We gave chase, but in dodging about the undergrowth our opponents had distinctly the advantage of us, and after innumerable croppers we only succeeded in capturing one prisoner. However, when morning broke we secured the lot, most of whom had spent the night hiding in the water, with only their heads above the surface. The slaves were released, the dealers sentenced to various terms of punishment, and their valuable cargo of ivory confiscated.

One way or another we succeeded at this time in liberating

THE SLAVE-DEALER'S ISLAND.

a large number of slaves. Owen, too, had, by a carefully arranged plan, surprised a large caravan on the borders of Unyoro as it was making its way to German territory, and had freed some slaves and captured a large amount of ivory.

But the slaves freed by such little expeditions were trifling as compared to the number of Lendus which we succeeded in liberating. These were Soudanese slaves whose status my predecessors had judged it well to leave alone for the time, however much they wished to see them freed. After the concentration of the Soudanese in Uganda, I took this matter in hand, and the means by which we not only secured the liberation of some two thousand slaves, but prevailed on the Soudanese themselves to urge this step, were simple in the extreme.

I promulgated a rule that a Soudanese soldier who possessed Lendu slaves was personally responsible that they were properly fed and did not misconduct themselves. This seemed a natural rule, and the Soudanese were perfectly content with what appeared to be a formal recognition of their proprietary rights to the Lendus. They soon, however, discovered that this property had its drawbacks. When a Lendu was caught stealing food, his Soudanese master received the flogging for the misconduct of his slave.

This soon made itself felt. The Soudanese found that so many mouths dependent on their scanty pay and allowances were a positive nuisance, and the new rule had not been in force many weeks before they were clamouring that the Lendus should be freed and made responsible for their own actions. Thus, at the earnest request of their quondam masters, they were set free, and encouraged to settle down on land allotted to them, and to enlist as free porters. This alteration in their status produced excellent results, and by the end of the year we had no difficulty in forming a Lendu porter corps on lower rates of pay than the regular Swahili received. These free Lendus proved very good men, and fully appreciated the change in their condition.

Time was now wearing on, and soon Smith and Martin arrived with a large caravan of cloth and stores for Uganda. They were pleased to express great surprise at the improved state of affairs which had taken place since their departure in the spring. After a brief stay, they again left for the coast to bring up more supplies.

I was now only awaiting the arrival of the four Arabic-speaking officers to commence operations against Unyoro, where Kabarega persisted in his spirit of hostility. The various details of this expedition were actually arranged. Owen was to lead the main body of two hundred and fifty Soudanese and a Waganda contingent by the direct route on Kabarega's capital, while Arthur, with one hundred and fifty Soudanese and another force of Waganda, was to strike at Mruli and get into the East of Unyoro between Kabarega and the Wakedi. Owen and I had even discussed the advisability of ascertaining the state of affairs at Wadelai before our return from Unyoro, for it was no part of my scheme to occupy the country permanently. I meant to overthrow Kabarega's force, drive him from his capital, do as much damage to his power as possible, and then return to Uganda, after giving our enemy due notice that the raid would be repeated if necessary unless he made peace, received a British agent and escort at his capital, opened his country to trade, and gave us a free and secure passage to Lake Albert.

CHAPTER XX.

UNYORO EXPEDITION.

Sir Gerald Portal had written to me just before his departure from Kavirondo congratulating me on my management of the Mohammedan and Soudanese troubles, and assuring me that he would do his best at the Foreign Office to prevent my being superseded. He told me that he had already written for four Arabic-speaking officers from England for duty with the Soudanese, and suggested how best, in his opinion, to utilize their services.

Thus, when Owen and I pushed on our work of organizing our small military force, and planned our future operations against Kabarega, who was unmistakably indicating that we need not expect peace proposals from him until we had shown our strength, we neither of us expected that a senior officer was already on his way from England to reap the advantages of our work.

However, it was so, and in November, 1893, Colonel Colvile, of the Grenadier Guards, arrived to take charge in Uganda.

He approved of our preliminary arrangements, appointed Owen Commandant of the Soudanese battalion, and made me his senior staff officer. Any lurking hope that Kabarega might make friends was finally dispelled by his sending an army against our friend Kasagama of Toru, and another to invade Usoga. So early in December Colonel Colvile declared war against Unyoro, while Owen was despatched with a small column to invade Bugangezi, and thus make a diversion in favour of Toru.

Unyoro, with which we were now at war, was a large Bantu kingdom lying north and west of Uganda on the elevated plateau between the equatorial lakes and the Victoria Nile. Though nominally tributary to Uganda, in recent years it had become practically independent, under the rule of Kabarega, who had taken full advantage of the opportunities offered by the long civil wars in the suzerain kingdom to extend his own power. Thus, though Unyoro proper consisted of thirteen large provinces, Kabarega had overrun and annexed the three additional provinces or petty kingdoms of Toru, Usongora, and Kitakwenda. The Wakedi, a Nubian tribe east of the Victoria Nile, were more or less under his influence, as were also the Shuli, a tribe who inhabited the country on the right bank of the Nile proper, south of Wadelai. Kabarega had also brought more or less under his rule certain of the tribes west of Lake Albert.

Kabarega had fostered trade with the Arab and Swahili traders of the east coast, but took care that these did not pass to the north of Unyoro; in fact, he kept this trade entirely in his own hands. He could obtain plenty of ivory, and at the rate of one small tusk for a musket he bought up a large supply of arms and ammunition. If he wanted more ivory, it could be easily obtained from the more unsophisticated tribes of the north, who were willing to pay three good tusks for a single gun, and for ammunition in proportion.

Kabarega had thus become wealthy and powerful, and retained, in addition to feudal levies, a standing army of three thousand Balasura. Unlike the kings of Uganda, he did not distribute these throughout his dominions, but located them in certain districts near his capital where they were under his immediate control. This was an excellent arrangement, as his strength was concentrated, and he could easily, by detaching a portion of his force, reduce any refractory provincial chief, as Rekwiamba of Mwengi had found to his cost.

Unyoro was first visited in 1862 by the illustrious travellers Speke and Grant, and two years later by Samuel Baker. These were friendly visits; but in 1872 we find Baker again in Unyoro at the head of an Egyptian expedition, with the task of bringing under the sway of the Khedive the countries of the Nile Basin. He found that Kabarega had seized the power, on the death of the former King, Kamarasi, but that a rival was still in the field in the person of Rionga of Magungu. Leaving a garrison in the latter's province, Baker marched to Kabarega's capital, which was then situated at Masindi. Kabarega received him with friendship, and agreed to place his country under the Egyptian flag. But the friendship was short-lived, and Kabarega tried to dispose of Baker's force by a lavish gift of poisoned beer. This dastardly attempt failed, and hostilities broke out. Baker, with his small force, gained more than one success, but finally want of food compelled him to retreat northwards towards the Nile. The Wanyoro harassed his march, and it was only after great hardships and considerable loss that Baker reached the friendly post in Rionga's country.

A few years later Gordon established some stations in Unyoro, and sent Emin Pasha to interview Kabarega. The result was that Emin deputed Casati to reside as his representative at Kabarega's capital, now at Nyamoga. Kabarega at first professed friendship, but ultimately seized Casati, and condemned him to death. Casati, however, escaped during the night, and reached the eastern shores of Lake Albert, where he was picked up by one of Emin's steamers in a state of exhaustion from starvation and hardships. Emin bombarded the coast town of Kibero, but as he did not send a punitive expedition into Unyoro, or otherwise interfere with Kabarega, the latter posed in native estimation as again victorious over the white men. His prestige was further increased when, after a few years, the last Egyptian stations in Unyoro were finally abandoned.

For some years after this little was heard of Kabarega, who was quietly consolidating and strengthening his power. When the Mohammedans of Uganda were expelled by the Christians in 1890, Kabarega welcomed them into his country, and in 1891 assisted them against Lugard. In the same year, when Lugard made his memorable expedition to Kavalli's, his northward march from Lake Albert Edward was opposed by Kabarega's forces.

When Lugard secured Selim Bey's Soudanese, and located them in his chain of five forts to protect Toru and Usongora, Kabarega more than once attacked the forts, and, although invariably beaten off, he did the garrisons no little damage by cutting up foraging-parties. After the forts were wheeled round and extended between Uganda and Toru, Kabarega became even more hostile, as he was thus deprived of four provinces, while two others were rendered desolate by the Soudanese raids for food.

In 1892 Captain Williams tried to make peace with Unyoro, but Kabarega declined his terms, and remained hostile as before. Early in 1893, when Sir Gerald Portal took over the Protectorate, the Soudanese raids were stopped; but Kabarega misinterpreted this action, and, encouraged by the abandonment of the most northern of Lugard's forts, directed another and still greater expedition against our garrisons in South Unyoro. As before, he was beaten off; but, by interrupting our communications with Toru, he greatly aggravated the food difficulty at Forts Nos. 3 and 4, and scored one small success by surprising and defeating a party of Soudanese led by Bimbashi Shukri.

The immediate effect of our concentration in Uganda, and the establishment of Forts Grant and Lugard within five days' march of Kabarega's capital, was good ; but the Unyoro King soon recovered from any temporary timidity, and now directly challenged us to show our strength. And there were many signs that the surrounding countries were watching with interest the approaching struggle between Unyoro, the enemy, and Uganda, the friend, of European progress.

I have already mentioned that Colonel Colvile approved of my preliminary arrangements and plans, but in one particular the latter were modified. Colonel Colvile contemplated more extended operations than I had allowed for, and so the simultaneous attack on Mruli, which had been part of my programme, had to be abandoned. Our whole strength was to be employed on the main attack upon Kabarega's capital.

I noted that Owen had been despatched to invade Bugangezi, and effect a diversion in favour of Toru. Needless to say, he carried out his mission with his characteristic energy. In seven days he had marched one hundred and ten miles, and collected his little column of three hundred men in the neighbourhood of the Unyoro border. A long and trying night march through a succession of difficult swamps placed him at dawn within striking distance of Chikakure's stronghold; and a succession of engagements commenced that did not terminate till sunset. Owen was sparing of ammunition, and drove the enemy from one position after another with the minimum of firing. By evening he was undisputed master of Bugangezi, and the news of his victory paralyzed the hostile attack on Toru—an attack which was afterwards hastily abandoned on the news that Colonel Colvile had declared war on Unyoro.

While Owen was keeping the enemy busy on the frontier, the main expedition was being rapidly organized at Kampala.

Colonel Colvile divided his force into two main bodies, the headquarter division under his immediate command, and the Waganda division under Kakanguru. The former consisted of eight Europeans, 450 Soudanese troops, two Maxims, 450 Government porters, about half of whom were armed, and a Waganda contingent, under the Kangao, of 400 guns and 1,200 spears. The second division mustered about 12,000 Waganda, of whom 3,000 carried guns.

On December 13th, 1893, the expedition started, the Government force marching viâ Fort Raymond, and the Waganda in a number of small columns by different roads. The concentration was to be effected on the border near our frontier forts, which covered the movement.

In thirteen days the concentration was completed at Kaduma's, a fertile district about seven miles across the Unyoro frontier, about a hundred and twenty-five miles from Kampala, and forty-five miles from Kabarega's capital. Everything had worked very smoothly, and without friction.

Colonel Colvile halted on December 27th to allow the various contingents to fall into their places, and on the 28th continued his advance towards the Kafu River, which was reached in two marches. The guides, however, had mistaken the track on the second of these marches, and we found ourselves at Usamba instead of at the Baranwa crossing, where the river was only about four hundred yards wide. At Usamba the Kafu had a width of a thousand yards, and as both banks were low and wooded, it was hardly a suitable place at which to force a passage. The only advantage of Usamba was that food was very plentiful, the new crops being ripe, but ungathered.

Colonel Colvile halted next day, and made the following dispositions. Owen was sent west with a company to search for the Baranwa crossing, and Captain Thruston was despatched with a similar force to look for a more favourable passage lower down the river. At the same time I was told off to superintend the construction of bridges or causeways about one and a half miles above our camp, the Waganda furnishing a working-party of seven thousand men.

At the point selected for our bridging operations, our bank had a slight command over that of the enemy, and a Maxim was ostentatiously brought down and mounted to cover the bridging operations. Of course, it could have done practically nothing, but its presence exercised a great moral effect on our own working-parties, who had implicit faith in the wonderful machine-gun.

Three bridges were commenced, and by afternoon were so far advanced that men could wade to the enemy's bank. Colonel Colvile accordingly ordered Arthur, with a hundred Soudanese and a thousand Waganda guns, across the river to cover the completion of the bridging operations. Owen had reported a skirmish at the Baranwa crossing, and Thruston had found the enemy watching passages lower down the river, but, strange to say, Arthur was unopposed.

By one p.m. next day two of the three bridges were ready, and the third was passable, so Colonel Colvile moved his whole force across the river. Two short marches then sufficed to place us in possession of the enemy's capital.

So far we had experienced nothing worse than a little very mild skirmishing, and we could not account for the timidity of the Wanyoro, who had displayed unexpected pluck in the preliminary fighting at Chikakure's. The reason for the lack of resistance we had encountered was apparently as follows. Kabarega had divided his force into four bodies. One was told off to attack Toru, a second to invade Usoga, and a third to mask our frontier forts, while Kabarega retained the fourth as a general reserve at his capital. He had calculated on our being fully occupied in defending Toru and Usoga, and had apparently overlooked the fact that we could equally well

—in fact, more easily—relieve the pressure on these outlying countries by a direct counter-attack on his capital. As soon as he knew what we intended, he had sent to recall the Toru and Usoga armies, but he did not allow for the rapidity of our movements. In 1891 it had taken Lugard a month to move a force about equal to our own from Mengo to the frontier, and Kabarega had not anticipated that in twenty-one days we should not only have reached the frontier, but be in possession of his capital. His Usoga army had not yet reached him; his Toru expedition had, indeed, returned the day we crossed the Kafu, but it was hardly in fighting trim, as it had suffered severely at the hands of Kasagama, and still more severely during its forced marches to rejoin Kabarega; his frontier force was much demoralized and disheartened by the rough handling they had experienced from Owen, and Kabarega did not feel strong enough with only a quarter of his army to contest the passage of the Kafu or defend his capital. To gain time and reorganize his force, he retreated north-east towards the Budongo forest, where he had numerous stores of food concealed.

Colonel Colvile followed in pursuit, and on January 4th, 1894, our advance guard of Waganda was checked by Kabarega's rear guard. Owen was at once sent out with a company of Soudanese to ascertain the enemy's strength, but found that the Wanyoro had already retired. Colonel Colvile judged from this that he had only a rear guard to deal with, so sent me ahead next day with a half-company of Soudanese to support the Waganda advance guard, with orders to at once drive in the enemy's rear guard if met with. His judgment was correct, for, sure enough, after marching about nine miles, we came on the enemy posted at the entrance to a defile in a belt of very thick jungle. I ordered an immediate attack, keeping the Soudanese in reserve. The Waganda rushed forward, and the fusillade that ensued was very creditable to the small numbers engaged, in volume, if not in accuracy. The weak force of Wanyoro was soon turned out of the forest; but further advance through the defile was somewhat checked by the enemy, who could command the pass from a rocky hill on the left. This we captured, and the position was ours.

As the Waganda lost touch of the enemy, Owen and I were sent out that evening to reconnoitre, and from the summit of a neighbouring hill we could make out a large camp of the enemy about seven miles off in the Budongo forest. This was good news, for we thought that at last the enemy meant to accept battle.

Next day we accordingly advanced in battle formation, the Soudanese and Maxims in the centre, and the Waganda in a line of parallel columns on each flank, the whole being covered by skirmishers. The bush proved very difficult, and though the enemy did not offer much resistance, it was late in the afternoon when we reached the hills of Bitiberi and overlooked Kabarega's camp, which nestled in a thick patch of forest about 2,500 yards away.

It was so late in the day that a victory would have been rendered ineffective, as darkness would have stopped a vigorous pursuit, so Colonel Colvile decided to postpone his attack till next morning, when we should have the whole day before us. But next morning we found the enemy had again retired still further into the foodless forest. To follow would have been futile, for Kabarega evidently did not mean to stand, and he could always retire faster than we could advance if deployed.

So Colonel Colvile resolved to try and tempt him to come out into the open, and with this object moved the whole force two days' march towards Mruli. This had the desired effect, and Kabarega left the forest and returned towards his former capital in high spirits at the way he had out-manœuvred the detested Europeans, who were apparently in full retreat towards Mruli. As soon as we heard he was well clear of the forest, a flying column was despatched under Owen to cut him off, while the main body stood fast. Owen very nearly succeeded in his mission, but his movement was prematurely exposed by the unauthorized action of some irresponsible Waganda, who pushed ahead and fell foul of one of Kabarega's outlying parties. Owen had to support the Waganda, and though he drove the enemy back, Kabarega gained sufficient time to once more take refuge in his favourite forest.

Colonel Colvile now altered his tactics. It was evident that Kabarega would not hazard a serious engagement, so it was decided to blockade him in the forest of which he was so fond. With this object, the headquarter column was to occupy Kitanwa, while the Waganda, under Kakanguru, moved to Kisibagwa. These dispositions would prevent Kabarega from drawing supplies from the fertile districts south of the Budongo forest. The districts to the east near Masindi had already been depleted by our movements after bitiberi; and thus Kabarega, once his concealed magazines were exhausted, must either come out into the open and fight us, or draw his supplies from Magungu. We hoped he would adopt the former course, but in case he attempted the latter, further dispositions were to be made.

On January 17th these new arrangements were carried out, and the headquarters reached Kitanwa. A brisk skirmish which took place on our right showed that Kakanguru was also at work, and that the enemy's foraging-parties were being hustled into the forest. The same night we occupied the prosperous town of Kibero.

Colonel Colvile considered that it would be desirable to keep open the road from Uganda to Lake Albert, and to this end we had proposed to build three forts: one at the Kafu

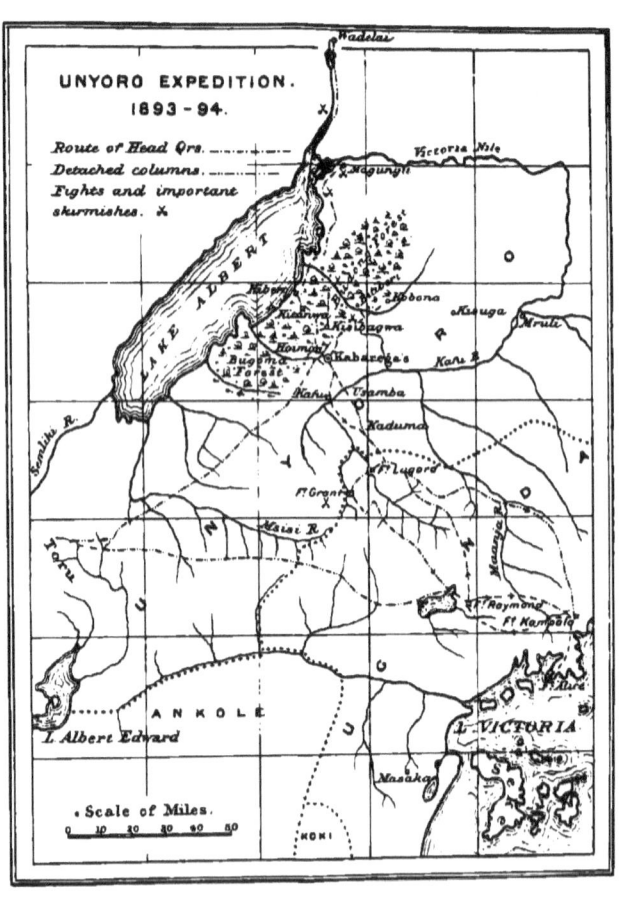

River, a second near Kabarega's capital, and a third at Kibero. The last was essential, as the steel boat was to be left afloat on the waters of the lake. But now we had arrived at Kibero we found there was no cultivation on the sterile shores of the Albert Nyanza; so a fourth fort became necessary at Kitanwa, to maintain our hold on that fertile district and feed the garrison of Kibero.

Accordingly, on January 18th a site was selected for the Kitanwa fort, and Villiers, with a company of Soudanese and a lot of Swahilis, was told off to construct it. The Waganda under the Kangao, the contingent with headquarters, also remained to assist Villiers. The remainder of the headquarter column moved to Kibero. The same day Arthur was sent south with the steel boat to capture canoes, and after a brisk skirmish he succeeded in securing a good many. The canoes of Lake Albert are not to be compared with those of Lake Victoria, being clumsy dug-outs, but they proved useful in a variety of ways.

On January 20th Owen was despatched with a column of three hundred men to occupy Magungu, and forbid to Kabarega the food-supplies of that district which lay north of the Budongo forest. At the same time Owen was to find out what was the state of affairs at Wadelai. To facilitate his passage of the Nile, the steel boat, under Purkiss, was to accompany him, keeping parallel to his column.

Colonel Colvile and the remainder of the headquarter column remained at Kibero, and commenced work on the mud fort which was to shelter our small garrison. At the same time the Kibero stream was deepened and trained to form a little harbour for the boat under the walls of the fort.

I need not describe the details of our work and life at Kibero, as my friend and late chief, Colonel (now Sir Henry) Colvile, has graphically portrayed them in his book, 'The 'Land of the Nile Springs.'

Suffice it to say that, while we were busy with our fort-building, Kabarega and his army were beginning to feel the results of Colonel Colvile's tactics. Food became scarce, and Kabarega moved to the southern edge of the forest, and endeavoured to obtain supplies. This led to frequent skirmishes between his foraging-parties and the Waganda, and invariably resulted in Kabarega's men being driven back into the forest. Once he attempted a partial night attack on the half-finished post at Kitanwa, but Villiers was equal to the occasion, and repulsed the assault with ease.

The scarcity of food made Kabarega still bolder, and messages from both Kakanguru and Villiers pointed to a more serious attempt on Kitanwa, so Colonel Colvile ordered Kakanguru to attack the enemy as they left the forest, rightly judging that Villiers could hold his own.

But before we heard the result of these dispositions we had fresh excitement in the return of the steel boat on January 31st. Purkiss and his crew had suffered severely, and had to report that all touch with Owen's column had been lost. They knew that Owen had defeated the enemy on January 23rd, and had pushed on towards Magungu, but the steel boat had found it impossible to penetrate the dense sudd and vegetation that blocked the mouth of the Victoria Nile. After spending several days in fruitless attempts to reach Magungu, Purkiss sailed fifteen miles down the Nile toward Wadelai, thinking that Owen might be marching northwards. But he heard nothing of that officer, and nearly lost the boat by the treachery of the Lurs at Iyar's. He had been attacked, and after days of semi-starvation returned to Kibero.

Colonel Colvile at once ordered me to select a fresh crew, and sail, the following morning, to find out the fate of Owen's force, and in any case to push on to Wadelai. But that night Owen turned up.

He had a second engagement with the Wanyoro on January 26th, at Magungu, when the camp, under Captain Thruston, was fiercely attacked at night. The result had been a second victory for us, and the enemy had abandoned the district. In the absence of the steel boat, Owen had found it impracticable to cross the Nile, and so reluctantly retraced his steps.

Owen was at once sent off with a picked crew in the steel boat to visit Wadelai; and as the forts at Kibero and Kitanwa were now complete and provisioned for months, a company of Soudanese was told off as garrison, while the headquarters marched to Hoima, and commenced work on what was to be the chief station of the Unyoro command.

At the same time we heard of the complete success of Kakanguru's movement against Kabarega. Kakanguru had left his standing camp at Kisibagwa on January 28th, and found Kabarega's forces distributed in three bodies. Feinting against the flanks, he moved to attack its centre division. But Kabarega, in ignorance of the proximity of the Waganda, also advanced, and the actual meeting was more or less a surprise for both parties. In the fight that resulted, the Waganda were victorious, and captured the enemy's camps and a good deal of booty. Kabarega himself had a narrow escape, but managed to get away.

On February 12th Major Owen returned from his adventurous journey to Wadelai. He had entered the Nile at dusk, and hoped to reach his destination before dawn. But when day broke, he was still some ten miles from his objective, and the natives turned out and opened an ever-increasing fire on the steel boat. Owen, feeling that if he returned their fire all chance of peace was lost, pushed stubbornly down-stream without firing a shot. In the neighbourhood of Wadelai a parley took place. The chief of that district made friends; a small force was enlisted locally to guard the British flag, which was hoisted on the abandoned Egyptian station; and Owen returned to Lake Albert in peace.

Arthur had meanwhile visited our frontier forts in Uganda, and returned with a convoy of stores; and as the fort at Hoima was rapidly approaching completion, the end of the war appeared in sight.

Colonel Colvile decided to form a confederation of some of the southern provinces of Unyoro under friendly chiefs, so Owen and Villiers were sent off with a small column to Toru. I may at once say that Owen was successful in his mission, and the provinces of Usongora, Mwengi, Kyaka, and Toru were formed into a confederacy under the leadership of Kasagama of Toru.

In nine days the fort at Hoima was completed and provisioned, so the headquarters moved to the Baranwa crossing of the Kafu. At the same time the Waganda, under Kakanguru, were permitted to return to Uganda, which they were glad to do, as small-pox had broken out in their camp and claimed many victims. Before their departure, Colonel Colvile sent me to overhaul their captives and release any Wanyoro prisoners. This was a troublesome job, but in the end about eleven hundred Wanyoro were sifted out and sent to their homes in peace. A large number of Waganda who had been carried off into slavery in Unyoro were recovered and liberated, and now returned to their own country with the Waganda army.

In four days the fort at the Kafu was built, and a bridge or causeway constructed across the river. This being done, Captain Thruston was left in command of Unyoro with three and a half companies of Soudanese, and the headquarter column recrossed the frontier of Uganda on February 27, 1894.

This closed the Unyoro expedition of 1893-94, and Colonel Colvile might fairly congratulate himself on the results achieved. Though the fighting had not been as severe as in the civil wars of Uganda, the power of Kabarega had been broken, and half his kingdom wrested from him. A road had been opened to Lake Albert, and our steel boat was afloat on the waters of the lake as a visible sign of our effective occupation.

Since then there has been further fighting in Unyoro, but each successive struggle on the part of Kabarega has only weakened him and more firmly established our power, until now Unyoro is included in the Uganda Protectorate.

* * * * *

This brief account of the Unyoro Expedition makes a fitting close to my narrative. After spending a few weeks in Uganda, to assist Colonel Colvile, I marched for the coast, with nothing more eventful to chronicle than peaceful meetings with Masai and a hostile encounter with a troop of lions. In due course I reached Mombasa, and, after a brief visit to Zanzibar, sailed for England in June, 1894, having spent about two and a half years in the interior of East Africa.

The reader who has followed me thus far will understand that it was with mingled feelings that I said good-bye to this savage but fascinating country, for the memories of past hardships were lost in the satisfaction that I had been privileged to play an important part in laying the foundations of its future prosperity. As Chief Engineer of the Railway Survey I had ascertained that a feasible line could be built at a cost of from two and a quarter to three and a half millions, according to the style of work adopted; and this railway, which will do so much to carry civilization and trade into the dark interior, is now being built on the basis of my preliminary survey and recommendations.

While inquiring into the events of the civil war between the Christians in Uganda, I was able to collect information that influenced Sir Gerald Portal in his momentous decision, that a British Protectorate was desirable. As Acting Commissioner of Uganda, it was my good fortune to crush once for all the last great effort made by Mohammedan barbarism to drive European influence, missionary enterprise and civilization from the land. And as Chief Staff-Officer to Colonel Colvile I was privileged to assist in the overthrow of Kabarega, which made our position in Uganda absolutely secure.

In this narrative I have all along endeavoured to give a plain and truthful account of events as they happened, and, in addition, to do justice to the work of others, instead of confining myself to a description of my own achievements. I trust it may have proved interesting to my readers as giving a more or less connected account of the stormy times that preceded the foundation of our new Protectorate in British East Africa.

GLOSSARY.

Askari (Swahili): soldier.
Bakopi (Uganda): plural of Mkopi, a peasant.
Balasura (Unyoro): soldiers.
Baraza (Uganda): durbar.
Bimbashi (Soudanese): major.
Boma (Swahili): a fort or defensive enclosure.
Donya (Masai): a hill or mountain.
Elmoran (Masai): warriors.
Ferruk (Soudanese): a gun-bearer.
Guash (Masai): a plain.
Guaso (Masai): a river.
Hongo (Swahili): blackmail or transit duty.
Kabaka (Uganda): royal title.
Kraal (South African): a village.
Leibon (Masai): a medicine-man.
Lagonani (Masai): a war-chief.
Mto (Swahili): a river.
Mubaka (Uganda): an envoy.
Mugabe (Uganda): a general.
Mulazim (Soudanese): a lieutenant.
Ngare (Masai): a stream.
Pagazi (Swahili): a porter.
Pombe (Swahili): beer.
Shamba (Swahili): a garden or cultivated property.
Shauri (Swahili): a council or meeting for deliberation.
Sifari (Swahili): a caravan.
Sime (Swahili): a leaf-shaped sword.

The following examples will enable the reader to understand the connection between the names of countries and their peoples:

	Swahili Language.	Uganda Language.
Name of a country:	Uganda, Sese.	Buganda, Sese.
A man of that country:	Mganda, Msese.	Mganda, Msese.
People of that country:	Waganda, Wasese.	Baganda, Basese.

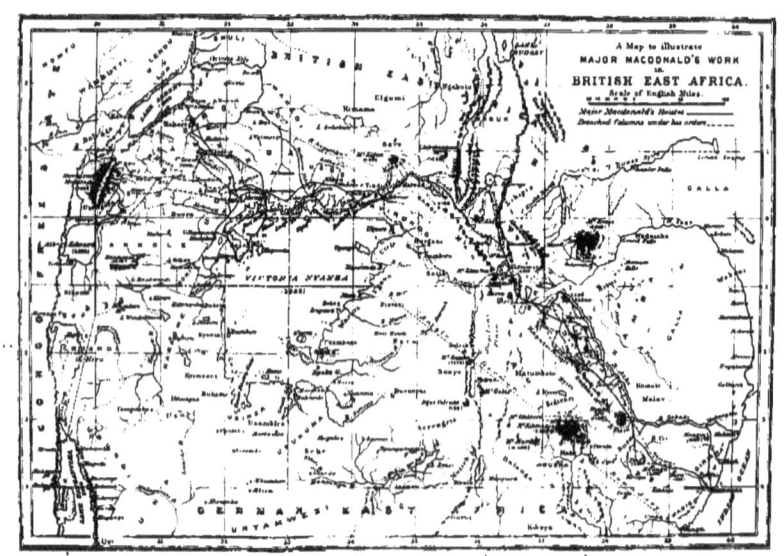

INDEX.

ABDOOL RASUD, 214
Agriculture, Wakamba, 30; Kikuyu, 56, 109
Ainsworth, Mr., 46; subdues Wakamba, 47, 102, 129
Ankole, 88; kingdom of, 136; asylum for Christians, 184, 187; route, 220, 231
Apollo, Protestant chief, 187; advance of, 188, 189; chases Karema, 190; Katikiro, 191; wounded at Vumba, 193, 200, 287
Arabs enter Uganda, 179
Arthur, Lieutenant, and Zanzibaris, 125, 240, 263; in Buddu, 270, 273; Kampala, 285; Kibibi, 287
Ashe, Rev. (C.M.S.), 134, 182
Athi River, 14; joins Sabaki, 23, 103; game on, 55; Masai, 102; Falls, 104
Athi, Stony, 55, 129
Austin, Lieutenant H. H., R.E., 4, 9, 25, 55, 60, 64, 68, 76, 97-107, 116, 119

Bagge, Mr., and steel boat, 84, 88
Bagwe, island in Lake Isolt, 240, 271
Baker, Sir S., 309
Baringo route, 64, 66; Lake, 72, 98
Baxter, Dr. (C.M.S.), 224
Baziba, 136; chief, 185
Bees and caravan, 18, 29; on Nzoi Peak, 31; in Kikuyu, 109
Berkeley, Mr. (I.B.E.A. Co.'s administrator), 7, 45, 127, 129, 227, 272
Bilal Bey, 279

Bondani pools, 43, 51
Bridge-building, 97-99, 313; on Kafu, 320
Brussi (in Busiro), 193; Chief of, 257
Bubonic plague, form of, in Uganda, 195
Buddu (south province of Uganda, 135), 84, 88; Wavuma raid, 149; given to Roman Catholics, 171; Ankole road, 185-188; desolate, 194, 206; Roman Catholic missionaries fly to, 216, 250; loyal, 240, 259, 270, 273; port in South Buddu, 291
Budongo Forest (Unyoro), 314-317
Bugangezi. *See* Chikakure
Bukoba, German station on Lake, 90
Bulamwezi, 135; Kangao of, 136, 194
Bulingugwe Island, 154; Mwanga's refuge, 83, 187, 193; capture of, 85, 207; loss in battle of, 87
Bura Hills, Wabura, 18
Busiro (province), 135; Mohammedans demand, 177, 220, 223; Mohammedans driven out of, 257
Busuju (province), 135; desolate, 194, 209; given to Roman Catholics, 284, 287; Mohammedans to remain in, 269, 275; Owen in, 287
Butambala (province), 287; Mohammedan, 209, 221, 257, 262, 284, 286; Kibibi in, 275, 292
Butunzi (province), 135; desolate, 194, 209; Chief of, 214; Pro-

testants receive, 284; Butabuzi rebels in, 288
Bwekula (district), 172, 176
Bwera (tributary to Buddu), 194
Bwinzau Mountain, 27, 32, 104

Caravan, start of, 10; contractor's, 21; attacked by bees, 18; ants, 21; rhinoceros, 53; Masai, 71, 128
Casati, 309
Chagwe (province), 135; in revolt, 84, 89; Wavuma raid, 151; headlands, 155, 208, 217, 244
Chikakure (chief of Bugangezi), 203, 299; chastised by Owen, 311
Colvile, Colonel Sir Henry, C.B., Commissioner in Uganda, 307; attacks Kabarega, 311; builds forts, 316
Congo Free State, Manyema slavers in, 231, 234

Dagoretti, Fort, 111; destroyed, 113
Damo, Mwanga beaten at, 186
De Winton, Mr., Kampala, 207; dies in Unyoro, 209; buried at Namerembe, 225
De Winton, Fort, 219, 232; Owen at, 275-283
Diamaluni Island, 155
Donkeys start, 10; in trouble, 17; a failure, 19
Dualla (Lugard's interpreter), 81, 85; goes to Mbogo, 211; Mbogo's surety, 212; escapes Masai, 101

Eldoma Ravine, Mau, 72, 99
Elgeyo Mountains, 64
Elgon, Mount, 74, 77
Elmenteita (salt lake), 68, 100
Emin Pasha, 198; and Kabarega, 309
Etakatok River, 97

Ferag reaches Kampala, 89
Fisher, Mr. (C.M.S.), 271
Foaker, Mr. (I.B.E.A. Co.'s transport officer), 17, 25, 49, 50, 54-56, 60, 64, 70, 72, 74, 76; ill, 93, 98, 104, 116, 118; to coast, 272
Food-supplies, 49; at Kikuyu, 56;

scarce at Kibwezi, 104; wanting in South Unyoro, 281
Forster, Mr. (C.M.S.), 264, 265, 268, 272
Fuladoya, 20
Futabangi, heathen Waganda, 79

Gabunga, commander of canoes, 136
Game, mysterious disappearance of hunters, 28; buffalo, 72, 103; cheetah, 52; elephants raid Singo, 194, 201; gazelle, 50; grouse, 67; hartebeest, 28, 50, 55, 103, 130; hippopotami, 22, 54, 60, 103, 154; klipspringer, 74; leopard, 51, 61, 103, 130; lion, 28, 52, 103, 129; mpalla, 103; oryx, 28; ostrich, 50; reed-buck, 133; rhinoceros, 51-54; warthog, 131; waterbuck, 23, 55, 103, 133; wildebeest in thousands, 103; zebra, 50, 100, 130
Gedge, Mr. E., 2, 64; *Times* correspondent, 166; I.B.E.A. Co.'s agent, 187, 197, 228; at Port Alice, 230, 239-250, 259, 264-273
George, Fort, guarding Salt Lake, 218-220, 231; evacuation of, 234, 293
Gibb, Captain, 168
Gilgil River, 68; camp in Masailand, 131
Giriama, 19
Gordon, General, sends Emin to Kabarega, 309
Gordon, Rev. (C.M.S.), 182
Grant, the explorer, 180, 309
Grant, Mr., raids Tunga's, 133; at Kampala, 153; with Lugard, 200; with Owen, 230-234, 262, 270, 274, 278-282, 284, 287, 297-299
Grant, Fort, on frontier of Singo, 301, 311
Guash Ngisho, 50; easiest route to Uganda, 65-67; pastures of, 74, 98
Guaso Masa, 'river of wealth,' 74, 97, 133, 272
Guaso Masai, 99
Guba, on lake, 85, 86
Gunther, Mr. (C.M.S.), 271
Guruguru, country of Waguruguru, 115-122

INDEX

Hall, Mr., and donkey caravan, 122; cultivates Masai, 126
Hannington, Bishop, 64; massacred, 181
Hirth, Monseigneur, at Bulingugwe, 84-87, 216; in Buddu, 250-273; interferes, 284
Hoima, headquarters in Unyoro, 319
Hyenas fond of donkey, 8, 56; bold in Masailand, 55

I.B.E.A. Co., protection of, 19, 45
Islam crushed in Uganda, 195

Jackson, Mr. (I.B.E.A. Co.'s officer), visits Uganda, 79; in Kavirondo, 187; opposes Protestant migration to Usoga, 8, 14, 22, 197; returns to England, 26
'Jiggers,' 245
Juma (Mohammedan chief) at Natete, 214, 229, 235; arrested, 246-250, 264; escapes, 273

Kabaka. See Uganda, officers of State
Kabarega, King of Unyoro, 209; tributary to Uganda, 136, 170; curbed by Lugard, 310; attacks forts, 90, 174; aids Karema, 191, 196, 208; active, 232, 285, 296; extends power, 308; defies British, 311; retreats, 314; blockaded in Budongo Forest, 316
Kafu River, 191, 201, 204; Colvile at, 312
Kagera River, 186; navigable, 291
Kaitabia, 201
Kakanguru defeats Futabangi in Chagwe, 88; Roman Catholics, 89; fights Wavuma, 152, 165; pursues Mohammedans, 257; recalled, 259, 270; joins Owen, 281; under Colvile, 312, 316; beats Kabarega, 319
Kalifi, Port, possible terminus of railway, 25
Kamania, warrior King of Uganda, 148
Kamarasi, King of Unyoro, father of Kabarega, 309
Kamasia range, 64, 66, 133
Kampala (I.B.E.A. Co.'s fort, Mengo), position of, 82; flies Union Jack, 217; in danger, 237, 241, etc.; Mbogo at, 246
Kampi Ambaruk, fight at, 71
Kamswaga, King of Koki, 289
Kangao, 317. See Bulamwezi
Kapote, Masai steppes, 32, 34, 36; watched by Wakamba, 41, 50, 103; railway route to, 105
Karakwanzi rejected by Wasongora, 218
Karema, Mwanga's brother, 153; made King, 184; unpopular, 187; flies, 190; rallies and re-enters Mengo, 191-193; beaten at Brussi, 194
Kasagama, King of Toru, 219, 230; friendly, 294; 'at home,' 299; opposes Kabarega, 314; leader of Toru, 320
Katikiro, court of the, 138
Katonga River, defeat of Christians on, 185, 288-290
Kavalli's, on Lake Albert, view of, 192; Lugard goes to, 207; Manyema devastate, 218; Soudanese in Unyoro plot a return to, 278
Kavirondo, 49; small-pox decimates, 76; Martin in, 62, 91; route, 66, 181; blocked, 152; opened, 75, 167, 187, 213, 273. See Mumias
Kawanda, ridge on Lugard's march, 201
Kawawa, camp on Lugard's march, 201
Kedong River, 57
Keite River, cultivation on, 30; mouth, 104
Kenani, near Masai war-path, 26; mail looted, 127
Kesubi, on Port Alice road, 253, 258-264
Kibero bombarded by Emin, 310; fort at, 316-319
Kibibi, Fort, 220, 224; evacuated, 234; Protestants reach, 270; Kakanguru, 275; junction with Owen, 287-289
Kibibi Island, 156
Kiboga Hill, double peak of, 192; Christian camp before Vumba, 192, 201
Kiboko River, 27, 101, 104; Masai

attack native caravan on, 36, 128
Kibwezi, 34, 128; food depot at, 4, 8, 101, 104, 105; Scottish mission at, 26, 27, 35
Kikabala, peak on Lugard's march, 202
Kikumbuliu district raided by Masai, 34
Kikuyu, 35, 47, 66, 96, 99, 101, 107, 128; on lake route, 49; Forest, 55, 102; Wakikuyu, 108; their arms, 109; treachery, 102, 111; punished, 122; invest Fort Smith, 125
Kilimanjaro Mountain, 26, 33
Kilungu, district of Ulu, 30, 36, 46; superstitions in, 39; Masai raid, 43; Nelson, 125
Kimbugwe. *See* Uganda, officers of State
Kintu, founder of Uganda, 134; his tomb, 135; example, 171; royal blood, 183
Kisibagwa, Kakanguru at, 316, 319
Kitakwenda district, 174, 218, 231; offered to Kasagama, 230; hostile, 284; overrun by Kabarega, 308
Kitangole, slavers at, 303
Kitanwa, fort at, 317, 317
Kitumbui River, 201-203
Kivari's (old Lugard fort), battle near, 282
Kiwewa, Mwanga's brother, made King, 183; deposed, 184
Koki, tributary to Uganda, 136, 139, 196, 288-292
Kome Island, furnished canoes against Sese, 84, 90
Kowar, battle of, 203
Kyadondo, province of old Uganda, 135
Kyaka, province of Unyoro, ravaged by Soudanese, 174, 196, 320
Kyangora River, Lugard beats Mohammedans at, 202, 207
Kyulu Hills, 26-28, 32

Lamu, port of, 5
Lecky, Mr. (C.M.S.), 258, 272
Lendus, Nubian tribe, porters, 274; set free, 305
Longonot, extinct volcano 57, 60

Loonga Forest, 292
Lorne, Fort, road from Fort Briggs to, stopped, 232; reopened, 276
Lubegi River, near Mengo, 200, 254
Lubwa (Usoga chief) murders Hannington, 152, 181; sends one hundred war-canoes, 166; holds review, 168, 298
Lubwa Fort, 301
Lugard, Major F. D., C.B., D.S.O., 66, 191, 228, 238, 267, 282, 314; forts on Sabaki, 8, 20; Machako's, 45; route to Uganda, 220; arrives, 196; reconciles Protestants and Roman Catholics, 79; fights Mohammedans, 200; wins Kowar, 203; to Kavalli's, 207; refuses Kabarega's friendship, 296; Toru Soudanese, 174; Soudanese at Kampala, 175; defeats Roman Catholics, 82, 85; 'victorious all along the line,' 90; his settlement of Uganda, 169-178; administration of Uganda, 62, 64, 75, 76, 212-214, 218, 310; leaves Kampala, 77; journey to coast, 93-101
Lugard Falls on Sabaki, 23
Lugard Fort, 202, 301, 311
Lumbwa, 65, 67
Lurs attack Purkiss, 318
Lutaia (Mohammedan chief), 289
Luwamba, old fort on Lake, 88

Maanja River, 190, 200; plains, 192
Machako's, fort in Ulu, 4, 8; arrival at, 33; importance of, 45, 101, 102, 104, 106, 129; Wilson fights his way to, 113
Machako's River Valley, 33, 34, 103
Mackay 'of Uganda,' 180; dies, 182; his old mission-house at Natete, 214
Mackinnon Road, 35
Macpherson, Dr., 200
Magungu, province of Unyoro, 309, 316; occupied, 317
Magungu, old Egyptian station, 318, 319
Mahdi, 195
Maka district, 36, 43, 45; Mountains, 52
Makangeni, on Sabaki, 8, 20; railway route to Kalifi, 25

INDEX

Maktub, Swahili headman, killed, 115, 119; avenged, 118
Makwenda, Chief of Singo, 200, 201, 210, 257, 286
Malindi, on coast, 23
Mangea Hill, on Sabaki, 20, 23
Manyema, slave-dealers on Semiliki, 218, 231, 233-235, 269, 281; attack Usongora, 293
Marching, night-floods, 14; hindered by rains, 204; improved rate of, 205
Martin, James, 64, 68, 73, 100, 105, 121, 125, 133, 306; discovers Guash Ngishu route, 65; meets us at Naivasha, 61, 88, 91; brings small-pox, 76; donkey-dealing, 107; ex-sailor, 303
Masai, 41, 102, 107, 109; warpaths, 15, 28; respect treaties, 35, 71; ruse against, 42; once defeated, 43; hongo, 50; hunting-grounds, 58, 132; troublesome, 63, 70; Elmoran fight, 68; kraals, 100; Hall's allies, 126; loot mails, 127; 'back door of Uganda,' 181
Masindi, Kabarega's old capital, 309, 316
Mata River, 201
Matamba Plateau, 201
Matiana, capital of Singo, 200, 238, 257, 285-289; garrisoned, 298; receives Toru immigrants, 299
Matundwe Ridge, near Mengo, 262
Mau escarpment, 61; forest, 72
Maungu Hill, 12
Mawakota, province of old Uganda, 135, 172; given to Roman Catholics, 176; road from, 227; swamps of, 264
Maxim guns at battle of Mengo, 83; Bulingugwe, 86; Sese, 90; against Wavuma, 152; unreliable, 213; wanted in Unyoro, 233; to Buddu, 270, 287; to Koki, 289; Kabarega, 312, 315
Mazamboni, Manyema devastate, 218
Mbogo, uncle of Mwanga, 153; becomes head of Mohammedans, 194; demanded by Lugard, 202; given up, 211; his sureties, 212; settlement round him, 216, 253;
loyal, 235, 263; sent to coast, 273
Mengo, capital of Uganda, only one King in, 137; chiefs attend at, 139; body-guard, 141; battle of, 82; smoking, 84; Mwanga back in, 91; Mohammedans beaten near, 190; Karema near, 193; prospering, 134; Catholic road to, 176; Toru immigrants, 219; concentration at, 243; slave-dealers, 303
Meridional Rift, 50
Mfu (Moffat's island), slavers captured in, 304
Miller, Mr. (C.M.S.), 272
Missionaries first invited by Mtesa, 180; 'in politics,' 144; re 'road,' 228
Missions have had good effect on Waganda, 143
Mkamba, Chief of Wakamba, 36
Moffat, Dr., Scottish missionary at Kibwezi, 26, 101, 167, 230, 264, 269, 273; braves Masai, 36; attends Portal, 224; holds Kampala, 247; tends wounded, 258, 260; commands troops, 265, 288; mentioned in despatches, 271
Mohammedans, rise of, in Uganda, 179; second war against, 199; beaten at Kowar, 203; advance on Uganda, 210; yield to Lugard, 211; reinstated, 171; unsettled, 177, 214; demand Busiro, 220; hatch plot, 226; driven out of Natete, 257; split up, 269; make for Salt Lake, 282; return of defeated, 283
Molondo, 88. *See* Kakanguru
Mombasa, capital of British East Africa, 7
Morendat River in flood, 97, 101
Mruli, 306, 311, 315
Msaka, C.M.S. station in Buddu, 89
Mtesa, Suna's greater son, 136; reign of, 179-181; islet prison, 155; fails against Wavuma, 150-152; population of Uganda, 194
Mubaka, King's commissary, 140
Mugema, Chief of Busiro, 200
Mujasi. *See* Uganda, officers of State

Mukasa, Protestant chief killed near Natete, 223
Mukotanyi, Baziba chief friendly to Christians, 185
Mumia's, station in Kavirondo, 93
Munyunyu, port of Mengo, 85, 153, 230, 235, 268, 269
Murchison Bay, fleet in, 153, 154; slave canoes, 303
Mwanga, King of Uganda, son of Mtesa, 181; cautious, 189; greedy, 166; murders Hannington, 181; retains Mackay, 182; deposed, 183; turns Roman Catholic, 170, 183; heads Christians, 186; joined by missionaries, 187; re-enters Mengo, 190; his faction popular, 191; flies to Bulingugwe, 193; at Mengo, 194; accepts I.B.E.A. Co., 198; escapes from Bulingugwe, 208; reinstated, 77
Mwebia, fertile district, 192, 202
Mwengi, province of Unyoro, 320

Naivasha, Lake, 50; round, 60, 97, 101; meet Martin at, 91; food depot, 131
Nako, ford on Maanja, 200
Nakuro, Lake, 71, 100
Nalukorongo River, near Mengo, 254, 262; Mohammedans jammed in fords of, 257
Namagoma, twin peaks, 194
Namasole. *See* Uganda, officers of State
Namaya River, 194, 257
Namirembe Hill, position of, 84, 254, 255; C.M.S. headquarters, 244
Nandi Hills, 98; three, 74, 133; Wanandi, 132
Natete, Mohammedan quarter at Mengo, 190; position of hill, 255; turbulent, 214; reinforced, 221, 236, 238; Mukasa killed near, 223; threatened, 240; Juma's letter to, 249; cleared out, 256
Ndabibi Plain, at foot of Mau, 61
Ndi, grain district, 13, 35, 104
Nelson, Captain, and Wabura, 13; punishes Wakainba, 46; at Fort Smith, 121; dies, 125
Newman, Smith's assistant, 65

Nile, 77, 92, 133, 317; ferry occupied, 240
Ngongo Bagas, 57, 111
Nolosegeli River, 74; bridged, 98
Ntebi, 264, 304
Ntuti, district, 192, 202, 204
Nyamoga, Kabarega's capital, 309
Nyoni Ntono, Christian leader killed, 185
Nzaze Island, Selim's temporary prison, 268, 273
Nzira, island of Uvuma, 149
Nzoi, district, 36, 44
Nzoi Peak, 25, 28; ascent of, 31
Nzoia River, 74; Falls, 75; flying bridge over, 133

Owen, Major E. R., D.S.O., 219; in Unyoro, 175, 240, 262, 269, 274; builds new fort in Toru, 176; in difficulties, 230, 235; assistance for, 270, 275, 281; quenches mutiny, 276-280; defeats Mohammedans, 281-283; marches for Mengo, 284-289; reports on country, 294-296; conducts evacuation of Toru, 297-300

Pigott, Mr., follows Sabaki, 23
Pilkington, Rev. (C.M.S.), 225, 244, 272
Pokino, chief of Buddu, 216
Port Alice, on Ntebi Peninsula, 167, 222, 240, 254, 258, 274, 277, 304; Selim arrives at, 235, 236; Reddie and Gedge at, 245-249; Selim expected from, 253; we move on, 261-267; new headquarters, 264, 285; Reddie at, 236, 289; Villiers, 292; Toru immigrants, 298; garrison of, 301; improvements at, 302
Port Reitz, 7
Portal, Sir Gerald, Commissioner in Uganda, 125, 144, 166, 230, 300; at Kampala, 169-177, 217-225, 310; and corvée, 140; increases Roman Catholic territory, 284; founds Port Alice, 264; leaves for coast, 226, 272, 274; recall of, 241; letters from, 233, 237, 271, 272, 293, 305
Portal, Captain Raymond, enlists

Soudanese in Unyoro, 175, 219, 230; his death, 177, 224
Pringle, Captain J. W., R.E., 4, 16, 31, 33, 60, 62, 76, 95, 97; to Salt River, 50-54, 101, 105; Kikuyu, 55-57, 98; captures Masai women, 63; through Sotik, 64; crosses Mau, 66; Kavirondo, 68; Mumia's, 75; ill, 93; in Guruguru, 116-119; Masai inquiries, 131
Protestants contemplate retiring to Usoga, 79, 244
Purkiss, 56, 101; probationer, 113; at Fort Smith, 115-126; attacked by Wyaki, 120; ordered to Uganda, 126; on Nile, 317

Rabai Hills, 6
Railway, staff, etc., of survey, 3; difficulties, 9; Taru and Sabaki routes compared, 24; route viâ Salt River Valley to Kapote Steppes possible, 105; success of, 106
Raymond, Fort, garrison of, 301
Reddie, Mr., cut off from Lugard, 88; in Unyoro, 218; Port Alice, 236, 240-250; assists in capture of Port Alice, 260-271; with Villiers, 289-291
Rekwiamba, chief chastised by Kabarega, 309
Rhodes, Colonel F., 271-273
Ribi, mission-station, 16
Rionga, rival of Kabarega, 309
Roman Catholics attempt to seize canoes, 84; get more territory and 'Catholic road,' 176, 220, 227
Roscoe, Rev. J. (C.M.S.), 244, 272
Rubaga Hill, Mengo, 82; position of, 254; Roman Catholic mission on, 245, 264; battle of, 256-258
Rubuga. *See* Uganda, officers of State

Sabaki River, 4, 103; route, 20-25
Salt Lake, not commercial success, 176; Company's caravans at, 174; Fort George, 218; to be evacuated, 234, 297; Mohammedans make for, 281
Salt River, 27, 53, 101, 104, 105

Sango Peninsula, 291
Sekebobo, chief of Chagwe, 258, 264, 266, 287
Sekiwala, sub-chief of Singo, 165, 238, 271
Selim Bey, Soudanese Commandant, 170, 246, 276-280, 284; won by Lugard, 207; treats with Mbogo, 209; Mbogo's surety, 211, 212; and Natete, 214; interferes, 215; supports Mohammedans, 223; becomes their accomplice, 227; 'an independent commander . . . invited by Captain Lugard,' 228; arrives at Port Alice, 235; opposes Reddie, 236; sends mutinous message, 238; taken unawares, 247; proclaims intentions, 249; expected, 253; arrested, 266; life spared, 267; sent to Nzaze, 268; dies on way to coast, 273
Selim Bey's Soudanese, 175, 207, 239; disarmed, 251; located in Kikuyu, 273; in Unyoro forts, 208, 210; raid, 214, 218; enlisted or unenlisted? 219; plot, 278; scourge of Unyoro, 294; unpaid by Company, 295
Semiliki River, Manyema stockade west of, 218, 231, 269, 281
Sentema, village on Maanja River, 200
Sese Islands, 85, 176; Mwanga flies to, 186; fleet supports him, 187, 188; expedition against Roman Catholics in, 90; Williams, 213; Wasese paddlers, 154, 156
Shukri, Soudanese officer, 233, 235, 293; killed in action, 232, 311
Shuli, tribe on Nile, 308
Singo, 172, 194, 289, 298; absorbed in Uganda, 135; Mohammedans in, 199, 208; Mohammedans leave for Mengo, 210; Karema takes refuge in, 190-193; part of, offered to Kasagama, 299
Slaves and slave-dealers, Makengeni settlement of runaway slaves, 21; Arab slavers in Ulu, 44; slave-raiding in Unyoro, 214; Lendus set free, 274, 305; slave-dealers at Mengo, 303; capture of

slavers, 303, 304; at Unyoro forts, 172
Smith, Mr. (C.M.S.), his porter shoots Wakoli, 93, 94
Smith, Mr. (C.M.S.), pioneer, murdered at Ukerewe, 180
Smith, Major Eric, 56, 64, 65, 68, 133, 303, 306; in Kikuyu, 113-115; to Uganda, 106, 121, 124, 134; assists Williams against Wavuma, 152-167; holds Kampala, 215
Smith, Fort, in Kikuyu, 45, 50, 101, 106, 119, 121, 129, 131; founded by Major E. Smith, 56; European vegetables at, 108
Snake, porter bitten by, 16
Sotik, 65; short route viâ, 49; populous, 67
Soudan, 148, 205; Soudanese offered return to, 229
Soudanese a fighting-machine, 300
Speke, great African explorer, 180, 309
Stanley, Mr. H. M., 73; with Mtesa, 180; aids Waganda against Wavuma, 149-152; leaves Emin's Soudanese in Equatoria, 80
Stewart, Dr., founder of Kibwezi Mission, 26
Stokes, Mr., trader friendly to Mwanga, 189; his yawl, 154-156, 186
Suliman wounded by Wakikuyu, 121
Suna, King of Uganda, subdued Usoga, 148; Mtesa's father, 136
Suswa, an extinct volcano, 57

Takaungu, Arab chief of, contractor, 21
Tana River, 44, 103, 108
Tanganyika, 231
Taru, 12
Teita, 12
Thomas, Sergeant, 18, 60, 61, 64, 116
Thomson, Joseph, 'Through Masailand,' 64, 75, 107; visited Kikuyu, 111
Thomsonii gazelle, 74
Thruston, Major A. B., 168, 311, 319; Hoima, 320
Tiwa River, 30, 34, 44
Toru, 173, 219, 230, 240, 277, 307-314; supplies from, 233; forts, 208; Soudanese interfere in, 174; Portal lets go, 234, 293; reoccupation of, 320
Tsavo River, 104; depot at, 4, 8, 101; stockade on, 14, 24
Tucker, Bishop, going to Uganda, 127, 128, 133
Tunga, 94, 133
Twining, Captain P. G., R.E., collects survey staff, 5; surveys Athi, 25; sick, 71-74; to complete survey, 76; collects supplies, 104; at Fort Smith, 116; *passim*, 1-106

Uganda, 134; founding and extension of, 135; officers of State, 136; chiefs' town-houses, 139; corvée, 139; arms, formation, etc., 142; Waganda off to the war, 153, 155; cause of civil war in, 81; redistribution of, by Lugard, 91; sects of, 170; population after civil war, 195; great progress in, 213, 217; brick houses, 302; swamps bridged, 133; unbridged swamps required, 137
Ugaya, Wavuma island, 145, 150; submission of, 166
Ukambani, or Ukamba, country of Wakamba, 34, 110
Ukerewe Island, 180
Ulu, fastness of Wakamba, 36, 50; fertile, 49; watch-towers of, 52
Ulukenia Hill, 129
Unyoro, 170, 177, 191, 192, 298; Mohammedans fly to, 194, 196; Lugard in, 204-206; De Winton dies in, 209; Reddie in, 218; Colvile in, 205, 301-322. *See* Owen, Kabarega
Unyoro, forts in, 88, 214, 220, 224, 232, 234; repulse Kabarega, 90; slave market at, 172, 214; enlistment at, 175, 219; unenlisted at, 222; alteration of, 176; two retained, 293. *See* Owen
Usamba, on Kafu River, 312
Usiri, Wavuma island, 145, 156-158
Usoga conquered by Mtesa, 136, 139; Hannington passes through, 181; cut off from Mengo, 88;

INDEX

Williams in, 75, 210, 211; Smith in, 94; Arthur returns from, 240; new half-company of Soudanese for, 300; Kabarega attacks, 313, *et passim*
Usongora, 218; alienated, 219, 230, 294; under Kasagama, 320
Uvuma Islands, 145; history of, 147-151; Williams subdues, 151-168

Villamaria, Roman Catholics' headquarters in Buddu, 290; Arthur at, 270
Villiers, Captain C. H. (Royal Horse Guards), 224, 230, 304; at Kampala, 222; Uganda, 271, 287; clears Koki, 289-292; conducts immigrants, 298; at Kitanwa, 318
Villiers, Lake, 291
Vumba, 191, 201, 203; battle of, 192

Wabura show fight, 13
Wadelai, 306, 308, 317; Owen reaches, 319
Waelgumi, 148
Wagiriama, courageous, 128
Waguruguru, relations of Wyaki, 114, 115; chastised, 117
Wahuma, 186, 291
Wakamasia, settlements of, 72
Wakamba, 27, 30, 34-48, 102; dress and marriage customs, 38; turn tables on Masai, 41, 43
Wakavirondo, 148; resist Mtesa, 136
Wakedi, 148, 306, 308; resist Mtesa, 136

Wakoli, 88, 94, 233, 293; assassinated, 93
Wakwavi, Masai, 66; raid caravan, 71
Walegeyon River, 99
Wandenge, friendly chief, 115, 119
Wanderobbo, 65
Wasamia rise, 95
Wasoga called out by Lugard, 94
Wasongora. *See* Usongora.
Wavuma, 145-168; intercept boats, 88
Wema, deserted island, 156
White Fathers arrive in Uganda, 181; brought to Kampala, 88; Pères Gaudibert and Guillermain, 272
Williams, Major, R.A., 77, 79, 214; his Soudanese, 199; maintains peace, 80; at battle of Mengo, 83, 213; at Bulingugwe, 85-87; captures Sese, 90; attacks Uvuma, 159; charges, 166; in Usoga, 75, 210; at Kampala, 172-176, 207, 212-217; rescues Smith, 94; makes overtures to Kabarega, 310; works wonders in Uganda, 94, 95
Wilson, Rev. C. T. (C.M.S.), 180
Wilson, Mr., 230, 251, 260, 272
Wilson, George, and Wakamba, 35; at Dagoretti, 112
Wolf, Herr Eugene, 122
Wyaki, Lugard makes blood-brothership with, 111; and Wilson, 112, 113; an amiable scoundrel, 114-120; sent to coast, 121; his village destroyed, 124

THE END.

www.ingramcontent.com/pod-product-compliance
Lightning Source LLC
Chambersburg PA
CBHW032034220426
43664CB00006B/469